UNPACKING the Competency-Based CLASSROOM

EQUITABLE, INDIVIDUALIZED LEARNING IN A PLC AT WORK®

Jonathan G. Vander Els **Brian M. Stack**

FOREWORD BY MIKE MATTOS

Solution Tree | Press

Copyright © 2022 by Solution Tree Press

Materials appearing here are copyrighted. With one exception, all rights are reserved. Readers may reproduce only those pages marked "Reproducible." Otherwise, no part of this book may be reproduced or transmitted in any form or by any means (electronic, photocopying, recording, or otherwise) without prior written permission of the publisher.

555 North Morton Street
Bloomington, IN 47404
800.733.6786 (toll free) / 812.336.7700
FAX: 812.336.7790

email: info@SolutionTree.com
SolutionTree.com

Visit **go.SolutionTree.com/PLCbooks** to download the free reproducibles in this book.

Printed in the United States of America

Library of Congress Cataloging-in-Publication Data

Names: Vander Els, Jonathan G., author. | Stack, Brian M., author.
Title: Unpacking the competency-based classroom : equitable, individualized learning in a PLC at work / Jonathan G. Vander Els, Brian M. Stack.
Other titles: Equitable, individualized learning in a professional learning community at work
Description: Bloomington, IN : Solution Tree Press, [2022] | Includes bibliographical references and index.
Identifiers: LCCN 2021053401 (print) | LCCN 2021053402 (ebook) | ISBN 9781952812453 (Paperback) | ISBN 9781952812460 (eBook)
Subjects: LCSH: Competency-based education. | Professional learning communities. | Teachers--In-service training. | Teaching--Methodology. | Educational change.
Classification: LCC LC1031 .V36 2022 (print) | LCC LC1031 (ebook) | DDC 370.11--dc23/eng/20220124
LC record available at https://lccn.loc.gov/2021053401
LC ebook record available at https://lccn.loc.gov/2021053402

Solution Tree
Jeffrey C. Jones, CEO
Edmund M. Ackerman, President

Solution Tree Press
President and Publisher: Douglas M. Rife
Associate Publisher: Sarah Payne-Mills
Managing Production Editor: Kendra Slayton
Editorial Director: Todd Brakke
Art Director: Rian Anderson
Copy Chief: Jessi Finn
Senior Production Editor: Suzanne Kraszewski
Content Development Specialist: Amy Rubenstein
Proofreader: Jessi Finn
Text and Cover Designer: Rian Anderson
Editorial Assistants: Charlotte Jones, Sarah Ludwig, and Elijah Oates

ACKNOWLEDGMENTS

This book, our second on this topic for Solution Tree, extends and expands on our professional work as educational leaders supporting the competency-based learning work of schools and school districts across the United States. We forever owe a debt of gratitude to the educators whom we have worked alongside and learned with along the way, including those closest to us in New Hampshire where we both got our start.

We are forever indebted to the staff at Solution Tree, including Douglas Rife for believing in our vision for this book and supporting our efforts to make it a meaningful and relevant tool for classroom educators. We would especially like to thank our editor Suzanne Kraszewski, designer Rian Anderson, and all the team members behind the scenes at Solution Tree. As with our first book, the influence of many of Solution Tree's authors is evident. We thank all of you for the tremendous work you have done in helping educators throughout the world understand ways to better support students and teachers everywhere and consider ourselves very fortunate to work alongside each of you in support of students everywhere.

We owe gratitude to countless professionals who work on competency-based learning at the national level for taking time to contribute, inform, and guide us through the development of this book, among them Eliot Levine and Susan Patrick of the Aurora Institute, Paul Leather from the Center for Innovation in Education, and the many practitioners we've worked with across the country. Thank you all for your guidance and feedback with our revised competency-based learning school design rubric. We would like to thank our many colleagues who have reviewed pieces of our work or who have provided valuable insight as professional practitioners. A special thank you to Dr. Karin Hess and Sarah Lench, who both continue to influence so many with the amazing, practical tools that they so willingly share to impact students and educators everywhere. Thank you to Rose Colby, a mentor and friend from the beginning of our journey, who selflessly continues to champion competency education and our work. And a very special thank you to the amazing educators who were willing to share their stories in this book: Tonya Howell and Damarr Smith, Chicago Public Schools, Illinois; Beth Blankenship and Elizabeth Dean from Madison High School, Fairfax County, Virginia; Dr. James Neihof from Shelby County, Kentucky; Dr. Josh Ray and Faith Short from East Pointe Elementary School in Greenwood, Arkansas; Sara Casassa, Barnard School, New Hampshire; Shannon Schinkel, Humanities/Drama Educator and Cofounder, Assessment Consortium of British Columbia, Canada; Ellen Hume-Howard from the New Hampshire Learning Initiative in Hampton, New Hampshire; Gail Bourn from Laconia School District in Laconia, New Hampshire; Steve Holmes, Samantha Fernandez, and Kasie Betton from Sunnyside School District, Arizona; Irene Stinson, a fifth-grade teacher from the Laconia School District in New Hampshire; Paul Butler, special educator from New Hampshire; Bill Dinkelmann and Dr. Michael Burde from the Kenowa Hills Public Schools in Grand Rapids, Michigan; Stan Williams and Emily Rinkema of the Champlain Valley School District in Vermont; Dr. Sarah Bond, instructional coach and former primary grade teacher, University of New Hampshire; Donald Conti, Elizabeth Szeliga, Lisa Woodruff, and Amanda Loder from Lincoln Akerman School, New Hampshire; Anthony Doucet, Souhegan High School, New Hampshire; Kirk Savage, Chilliwack School District, British Columbia; Donna Couture, Winnacunnet High School, New Hampshire; Erica Pappalardo of the Inter-Lakes School District in New Hampshire; Crystal Bonin of the Winnisquam Regional School District in New Hampshire; and Dawn Olson of Seabrook Middle School in New Hampshire.

And of course, we are forever lifted up by our family and friends who have stood beside us through our professional journeys, those in the schools we've worked in, as well as the incredible networks we're humbled to be a part of now who continue to consider what could and should be in our collective quest to promote change in support of *all* learners.

From Brian: To my wife, Erica, you have always stood by my side and been my biggest advocate to take risks and follow my heart. To my children, Brady, Cameron, Liam, Owen, and Zoey, may this book be a living example and proof that you should follow your dreams and remember that your future has not been written yet—no one's has. Your future is whatever you make it, so make it a good one! To the countless colleagues, students, friends, and family members who have helped me frame my beliefs and values about education, you forever have my gratitude for helping me internalize my why for this work.

From Jonathan: Thank you to the many colleagues I have the great fortune to learn from and with on a daily basis. Ellen, Kathy, Carolyn, Mariane, and Debbie, being able to support schools in New Hampshire with all of you is a privilege. And to those national friends and colleagues from Solution Tree and from Communities of Practices like the Assessment for Learning Project who continue to push my thinking about what is possible and who always put students first, I am honored to have the opportunity to learn from you.

Most importantly, thank you, with my utmost love and affection, to Stephanie. You've always believed in me unequivocally. This support is truly what has allowed us to take chances and for me to follow my passion. And to our three beautiful children, Grace, Garrett, and Will: watching you grow into the amazing people you are fills me with wonder and an excitement anticipating the incredible things you will do as you follow your hearts. Thank you, as well, to my sisters Wendy and Amy, and to Brian, Nathaniel, David, James, and Judith. And to my dad and mom: Through your selfless example, as our parents, and now for you, Mom, as Gram to our kids, and as lifelong educators yourselves, you've touched the lives of so many, a gift that will carry on in perpetuity.

Solution Tree Press would like to thank the following reviewers:

Jed Kees
Principal
Onalaska Middle School
Onalaska, Wisconsin

Melisha Plummer
Assistant Principal
South Atlanta High School
Atlanta, Georgia

Pamela Liebenberg
Director of Curriculum & Instruction
Tuscaloosa County School System
Tuscaloosa, Alabama

Paige Raney
Chair, Division of Education
Spring Hill College
Mobile, Alabama

Visit **go.SolutionTree.com/PLCbooks** to download the free reproducibles in this book.

TABLE OF CONTENTS

Reproducible pages are in italics.

About the Authors xi

Foreword by Mike Mattos xiii

Introduction 1
   About This Book 2
   A Laser-Like Focus on Learning 3

1 The Seven Components of the Competency-Based Classroom 5
   Why Now? 6
   Trends in Necessary Employability Skills and Dispositions 7
   Competency-Based Learning: A Definition 9
   The PLC and Competency-Based Learning Connection 15
   Equity, Social Justice, and Competency-Based Learning 15
   Evolving Policy 18
   Anytime, Anywhere Learning 21
   Reflection Questions 24

2 Collaborative Teams: The Structures That Support Competency-Based Learning 27
   Shared Leadership 29
   A Strong Foundation 31
   The Three Big Ideas: Guiding the Work of Schools 36

The Four Critical Questions of a PLC and Competency-Based Learning 41
Reflection Questions 45

3 Competencies, Essential Standards, Learning Targets, and Learning Progressions 47

Refining the Curriculum 49
What Are Competency Statements? 49
What Are Essential Standards? 58
What Are Learning Targets? 61
What Are Learning Progressions? 62
What Is the Role of Metacognition? 62
Putting It All Together 65
Reflection Questions 69

4 Meaningful, Balanced Assessment 71

Components of a Balanced Assessment System 72
Formative Assessment as a Classroom Practice 73
Ambitious Teaching and Formative Assessment 77
The Role of Student Self-Assessment 78
Common Formative Assessment: Measuring Where Students Are 80
Summative Assessment: Seeking Evidence of Transfer 82
Reassessment 86
Rigor, Complexity, and Cognitive Demand 86
Rubrics 87
The Unit Planning Template 91
Reflection Questions 99

5 Structures and Systems to Support Instruction 101

Shaping Structures to Support Personalized Learning 104
The Three Tiers of RTI 104
Planning Weekly Lessons That Empower Learners 119
Choosing School Experiences That Support a Competency-Based System . . . 121
Reflection Questions 126

6 Structures for Feedback 129

Why Do We Grade? 129
What Should We Grade? 132
Should We Separate Academics From Skills and Dispositions? 134
What Grading Scale Should We Use? 135

    Grading What Is Learned, Not Earned 149
    Reflection Questions 151

7 The Design Rubric 153

    Planning Your Transformation 155
    Design Principle 1: Student-Centered Learning 157
    Design Principle 2: Meaningful Assessment 160
    Design Principle 3: Differentiated Support for All 163
    Design Principle 4: Mastery Based on Evidence (Not Seat Time) 165
    Design Principle 5: Active Learning With Multiple Pathways and
        Varied Pacing 168
    Design Principle 6: Strategies to Embed Equity Into the System 171
    Design Principle 7: Rigorous, Common Expectations for Learning 175
    How to Use the Rubric Tool 178
    Final Thoughts 182

Appendix 183

    Competency-Based Learning School-Design Rubric: Principle 1 . . . . *184*
    Competency-Based Learning School-Design Rubric: Principle 2 . . . . *186*
    Competency-Based Learning School-Design Rubric: Principle 3 . . . . *188*
    Competency-Based Learning School-Design Rubric: Principle 4 . . . . *189*
    Competency-Based Learning School-Design Rubric: Principle 5 . . . . *191*
    Competency-Based Learning School-Design Rubric: Principle 6 . . . . *193*
    Competency-Based Learning School-Design Rubric: Principle 7 . . . . *195*
    Performance Assessment Template *197*
    Rubric Template *199*
    Performance Assessment and Unit Feedback Protocol *200*
    Student Work Calibration Protocol and Rubric Analysis Tool *202*
    Resource for Common Formative Assessments *204*
    Tool 1 in Hess's Rigor Matrices *205*
    Tool 2 in Hess's Rigor Matrices *208*
    Tool 3 in Hess's Rigor Matrices *211*
    Tool 4 in Hess's Rigor Matrices *214*
    CBL Weekly Lesson Planning Template *217*
    SMART Goal Team Planning Tool *218*
    Making Meaning of Assessment *219*

References and Resources 221

Index 227

ABOUT THE AUTHORS

Jonathan G. Vander Els, EdS, specializes in supporting teachers and administrators in schools and districts across the United States in developing, sustaining, and enhancing structures to support all learners. As a practitioner, Jonathan is able to blend his experience and expertise to meet educators where they are and assist them in developing practical next steps to ensure high levels of learning for students in their school.

Jonathan has consulted, coached, and presented at conferences and PLC at Work® Institutes throughout the United States on building highly effective professional learning communities (PLCs), implementing competency-based and personalized learning, and developing balanced and rigorous assessment systems. He is the coauthor of *Breaking With Tradition: The Shift to Competency-Based Learning in PLCs at Work®*, written with Brian Stack.

Jonathan serves as a project director for the New Hampshire Learning Initiative, overseeing and participating in the personalized and competency-based work throughout the State of New Hampshire. Formerly, Jonathan was principal of Memorial Elementary School in Sanborn Regional School District in Kingston, New Hampshire. Under his leadership, Memorial School became a nationally recognized model PLC and competency-based learning elementary environment.

Jonathan has an education specialist degree from the University of New Hampshire in educational administration and supervision, a master's in elementary education, and a bachelor's in history. Jonathan is currently enrolled at the University of New Hampshire in their PhD Educational Leadership and Policy strand, with a focus on competency-based learning. Jonathan lives with his wife and three children on the New Hampshire Seacoast.

To learn more about Jonathan's work, follow @jvanderels on Twitter.

Brian M. Stack, CAGS, is the principal of Sanborn Regional High School in Kingston, New Hampshire, and a professional development provider supporting educators in schools and districts around the world. Since 2010, Brian has been a member of the research, design, and implementation team for his school district's internationally recognized K–12 competency-based learning system. An educator since 2001, Brian was a high school mathematics teacher, curriculum director, high school administrator, and school board member in three different school districts in New Hampshire and Massachusetts. He has worked as a consultant and expert coach for a number of schools, school districts, and organizations engaged in personalized and competency-based learning across the United States and beyond. He is coauthor of *Breaking With Tradition: The Shift to Competency Based Learning in PLCs at Work*® with Jonathan Vander Els.

Brian is a member of the New Hampshire Association of School Principals. He received the 2017 New Hampshire Secondary School Principal of the Year award from that organization. In 2010 and again in 2013, he was recognized with the Outstanding Role Model award, also from that organization. He is a strong advocate of personalized learning, competency-based learning systems, and high school redesign for the 21st century. He has presented his education reform and redesign work in workshops and conferences across the United States.

Brian received his bachelor's degrees in mathematics and mathematics education from Boston University and a master's degree in education administration from the University of Massachusetts at Lowell. He received his CAGS in educational leadership from New England College. He lives with his wife, Erica, and their five children—Brady, Cameron, Liam, Owen, and Zoey—on the New Hampshire Seacoast.

To learn more about Brian's work, follow him at @bstackbu on Twitter.

To book Jonathan Vander Els or Brian Stack for professional development, contact Solution Tree at pd@SolutionTree.com.

FOREWORD

By Mike Mattos

At the risk of sounding boastful, I must admit that as a student, I was truly gifted at playing the game of school. My parents—not my teachers—set the ultimate goal of the competition. Their academic expectation was quite simple: "get Bs or better on your report card." Earning As was preferred, but Bs were acceptable. Scores on individual assignments did not matter as much, so long as my marks at the end of each grading term met this minimum standard. If I achieved this goal, I would stay in my parents' good graces and enjoy more freedom during my time outside of school. Every mark below a B, however, directly restricted my free time—and my happiness—until I rectified the situation. One C wasn't too bad. It usually meant an uncomfortable conversation, a pinch of guilt, and a clear directive that things better improve on the next report card. A grade of D included all the consequences of a C, plus my parents monitored my time after school more closely to ensure I was getting my work done. Multiple marks below a B and my life went into DEFCON 1—total lockdown. No car, no video games, and no hanging out with friends. With so much at stake, I set out each school year with one clear objective: earn at least a B in each subject while exerting the absolute minimum amount of effort possible.

While my parents set the goal, my teachers created the rules to the game. Most of them based the competition on the same currency—collecting these imaginary things called *points*. In all my years, I have never actually seen a point or held one in my hand. But each teacher had a way of knowing how many of these invisible units I had at any given time. The more points you collected by the end of the term, the higher the letter grade on your report card. The tricky part was that every teacher had their own rules regarding how to earn points, how to lose them, and how many it took to earn each letter grade. Within these ever-changing ground rules, I developed my true gift: gathering points. Through trial and error, I learned the following keys to success in school.

- Most teachers used a hundred-point scale. Because my parents expected at least a B, I could lose roughly two out of every ten points and still win. I say "roughly" because some teachers rounded up (a 79 percent to a B–), while other teachers had a crazy hard grading scale where an 80 percent was a C+.

- Generally speaking, I earned more points for shoddy work turned in on time than I did for exceptional work turned in late. That is because most teachers cared much more about punctuality than correctness. This was especially the case in high school, where I had many teachers who would not accept your work at all—and give you no points—for an assignment turned in even minutes late.

- Some teachers did not actually read most of what I submitted for homework, so I did not care what I wrote in their classes; I just turned something in to get the points. The mere appearance of effort was enough.

- I loved teachers who gave opportunities for extra credit. Bonus points! And better yet, earning extra points often had nothing to do with learning the course curriculum. Over the years, I received extra credit for such nonacademic tasks as attending school sporting events, bringing in boxes of tissues, buying items at the book fair, straightening desks after class, and merely raising my hand in class. The extra-credit bonanza was Thanksgiving—a true cornucopia of bonus points. My school held a yearly canned-food drive, and almost every teacher offered extra credit for bringing in nonperishable food items. This meant if I did poorly on a test during the second quarter, no worries! Bring in ten cans of soup and all was good.

- I also strived for partial credit. Leaving questions blank on a test killed your score—no points! If the test was multiple choice, you usually had a 25 percent chance at points if you were lucky that day. If it was a short-answer or essay test, and you were clueless after reading the question, the key was to try to earn partial credit. Write something—anything—using words from the question. Teachers rarely gave no points for trying. I also learned that for some teachers, if you did not know the answer but could write something that made them laugh, they would give you points and a smiley face.

- Some teachers graded on a curve, meaning the highest grade on a test or assignment set the top score of the scale, with all other grades ranked from there. I found grading on a curve to be a double-edged sword. If I was in a regular class, such as English 9, it worked in my favor. I could get a 72 percent on a unit test and often get a B. This is because I might not have learned 28 percent of the content, but luckily, most of my peers had learned even less. (When two people find themselves face-to-face with a wild bear, they don't have to be faster than the bear—just faster than the other person.) But when I started qualifying for honors classes, curving became a nightmare. I had a dear friend, Dolores, in most of my advanced coursework. She was an exceptional student and a true curve wrecker. When the teacher returned a graded assignment, the first thing my classmates and I asked was "What did Didi get?"

I became so adept at playing the game I was consistently on the school's honor roll, graduated high school ranked tenth in my class, and was voted "most likely to succeed" by my peers (along with Dolores, of course). Yet despite my point-gathering prowess, I intuitively felt it was a deeply unfair system. I remember asking my teachers questions like, "How can a 79 percent be a B in my English class, but the same score is a C+ in your class? It makes a big difference in my GPA." The answer was almost always the same: "That's how it is in the *real world*, Mike—you'd better get used to it."

As I trusted my teachers, I became resigned to the idea that they must be right, and that my proficiency at earning points was bound to serve me well in my adult endeavors. Over the next two decades, I earned a college degree and teaching credentials, joined the teaching ranks, replicated the same point-based grading practices in my classroom, and tried my best to help students succeed in the game of school.

I am now fifty-seven years old—an age that has earned me a lot of gray hair and a little bit of wisdom. While I have no doubt that my teachers had good intentions, I cannot say that their claim of "preparing me for the real world" has proven accurate. Here is what I have learned over the years, living in the real world.

- Points have virtually no value outside of school. Regardless of how many I earned in school, I could not redeem them for anything I needed in the real world—not a latte at the coffee shop, and certainly not money to pay the rent.

- In my job interviews, nobody asked me how many points I earned in a single class. Instead, the questions were about what I could actually do. My marketability and employment were based on the knowledge, skills, and behaviors that I could successfully demonstrate and apply to the job at hand.

- The real world cares much more about the quality of my work than about promptness. Don't get me wrong, deadlines are important, but think about this: When you hire a contractor, what do you care most about—that the job is done quickly and on time, or that the job is done well, if perhaps a bit behind schedule?

- My performance in the real world is not based on a hundred-point scale—it is judged against a standard of performance. For example, as a teacher, I had the required job responsibility of submitting grades for my students. Can you imagine me asking the principal, "What percentage of grades do I need to submit to pass my yearly evaluation? Can I turn in 80 percent of my student grades correctly? Will that be sufficient?" I am sure the principal would have chuckled and thought that I must be joking. I was expected to meet the standard for my job and successfully submit accurate grades for all my students.

- In the real world, my efforts are almost never graded on a curve. Instead, I am judged against a standard of performance. For example, my principal never told me the following after formally observing me: "I found that you did not engage your students well during the lesson, but fortunately for you, I observed Mr. Smith this week too, and he was even worse! So you are off the hook." He didn't share the opposite either: "Mr. Mattos, that was an incredible lesson—one of the best I have ever seen in all my years in education. But unfortunately for you, I also observed Ms. Anderson this week, and I found her methods to be just a bit more effective. Since I evaluate employees on a curve, I must score you lower." Rather, my efforts were evaluated against the standards of being a professional and effective educator, and not against my peers' average.

- I have never been allowed to bring in cans of soup in place of finishing job tasks.

Looking back at my years as a classroom teacher, I feel regret about most assessment and grading policies I implemented in my classroom. Yet I did not perpetuate these traditional practices out of malice or indifference. I did the best I knew at the time, believing the educational mythology that these practices would prepare my students for future success. Luckily, as a profession, we educators now know better ways to assess our students, using practices that more accurately measure what students can actually do. We know how to target their next steps in learning, motivate their efforts, and better prepare them for future success. That is the purpose and content of this outstanding book.

The authors, Jonathan G. Vander Els and Brian M. Stack, are globally recognized experts in the field of competency-based education. As site practitioners, they have worked on the front lines of education. Their recommendations are firmly grounded in research, refined through application, and validated in schools and districts across the United States. Because most teachers, like me, succeeded as students based on collecting points, creating a competency-based classroom will require educators to learn and apply new practices. To this end, I commend the authors for grounding this book in the Professional Learning Communities at Work® process (DuFour, DuFour, Eaker, Mattos, & Muhammad, 2021). When a school or district functions as a PLC, staff embrace that the key to increasing student learning is through the continuous, job-embedded learning of adults. This book is far more than some tips and activities to try in your class; it reveals a whole new way of thinking about how we instruct, assess, and motivate student learning.

I cannot promise you any points for reading this book, nor will you earn any extra credit. Likewise, applying what you have learned will not be graded on a curve, and there is no strict deadline to when you must complete this work. What I can promise is that the practices this book details can drastically improve your knowledge, skills, and competencies as an educator, which in turn will better prepare your students for future success. In the end, students should succeed in the game of life because of the methods we utilize in our classrooms, not in spite of them.

Reference

DuFour, R., DuFour, R., Eaker, R., Mattos, M., & Muhammad, A. (2021). *Revisiting Professional Learning Communities at Work: Proven insights for sustained, substantive school improvement* (2nd ed.). Bloomington, IN: Solution Tree Press.

INTRODUCTION

While we were educators in Professional Learning Communities at Work® (PLC at Work) schools, we attended many PLC at Work professional development events. At those events, Richard DuFour, the architect of the PLC process along with Robert Eaker, would often remind participants of the three foundational beliefs that must be at the center of our work:

1. We accept learning as the fundamental purpose of our school and therefore are willing to examine all practices in light of their impact on learning.

2. We are committed to working together to achieve our collective purpose. We cultivate a collaborative culture through the development of high-performing teams.

3. We assess our effectiveness on the basis of results rather than intentions. Individuals, teams, and schools seek relevant data and information and use that information to promote continuous improvement.

In this book, we will demonstrate how a competency-based learning system, when implemented at both the classroom and school levels, allows educators to realize Rick's vision for all educators.

Since 2010, competency-based learning systems have grown in popularity. According to Natalie Truong (2019), forty-nine of fifty states in the United States currently have policies around moving their state to a competency-based system of learning, recognizing the need to adequately prepare learners for a changing world. When students have *competency*, they have the ability to apply or transfer learning, rather than just the ability for rote memorization of facts. Critical, innovative thinking and problem solving are crucial components of competency-based learning.

A focus on capturing evidence of learning anywhere, anytime, is critical, whether in school with teachers, or at home (like during the COVID-19 pandemic) where learning can happen.

Much of the early work in competency-based learning grew from a nationally recognized 2011 definition published by the Aurora Institute (then known as the International Association of K–12 Online Learning [iNACOL]) based on input from over one hundred practitioners in the field. The 2011 definition provided a common understanding of the important features needed in competency-based systems to schools and school districts. This definition was the basis for our 2018 book, *Breaking With Tradition: The Shift to Competency-Based Learning in PLCs at Work*.

In 2019, the Aurora Institute released an updated definition that reflects the evolution of competency-based learning in the field as the model has grown. It includes new features that place an emphasis on equity, student agency, and different pathways for student success. In the updated definition, student agency is directly tied to learning pathways.

As our society has evolved and become more and more complex, so too have the needs society has placed on our schools. Now more than ever, we need schools that personalize learning to high degrees for all students at all grade levels.

About This Book

In this book, we unpack the competency-based learning approach. We walk educators through what they need to know about this philosophy in order to effectively implement the model in their classrooms and schools. We highlight the PLC process as the backbone organizational structure to advance the work and help educators and school leaders make student learning the center for all work that the school does.

The chapters that follow will also help school leaders understand how to sustain the change process to this model; how they can support educators in their efforts to develop the curriculum, instruction, and assessment frameworks that will guide them on their competency-based learning journey; and how the PLC process supports the overall work of a competency-based learning system.

Chapter 1 presents a framework and a foundation for the rest of the book by outlining Aurora Institute's seven-part definition for competency-based learning and showing how competency-based learning has permeated state educational policy across the United States and also influenced educational models across the globe.

Chapter 2 focuses on collaborative teaming, specifically on how the PLC at Work process, in which educators work collaboratively in recurring cycles of collective inquiry and action research to achieve better results for the students they serve, truly supports a competency-based learning model.

Chapter 3 focuses on the relationship between competencies, essential standards, and learning targets, and how they connect to the first of the four critical questions of a PLC: What is it we want students to know and be able to do? (DuFour, DuFour, Eaker, Many, & Mattos, 2016).

Chapter 4 focuses on assessment in a competency-based learning system, and how educators can ensure that students experience consistent, competency-friendly practices from classroom to classroom and teacher to teacher, and how those practices have to support the competency-education model.

Chapter 5 explores what effective, quality instruction looks like in a competency-based classroom. Specifically, readers will discover how instruction can be differentiated, focused, rigorous, and aligned with learning progressions that are based on essential standards and competencies.

Chapter 6 looks at structures for feedback, specifically the role of grading and reporting in a competency-based classroom. We focus on beginning with the end in mind, referencing the four pillars of a PLC at Work (DuFour et al., 2016) as a foundational component for the change process. Specifically, a collaboratively developed mission and vision are imperative, and the teacher leaders in a school play a critical role. It is through this lens that effective classroom grading and reporting strategies will be presented.

In chapter 7, we introduce a tool that educators can use to self-assess, reflect, and plot a course for their future work to advance competency-based learning in their classrooms and schools. Readers will be able to determine what their current reality is within each of the seven design principles of competency-based learning. This chapter will focus on how to move forward in each of these areas and provides specific next steps.

Embedded throughout the book are examples of competency-based learning in the field in various schools and districts. These Practitioner Perspectives offer the reader practical examples of how to turn theory into practice.

A Laser-Like Focus on Learning

As you undertake the work of transformation to competency-based learning, it may prove to be some of the hardest of your career, but you will find it to be some of the most rewarding because your school will truly become laser-focused on student learning. Students' engagement, ownership of learning, and career and college readiness will be the ultimate, tangible outcomes from this work.

CHAPTER 1

The Seven Components of the Competency-Based Classroom

On an early fall morning somewhere amidst the rolling hills and pastures of the bluegrass region in northern Kentucky, Jada, a middle school mathematics teacher, is making her way to the school for the first day of the new school year. As the sun starts to peak over the hills, a breeze begins to rustle the leaves and stir the horses on this crisp but otherwise typical September day. Across the community, the sunrise has prompted Jada's students to stir from their beds and start their before-school routines with their families. Parents are taking pictures of their nervous, but excited preteens as they wait for the bus, taking advantage of every opportunity to capture the moment for their social media feed. Unbeknownst to Jada's students and their parents, they are about to be part of one of the greatest transformations their community has seen. Jada and her team are committed to building their work on the vision of learning for all, whatever it takes. Jada is committed to implementing a competency-based learning structure in her classroom, and she is hopeful that her efforts and those of her teammates will become groundbreaking work that other colleagues and coworkers at her school will soon join her and her team in.

Like many who have been in her shoes, Jada is going to rely on her optimism, her dedication to her students, and a little bit of faith to help her reach her goal. With the right support and background, we have no doubt she will be successful in her efforts, and you could be, too.

Why Now?

Jada's decision to start a classroom transformation bodes the question, why now? We believe it is because her students cannot wait any longer. The world is changing at a fast and furious pace, and when it comes to creating deep and meaningful learning opportunities for students, we as educators must stay current. To understand just how quickly things change, consider the significance of the date June 29, 2007 (Chen, 2009). On this day, the first iPhone was made available to consumers worldwide. This product, a popular example of a first-generation smartphone, ushered in a new era for our world. In the coming months and years, every aspect of our lives began to evolve as over 1.4 billion of these devices were sold worldwide in the decade that followed. The smartphone became the ultimate multitasker, keeping notes, contacts, and calendar appointments; providing an alarm clock and a digital camera; and acting as a GPS device. It became nearly as powerful and useful as a desktop computer, and led to the rise of multibillion-dollar companies that didn't exist before the invention, such as the ride-sharing apps Uber and Lyft, or the food-delivery service Grubhub. We bank, shop, and socialize, all from this multitasker. When you really stop to think about it, there isn't a single aspect of our daily lives that hasn't been in some way impacted by the rise of the smartphone.

What else happened in June of 2007? High school seniors from the Class of 2021 were about to enter preschool, a milestone that for many would be their first experience in a formalized schooling environment. How many of these students entered a classroom where their teacher knew how best to prepare them for life in 2021, a world changed dramatically by the introduction of a pocket-sized piece of technology with a white apple on it? Was the teacher looking to future trends in society in order to determine which instructional strategies to employ or what skills to focus on? Did the teacher's school have a vision to support deep, meaningful, relevant learning in a way that would set these students up for future successes? Was the teacher skilled at predicting the future?

Predicting the future is never a perfect science. To quote fictitious character Dr. Emmett Brown from one of Brian's favorite movies, *Back to the Future III* (1990), "Your future is whatever you make it, so make it a good one." While we can't say for certain what the future will hold, we can look to trends to help us stay on the right path and influence our future choices. The advent of the iPhone was huge. It didn't take long for smartphones to get smaller, faster, and ultimately smarter. As they did, our appetite for real-time access to data and information drove an upsurge in smartphone applications that revolutionized how we interact with our world, how we act as consumers, and even how we socialize. With this evolution came a need for individuals to possess a deeper toolbox of higher-order thinking and problem-solving skills, and this has started to drive educators to a pursuit of how to help students grow and develop these skills, from ages as early as preschool.

Trends in Necessary Employability Skills and Dispositions

In 2019, we worked with a community to develop a portrait of a graduate document that would identify the important skills and traits that every graduate in the school must possess by graduation. This strategic-planning process involved soliciting feedback from a variety of stakeholder groups, including educators, students, parents, and business and community leaders. It was this last group that yielded some of the most profound results. When asked what skills and traits were most important for graduates, business and community leaders only talked about the critical need for what many of us call "soft skills" or "employability skills." No one mentioned content standards—not a single person.

This should come as no surprise to those who follow organizations such as the World Economic Forum, as they regularly track which skills are playing an increasing (as well as a decreasing) role in our society. According to a report by the World Economic Forum (2016):

> In many industries and countries, the most in-demand occupations or specialties did not exist ten or even five years ago, and the pace of change is set to accelerate. By one popular estimate, 65% of children entering primary school today will ultimately end up working in completely new job types that don't yet exist. In such a rapidly evolving employment landscape, the ability to anticipate and prepare for future skills requirements, job content and the aggregate effect on employment is increasingly critical for businesses, governments and individuals in order to fully seize the opportunities presented by these trends—and to mitigate undesirable outcomes. (p. 3)

According to Saadia Zahidi, Vasselina Ratcheva, Guillaume Hingel, and Sophie Brown (2020) of the World Economic Forum, the changes we are experiencing are a result of "growing income inequality, concerns about technology-driven displacement of jobs, and rising societal discord globally" (p. 3).

Employees need different skills today than they needed yesterday. The skills they will need for tomorrow will be different still. This need is creating downward pressure on schools to constantly evolve and adapt their focus in an effort to help all students be college and career ready.

To best illustrate this change, consider figure 1.1, a comparison from the World Economic Forum of the ten skills you will need to thrive (Gray, 2016; Zahidi et al., 2020).

2020		2025	
1	Complex Problem Solving	1	Analytical Thinking and Innovation
2	Critical Thinking	2	Active Learning and Learning Strategies
3	Creativity	3	Complex Problem Solving
4	People Management	4	Critical Thinking and Analysis
5	Coordinating With Others	5	Creativity, Originality, and Initiative
6	Emotional Intelligence	6	Leadership and Social Influence
7	Judgment and Decision Making	7	Technology Use, Monitoring, and Control
8	Service Orientation	8	Technology Design and Programming
9	Negotiation	9	Resilience, Stress Tolerance, and Flexibility
10	Cognitive Flexibility	10	Reasoning, Problem Solving, and Ideation

Sources: Gray, 2016; Zahidi et al., 2020.

Figure 1.1: Top ten skills—A comparison from 2020 to 2025.

What does this all mean for Jada and her students? Jada knows that she must find ways to better integrate these employability skills into her daily instruction. She must seek out opportunities to engage her students in deeper learning in an effort to help them transfer their knowledge and skills in new situations. Yet she knows the system that she works in doesn't allow her to do that effectively or consistently. She sees herself handcuffed by a system with policies and procedures that get in the way of this. She must free herself from it all if she is to better help her students succeed.

If all of this isn't reason enough to justify Jada's actions, consider this: even if we could have predicted the rise of technology and how it would ultimately change our society (including our schools), life can still throw us curveballs. For example, in 2020, the COVID-19 pandemic took educators around the globe by surprise, and seemingly overnight it upended our traditional educational models and systems. In mid-March 2020, Brian remembers having a normal Wednesday afternoon meeting with his high school staff. By the very next morning, however, he received a message from his superintendent alerting him to the fact that he was going to need to work quickly with his staff to identify a plan for remote learning because by the end of the week, it was likely the school would be forced to move to such a model for a short time. As everyone in education would soon discover, that "short time" went from days to weeks to months. Suddenly, Brian and his fellow educators had to find new ways to support students in their learning with the absence of an in-person experience. Everyone seemed to be on a steep learning curve to figure it out.

Brian's experience as an educator during the pandemic mirrors the experiences of many in classrooms across the globe. As educators reflect on lessons learned during the COVID-19 pandemic, new priorities have emerged about how best to support student learning. Suddenly, educational strategies and models that could deliver flexible, personalized, and student-centered approaches have taken on increased meaning for all.

It is not surprising why the years following the global pandemic that began in 2020 will likely be viewed as the time of the greatest advancement of the competency-based learning model in schools.

> **As educators reflect on lessons learned during the COVID-19 pandemic, new priorities have emerged about how best to support student learning. Suddenly, educational strategies and models that could deliver flexible, personalized, and student-centered approaches have taken on increased meaning for all.**

Competency-Based Learning: A Definition

Over the years, competency-based learning, defined as a comprehensive learner-centered system that allows students to move on upon demonstrated mastery of transferable learning objectives and skills, has become a prevalent phrase in education reform dialogues. It is born from the notion that elementary schools, secondary schools, and institutions of higher education cannot be confined by the limitations of "seat time" and the Carnegie Unit (credit hours) when organizing how students will progress through their learning. In competency-based learning, learning is organized by a student's ability to transfer knowledge and apply skills across content areas. Students refine their skills based on the feedback they receive through formative assessment and, when they are ready, demonstrate their understanding by performing thoughtfully developed summative assessment tasks.

> **In competency-based learning, learning is organized by a student's ability to transfer knowledge and apply skills across content areas. Students refine their skills based on the feedback they receive through formative assessment and, when they are ready, demonstrate their understanding by performing thoughtfully developed summative assessment tasks.**

Chris Sturgis (2015) provides one of the first clear and concise definitions for competency-based learning, and it influenced our book *Breaking With Tradition: The Shift to Competency-Based Learning in PLCs at Work* (Stack & Vander Els, 2018).

According to Sturgis (2015), in competency-based learning:

- Students advance upon demonstrated mastery
- Competencies include explicit, measurable, transferable learning objectives that empower students
- Assessment is meaningful and offers a positive learning experience for students
- Students receive timely, differentiated support based on their individual learning needs
- Learning outcomes emphasize competencies that include application and creation of knowledge, along with the development of important skills and dispositions (p. 8)

These traits provide a foundation for schools that were starting to implement early competency-based models. Since this time, however, we have learned quite a bit as a profession as the movement has grown. Since 2010, competency-based learning became one of the fastest growing education reform initiatives of the decade. The Aurora Institute has tracked this progress over time by studying state-adopted policies and procedures that support the model. Consider figure 1.2 from Aurora Institute (Truong, 2019), a 2012 map of the United States denoting which states had committed to policies that support competency education that were considered to be emerging, developing, or advanced.

In 2012, Aurora Institute classified just four states (Maine, New Hampshire, Iowa, and Oregon) as having advanced policies in place to support competency-based learning systems, while twenty-four states had yet to adopt any policies in this area. Advanced states received this rating due to "comprehensive policy alignment" or because the state has "established an active state role to build educator capacity in local school systems for competency education" (Truong, 2019). Similarly, a developing state "has open state policy flexibility for school districts to transition to competency education" (Truong, 2019). Finally, an emerging state has "limited state policy flexibility and, usually, the state requires authorization for school systems to shift to competency-based education" (Truong, 2019).

Fast forward to 2019, and a similar Aurora Institute review of state policies identified significant movement in the field in nearly every state. Consider figure 1.3 (page 12) from Aurora Institute (Truong, 2019), a 2019 revised map of the United States,

The Seven Components of the Competency-Based Classroom   11

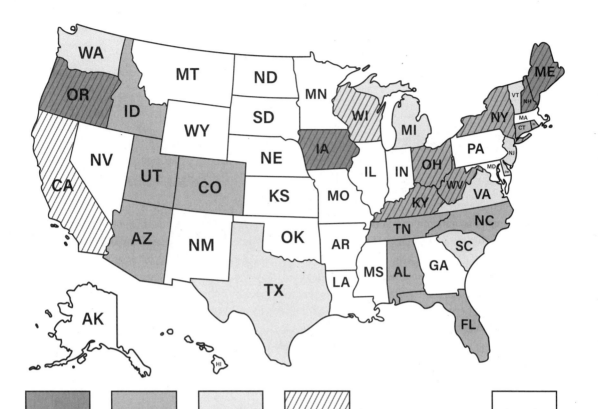

Advanced States

Those states with clear policies that are moving toward proficiency-based; more than just an option

Developing States

Those states with pilots of competency education, credit flexibility policies, or advanced next gen policies for equivalents to seat time

Emerging States

Those states with waivers, task forces

ILN States

Since its inception, the Innovation Lab Network (ILN) engaged schools, districts, and state education agencies working to identify through local efforts new designs for public education that empower each student to thrive as a productive learner, worker, and citizen. The state's responsibility is to establish conditions in which innovation can flourish and to develop capacity to sustain and scale what works through policy. The Council of Chief State School Officers (CCSSO) facilitates this network of states to support programmatic, policy, and structure design work within each participating state and across the network.

No Policies in Competency Education

States with seat time and no competency education policies

Source: Aurora Institute (Truong, 2019). Adapted with permission.

Figure 1.2: 2012—A snapshot of competency-based learning policy across the United States.

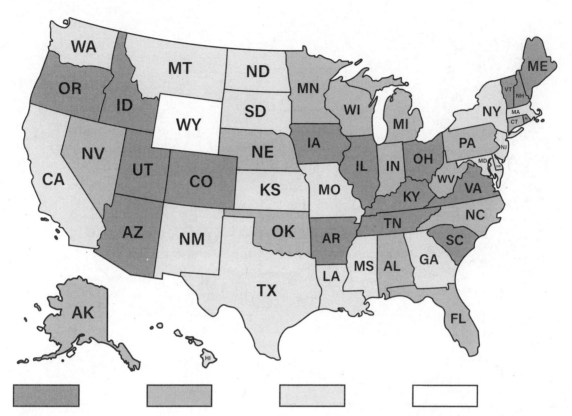

Advanced States

Those states with comprehensive policy alignment and/or an active state role to build capacity in local school systems for competency education

Developing States

Those states with open state policy flexibility for local school systems to transition to competency education

Emerging States

Those states with limited flexibility in state policy—usually requiring authorization from the state—for local school systems to shift to competency education, for exploratory initiatives and task forces, and/or minimal state activity to build local capacity

No Policies in Competency Education

States with no state-level activity and enabling policies for competency education. Significant policy barriers may exist, such as inflexible seat time restrictions

Source: Aurora Institute (Truong, 2019). Adapted with permission.

Figure 1.3: 2019—A snapshot of K–12 competency-based learning state policy across the United States.

denoting which states have committed to policies that support competency education that are rated to be emerging, developing, or advanced.

From 2012 to 2019, the number of advanced states increased from three to seventeen. Another fourteen moved into the developing category. Most notably, nearly every state made some growth in the area of policy development to support competency-based learning models. State-by-state progress with policy development was motivated primarily by an increased need for educational equity for all students. For many schools, the need for "all means all" policies continues to increase, looking to better address gaps experienced by students of color, students with disabilities, economically disadvantaged students, and other disadvantaged populations. Since 2012, the field of education has grown its capacity to understand and react to this growing need.

As competency-based learning has expanded across the United States, a parallel shift has taken root in several countries across the globe. A study of these international shifts (Bristow & Patrick, 2014) finds:

- Finland has initiated comprehensive education reform over the past forty years. High scores across most PISA exam cycles include unparalleled equity in performance, and its systemic approach to greater individualization in the tenth through twelfth grades can inform our thinking about high school redesign.
- British Columbia showcases the policy language of competency and personalization, innovates with pedagogical architecture, and enables student choice in the classroom through a flexible core curriculum.
- New Zealand has well-articulated competency frameworks, features the most autonomous schools in the OECD and strongly supports self-evaluation for principals, teachers, and even students.
- Scotland has been phasing in most components of competency education at the policy level for more than eleven years. National standards encourage teacher autonomy, formative assessment is the norm, and classroom supports focus on the whole child rather than solely academic performance.

According to the National Equity Project (n.d.), educational equity happens when "each child receives what he or she needs to develop to his or her full academic and social potential." The organization goes on to note the following.

> Working toward equity in schools involves:
> - Ensuring equally high outcomes for all participants in our educational system; removing the predictability of success or failure that currently correlates with any social or cultural factor;

> Interrupting inequitable practices, examining biases, and creating inclusive multicultural school environments for adults and children; and

> Discovering and cultivating the unique gifts, talents, and interests that every human possesses.

This definition is a call to action to schools to examine not only their culture for learning, but the ways in which they ensure high levels of rigor and understanding for all and how they work to support students individually to meet this high bar. Ultimately, this culminated in the need for revisions to the founding principles of competency education. The Aurora Institute spearheaded this work in 2018, releasing their results one year later. According to Levine and Patrick (2019), the following is a revised definition for competency-based learning that outlines seven design principles.

1. Students are empowered daily to make important decisions about their learning experiences, how they will create and apply knowledge, and how they will demonstrate their learning.

2. Assessment is a meaningful, positive, and empowering learning experience for students that yields timely, relevant, and actionable evidence.

3. Students receive timely, differentiated support based upon their individual learning needs.

4. Students progress based on evidence of mastery, not seat time.

5. Students learn actively using different pathways and varied pacing.

6. Strategies to ensure equity for all students are embedded in the culture, structure, and pedagogy of schools and education systems.

7. Rigorous, common expectations for learning (knowledge, skills, and dispositions) are explicit, transparent, measurable, and transferable.

Levine and Patrick (2019) call on educators to find ways to implement all seven design principles in their classrooms and schools. They stress that strong implementation requires "policies, pedagogy, structures, and culture that support every student in developing essential knowledge, skills, and dispositions." They make it clear that competency-based learning is a radical philosophical shift from a traditional system, one that is driven by "the equity-seeking need to transform our educational system so all students can and will learn through full engagement and support and through authentic, rigorous learning experiences inside and outside the classroom."

The PLC and Competency-Based Learning Connection

Equity is a fundamental driver for the move to competency-based learning, and it is for this reason that such a move is best supported in a school that functions as a PLC. Educators within PLCs believe that *all students can learn*; PLCs shift the focus from teaching to learning. Educators in a PLC believe in three big ideas (DuFour et al., 2016).

1. **A focus on learning:** The purpose of our school is to ensure all students learn at high levels.

2. **A collaborative culture and collective responsibility:** Helping all students learn requires a collaborative and collective effort.

3. **A results orientation:** To assess our effectiveness in helping all students learn we must focus on results—evidence of student learning—and use results to inform and improve professional practice and respond to students who need intervention or enrichment.

It is through this lens of having a focus on learning, a collaborative culture and collective responsibility, and a focus on results that PLCs can best implement and support the seven design principles of competency-based learning. Competency-based learning provides the framework for educators in a PLC to realize equity for all students. In PLCs, educators have the flexibility to develop learning environments around the varying needs of their students. Student growth is closely monitored, and students are provided with multiple pathways and opportunities to produce evidence to demonstrate their learning. The deliberate and calibrated efforts by all educators in a competency-based school, combined with an open and transparent communication of both learning expectations and assessment results, ultimately leads to the creation of a schoolwide culture of learning and accountability that exists in highly effective PLCs.

Equity, Social Justice, and Competency-Based Learning

Equity also leads to an increased focus on matters of social justice, leading to classrooms where teaching and learning can be designed to increase the understanding of differences and their value to a respectful and civil society. This fosters an environment that allows students to address stereotyping, bias, and all forms of discrimination.

Tonya Howell, social and emotional learning integration specialist, and Damarr Smith, competency-based education senior program manager from the Chicago Public School System share how competency-based learning, and a focus on social-emotional learning and performance assessment with a lens toward social justice have been a catalyst for change in their large, urban district.

> **Practitioner Perspective**
> **Tonya Howell, Social and Emotional Learning Integration Specialist, and Damarr Smith, Competency-Based Education Senior Program Manager, Chicago Public Schools**
>
> Chicago Public Schools (CPS) began its journey to competency-based education (CBE) in July of 2016 when Illinois passed the Postsecondary Workforce Readiness Act allowing districts to implement the practice. By 2017, CPS became one of the first districts to join the state pilot, aiming to better prepare students for college and careers by emphasizing academic and metacognitive skills.
>
> The CPS pilot brought together a unique collection of neighborhood schools, selective enrollment schools, and alternative and transitional high schools from different city areas. Establishing aligned goals, expectations, frameworks, and commonalities for the group was critical, but one consistent thread stood out from the inception of the pilot: each school viewed the intentional development of foundational skills as an essential reason for transitioning to competency-based learning.
>
> After the first year of implementation, there was a resounding consensus across the pilot schools that targeted support was necessary to aid the collaborative in infusing metacognitive skills into each school's environment and instruction.
>
> Since then, ten CPS high schools within the pilot have received that much-desired targeted support for implementing essential competency-based education components, integrating social and emotional learning into their curricula and daily practices, and designing performance-based assessments focused on student voice and choice. Ultimately, the CBE schools in Chicago aim to provide the rigorous, student-centered instruction necessary to ensure students have the academic skills and the life skills needed for success in school, college, career, and civic life. The aim is to build future leaders who will positively impact their communities and the world.
>
> The competency-based schools in Chicago are diverse in terms of student population and needs. By allowing students to work at their own pace and follow individualized learning pathways with the proper interventions and supports in place, issues around equity and access can be addressed and tackled. Chicago's competency-based schools regularly collaborate to share and codify best practices. They problem solve to identify and implement responsive strategies to meet school, staff, student, and family needs. They utilize an adaptive pacing tool (see figure 1.4) that uses the following guiding principles as the foundation of the work: (1) learning environment, (2) clear, shared learning outcomes, (3) multiple learning pathways, (4) student agency, (5) performance-based assessment, (6) practice and feedback, and (7) supports, intervention, and extension.

The Seven Components of the Competency-Based Classroom

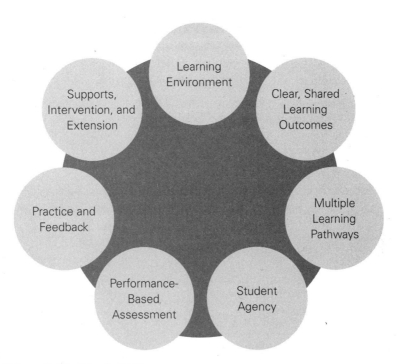

Source: *Chicago Public Schools, 2019.*

Figure 1.4: CPS adaptive pacing model.

Using the common language from the adaptive pacing tool has allowed for productive and meaningful discussions among school leaders that help to push practice and promote academic growth and overall student success. Another common thread in the work in Chicago falls under the umbrella of social and emotional learning. Through the lens of social-emotional learning, schools emphasize adaptive or nonacademic competencies of agency, collaboration, adaptability and flexibility, and leadership, and support students to develop healthy identities and promote a collective mindset to have a positive impact on their school and larger communities.

One way that CPS incorporates the adaptive competencies into teachers' regular practice is through supporting teachers with the development of performance-based assessments grounded in social-emotional learning, the adaptive competencies, and social justice to bring students' lives into the classroom and create engaging, meaningful learning experiences that have real-world applications and implications. Some teachers in Chicago tasked students with presenting change projects to their school's administrators to promote attending to the mental health of students at the school, which included research and innovative solutions to real-world problems. Others designed multidisciplinary art projects that connected to students' identities and personal struggles as well as to work from other artists who use self-expression as a form of healing and as a creative outlet. Students often choose to learn about topics that affect their communities and bring awareness to social issues that matter to them. Allowing for student choice and for students to share their perspectives and experiences with others increases engagement and gives so much

> more meaning to the final projects that require hard work, perseverance, creativity, and innovation. Through performance-based assessment, teachers can offer support and provide feedback on the academic standards or competencies necessary for success in a particular course of study and the adaptive competencies that we know are important for life beyond the classroom. CPS can ensure students leave its schools with the skills needed to advocate for themselves and others, collaborate and communicate effectively, adapt to changes or respond to constructive feedback productively, and take the initiative or lead when they are so inspired or called to take action. The goal is to ensure students have a seat at the table and that their voices are informed and heard.
>
> In CPS, we have seen that by connecting academics to the social-emotional learning, adaptive competencies, and social justice aspects of the work, we can bring out the excellence in staff, students, and families that will help make this world a better place. After all, isn't it our role as educators to uplift and empower young people to take charge ethically and responsibly in this fast-paced and ever-changing world? Competency-based education, focusing on the whole child, rigorous learning targets, 21st-century or foundational skills, social justice, and social and emotional learning, allows students to sit in the driver's seat of their educational journey, take charge of their learning, and pursue their passions.
>
> (T. Howell, D. Smith, personal communication, July 14, 2021)

Evolving Policy

According to ExcelinEd and EducationCounsel (2017):

> Effective implementation of competency-based education demands attention to an intricate array of education policies, practices and systems at the federal, state and local levels. Some decisions can be anticipated in advance (e.g., the need for flexibility from time-based credits and requirements) while others will only become apparent during implementation (e.g., challenges logging competency-based credits into time-based databases and IT systems). (p. 5)

The best thing that states can do (and have done) is to create opportunities for innovation—a way that schools and school districts can explore and adopt various competency-based models that work within the confines of the state laws, policies, and procedures. According to ExcelinEd and EducationCounsel (2017), "Innovation programs and pilots provide a reasonable and actionable first step for policymakers. They also provide an important opportunity to work through challenging issues and strike an appropriate balance of state and local responsibilities" (p. 5).

Many states in the United States have begun or advanced their work in competency education by way of an innovative program or project that falls into the category of one or more of the following six strategies.

1. Policy language that provides flexibility from time-based systems

2. Policy language that supports the transition to competency-based diplomas
3. Policies that recognize anytime, anywhere learning
4. Policies that allow for the acceptance of competency-based diplomas and credits by higher education institutions
5. State assessment systems that support competency-based education
6. Accountability systems that have been evolved to support competency-based learning

One of the earliest and most notable innovative projects to advance competency-based learning on a national scale first happened in New Hampshire and is known as Performance Assessment of Competency Education (PACE). The PACE pilot received a waiver from the U.S. Department of Education starting in the 2014–2015 school year, with four school districts part of the initial work. PACE is considered to be an innovative program because it is based on a performance assessment accountability system where performance tasks are created collaboratively by PACE school classroom teachers, administered to students as part of their regular classroom assessments, and then scored at both the local and state levels. These tasks are used to help determine student proficiency in some federally required grades and subjects instead of a more traditional achievement test. Evans (2019) studied PACE scores in the four pilot districts relative to peer districts that used traditional testing measures and concluded, "Findings suggest that students in PACE schools tend to exhibit small positive effects on the grades 8 and 11 state achievement tests in both subjects in comparison to students attending non-PACE comparison schools." This research supports with empirical evidence efforts being made by other states to implement similar innovative programs and strategies.

Innovative policy changes have taken different paths. By 2018, states like New Hampshire, Michigan, Oregon, and Utah had instituted policies that allow for flexibility from time-based systems. During that same time period, states like Vermont, Michigan, and Maine had enacted state policies to support competency-based diplomas. Louisiana and Florida started anytime, anywhere pilot schools. Florida, New Hampshire, and Virginia instituted state assessment systems that support the work of competency-based learning. Idaho and Ohio each had started innovation pilots focused on competency-based learning. Also in that same time period, Colorado and Georgia had started general innovation programs. These states continue to advance their work, and many more states have enacted similar programs since this time.

In neighboring Canada, competency statements have become a foundational structure of many provincial curriculum documents. In British Columbia, for example, the Ministry of Education (2016) defines its three core competencies of communication, thinking, and personal/social as "sets of intellectual, personal, and social and emotional proficiencies that all students need in order to engage in deep, lifelong learning." The Ministry goes on to state that they are "central to British Columbia's K–12 curriculum and assessment system and directly support students in their growth as educated citizens." The British Columbia core competencies are supported by smaller subcompetencies. Each subcompetency is made up of a handful of facets (unique and interrelated components), six profiles (descriptors of students' subcompetency development), and illustrations (examples of how students demonstrate their learning). What makes the British Columbia model stand out is the emphasis it places on student reflection on their growth and development of their learning throughout the learning process, by way of the profiles and their connections to the facets.

In the United States, policy work in the state of Virginia has opened doors for the work to flourish in its schools. Beth Blankenship, English teacher, and Elizabeth Dean, instructional coach, have been a part of their school's transformation and share how Madison High School in Fairfax, Virginia, got started.

Practitioner Perspective
Beth Blankenship and Elizabeth Dean, Madison High School, Fairfax County, Virginia

Our high school's journey to build a more equitable system for our students started in 2016. The discussion of fair grades was a trending issue in 2016 among our district office leadership, and after a two-year countywide committee process resulted in minor policy changes, there was little inspiration to make any grading changes at all. It wasn't until our school's leadership council decided to look closely at our current grading system from the perspective of students when inspiration to change arrived. Examining the system from the student perspective revealed many of the inaccuracies and inequities of our traditional approach to grading. The leadership council established a three-year goal to improve our system by transitioning from the 100 point scale to the 4.0 scale. Learning more about fair, accurate, and equitable grading practices was a part of these early years in our journey. In order to learn more about grading for equity, standards-based grading, and the 4.0 scale, we hosted teacher-led book groups, attended online courses, and reached out to other schools to learn from their experiences. Throughout our journey we had many "Aha!" moments.

One of our most important "Aha!" moments occurred at the iNACOL (now Aurora Institute) Conference in the fall of 2019 where we learned more about implementing competency-based grading at a preconference session our building leadership team all attended together. At that session, we realized two important ideas: grading for equity could be best enacted through competency-based learning, and that our school staff, while they had been developing a 4.0 scale, did not have a shared, basic understanding of the philosophical underpinnings of competency-based learning and assessment. We realized that if we wanted to truly be grading for equity, we needed to continue to learn together and get support in the process.

And then 2020 happened. To say that the situation was challenging is an understatement. In the midst of all the change, the focus on equity became the lens through which we saw the many problems of our school's grading, teaching, and assessment system. The moment demanded action. Even though a lot of change was happening each day, our administration knew that in order to better enact the 4.0 scale and a rolling gradebook throughout our school in the 2020–2021 school year, we needed more discussion and training around competency-based grading and assessment.

In the summer of 2020, our administrative and coaching staff read and discussed *Breaking With Tradition* (Stack & Vander Els, 2018). The text helped us develop a shared understanding of the what of competency-based learning and grading and how it intersected with the shifts we were already attempting. Throughout that summer, we planned an introduction to competency-based learning presentation for our entire staff at the beginning of the school year. While planning for that presentation, our discussions as an administrative team focused on identifying and naming the why of the competency-based system, to include assessment, grading, and learning. Through those discussions, we collectively noticed that the why was directly tied to our grading for equity work; everything was connected. Competency-based learning and assessment could ensure that every student is valued for their abilities, strengths, and developing understanding, while attending to each student's learning needs and interests as a learner. This pushed us to think beyond the formal gradebook process of the rolling gradebook, and beyond the 4.0 numbering system, and reminded us to focus on the most important element of learning: the student's needs and developing understanding.

As the 2020–2021 school year unfolded, we had many solitary and online collective "Aha!" moments that helped our staff and students experience the benefits of competency-based learning. Through it all, we deliberately continued to return to the why of student-centered learning and equity as the reason for our shift to competency-based learning and assessment. While we can honestly report that we do not have the perfect competency-based learning system in place at our school, or that every single staff member at our high school has a deep understanding of how to implement it with fidelity (yet!), we do have a shared mission for our daily work: we believe in equity and the value of each student's voice and learning journey. That belief and our larger community of competency-based learners with whom we network, inspire us every day to continue our journey toward competency-based learning for equity.

(B. Blankenship and E. Dean, personal communication, July 12, 2021)

Anytime, Anywhere Learning

Of all the design principles for competency-based learning, none are more famous (or infamous) than the notion of anytime, anywhere learning. When the model first came on the scene in the early 2000s, it was justified as a way to move away from the outdated Carnegie Unit (seat time) where learning was measured by the amount of time a student spent in a classroom in favor of a model based on what students actually learned (competencies). Early proponents saw such a system as more authentic and better calibrated to student achievement. Opponents at the time worried that it would create a culture whereby students would skip steps, take shortcuts, and look to "test out" of certain learning situations and courses. For many years, the idea that students could move at their own pace through curriculum or a course sequence was one that many schools feared to take on. Doing so would disrupt many of their operational models in their school, including how they build their calendar, schedule classes, and use their staffing resources. For the first few years, "move when ready" models stayed well under the radar, but this just provided time for the model to be perfected by those bold enough to take it on.

Since 2010, a variety of anytime, anywhere flexible models have found their way into mainstream schools. Following are some examples.

Online Self-Paced Schools and Programs

Schools such as the Florida Virtual School (FLVS) and the Virtual Learning Academy Charter School (VLACS) in New Hampshire have turned the educational model on its head by offering self-paced courses to students at all grade levels, facilitated by real teachers who use a scripted curriculum that is built by the school in advance. Typical teacher teaching loads mirror what they would be in traditional schools in terms of number of students managed and number of grade levels or courses taught, but teachers do not have to spend their time developing curriculum and building lesson plans. Rather, they spend their time providing reteaching and intervention to students as they work, and provide a critical communication link between the student, school, and home. Schools like FLVS and VLACS market themselves as flexible, competency-based approaches that allow students to learn anytime, in any place, at their own pace. Many schools allow students to pursue programs such as these and then transfer them into their school courses of study. This ability for students to mix and match increases scheduling opportunities and allows students to pursue passions in areas that the school may not have the capacity to offer. Some students never leave the online environment and are able to finish their programs completely through schools like FLVS and VLACS.

Extended Learning Opportunities

In many competency-based schools, students have the ability to earn credit for learning experiences that happen outside of the classroom. For example, in the state of New Hampshire in the United States, these are categorized as extended learning opportunities (ELOs). ELOs are often developed collaboratively by a student and a teacher so that a student can pursue a personalized experience. A business or community partner enters into an agreement to host the student for a period of time and is given a series of management or supervision tasks with the student, most commonly referred to as an internship. The school oversees and assesses the student's progress, and, ultimately, whether or not the student was able to meet the competencies identified at the start for the experience. Similarly, a student may wish to pursue a passion project on their own time. For example, a student may wish to engage in a specific long-term scientific study that is outside of the scope of a school science course. They could be matched up with a science teacher at the school or perhaps a lab scientist from a local college or university. Again, in this ELO experience, the student develops a set of competencies at the beginning and work toward reaching proficiency by the end of the experience. Since every ELO experience is unique, ELOs are often considered to be independent of time and are instead self-paced.

At the Singapore American School, extended learning opportunities are offered through the school's Catalyst Project. There, students have the flexibility to select a project in any field of interest with the support of their teachers. Students are assessed according to the school's competencies in the areas of character, collaboration, communication, creativity and innovation, critical thinking, cultural competence, and self-awareness. They do this by designing their own learning experience. Teachers provide guidance to students, but ultimately, the students are the drivers for their work. They are encouraged to network and collaborate with industry experts and other outside partners. These individuals provide a high level of mentorship to students to give them meaning, purpose, and insight throughout their learning process. There are commonalities in the examples from the United States and Singapore:

- The schools have a way to recognize and award credit for learning that takes place outside of the classroom.
- Students are encouraged to engage in learning that they are passionate about.
- Learning is connected to multiple competencies.
- Outside individuals play a critical mentorship role for students throughout their learning journeys.

Blended or Hybrid Learning

The COVID-19 pandemic brought blended learning or hybrid learning to the forefront. With these types of courses, students have access to a classroom teacher (either in person or remotely) as they work through a self-paced curriculum. In a hybrid approach, the teacher provides just-in-time-learning instruction in short bursts on a regular basis to students as they work through the curriculum. Formative assessment is conducted regularly so that the teacher is aware of what supports the student needs to help them be successful. In some cases, students are actually grouped in a learning community with access to multiple teachers, and teachers work collaboratively to group students to provide supports and instruction based on need.

Blended or hybrid learning models like these were relatively rare in schools until the COVID-19 pandemic, which forced schools into using these models without teachers having the necessary experience or training. Such professional learning had to come (and will continue to come) later as schools realized the importance of having blended and hybrid options that allow students to move flexibly in and out of the classroom. Such models dovetail well with the notion of a move-when-ready system.

Levine and Patrick (2019) caution schools looking to embed move-when-ready models from compromising rigor. They note that a common misconception by educators looking to move to such a model is to adopt a "checklist mentality" (p. 7) whereby students are passed through a series of learning activities that lack challenge and rigor. Competency-based learning "emphasizes deeper, contextualized, and interconnected learning and diverse assessments that include performance-based demonstrations of mastery" (p.7). When implemented with an appropriate understanding of rigor and how to hold all students accountable to high standards, move-when-ready models can provide effective ways to help the school provide flexibility in their efforts to help every student succeed in a competency-based system.

Every transformation has to start with an idea and someone to lead the charge. For Jada, her passion is with a new educational model that guarantees a deep and rigorous educational experience for all of her students. Jada is committed to starting her transformation for her students and her community, and she is hopeful that by taking a big risk to step out of her comfort zone, others will follow. When it comes time for action, will you be ready to answer the call? If she and her team can do it, so can you.

Reflection Questions

Consider these questions with your team.

1. The reasons educators are drawn to competency-based learning models varies from school to school. What is your team's why for engaging in this work?

2. Employability skills and dispositions are critical to today's employers. What do you see as the most important skills and dispositions students must master in order to be successful in tomorrow's global economy? How would you assess them?

3. There are seven design principles for competency-based learning. Which one or ones do you see as a priority for your team's work and why? Which will be the hardest for you to implement and why?

4. Policies on competency-based learning vary from place to place. What are the policies in your state or province, and how will they help you advance competency-based learning with your team?

5. Anytime, anywhere learning plays an important role in the competency-based learning model. What are some ways that students have the opportunity to learn anytime, anywhere in your classroom or school?

CHAPTER 2

Collaborative Teams: The Structures That Support Competency-Based Learning

A school in which teachers work in isolation will never accomplish alone what they may be able to do if they purposefully work together. Teachers working collaboratively is what allows a school to ultimately attain its vision. The processes for collaborative teaming are of paramount importance in ultimately meeting the needs of *all* students in a school. DuFour and his colleagues (2016) define a PLC as "an ongoing process in which educators work collaboratively in recurring cycles of collective inquiry and action research to achieve better results for the students they serve" (p. 10). PLC isn't what you *do*, it's who you *are*. The PLC process is the single best support structure that districts and schools need to have in place to successfully implement competency-based learning. When implemented correctly, the PLC process cultivates teacher leaders who become collectively responsible and mutually accountable for the learning for all students in the entire school.

> The PLC process is the single best support structure that districts and schools need to have in place to successfully implement competency-based learning. When implemented correctly, the PLC process cultivates teacher leaders who become collectively responsible and mutually accountable for the learning for all students in the entire school.

For Jada and her team, their work as a collaborative team with a singular focus aimed at supporting their students' attainment of high levels of learning allows them to learn together, make mistakes together, and ultimately grow together. Each member of the team recognizes that they would not be able to accomplish individually what they are able to accomplish as a team, and this recognition has been instrumental in their continued work within their PLC.

Teachers become supports for each other, and teacher teams become an integral part of both the decision-making process and instructional leadership for competency-based learning in the school. The work of the school and the collaborative teams within it is transparent. Student learning, a collaborative culture, and constant reflection and refinement become the norm, and these are the levers that will affect change through the work of the PLC.

A systems change on the magnitude of shifting to competency-based learning requires hard work and the dedication of the entire staff. It also requires a clear vision and a deep understanding of why the change is necessary. It is imperative to have the foundational structures in place to allow for this meaningful dialogue and subsequent action to occur, for collective decisions to be made, and for the requisite collaboration to occur within the school. Again, the PLC process is the vehicle for this change to a competency-based system.

As we argue in *Breaking With Tradition* (Stack & Vander Els, 2018), if high levels of learning for all learners is the *why* and competency-based learning is the *what*, then PLCs are the *how*. There are critical structures within PLCs that must exist for highly effective collaboration to achieve its intended results. Either prior to, or in conjunction with, delving into these structural components, the first step for a school is to develop a guiding coalition, a team comprised of teachers and administrators that acts collaboratively to affect change within the school. Some schools refer to this as "team leaders" or a "building leadership team" (BLT).

Often when educators think of leaders, they think of administrators—superintendents, principals, assistant principals. Anthony Muhammad and Louis Cruz (2019) define leadership as "a set of actions that positively shape the climate and culture of the working environment" (p. 2). When we speak of leaders and leadership teams in this book, we do not refer to traditional types of leaders only; we refer to an environment like the one James Burns (1978) envisions, one in which "leaders and [their perceived] followers [are] rais[ing] one another to higher levels of motivation and morality" (p. 20). This collective group of leaders works together to transform their school, resulting in everyone within the school seeing themselves as a leader, regardless of their role in the school.

In this chapter, we explore how the key structures in the PLC process, when implemented with fidelity, act as guardrails for the competency-based learning work in your school and within collaborative teams. We explain how effective teaming processes, ones in which educators engage together collaboratively in PLCs, in recurring cycles of collective inquiry and action research to achieve better results for the students they serve (DuFour et al., 2016), are *critical* for establishing a highly functioning competency-based system of learning.

Shared Leadership

John Kotter (2012) explains that "because major change is so difficult to accomplish, a powerful force is required to sustain the process" (p. 53). Therefore, there must be a clear structure of shared leadership. Richard Elmore (2000), a former professor of educational leadership at Harvard University, proffers a vision for "distributed leadership" that outlines the following.

> In a knowledge-intensive enterprise like teaching and learning, there is no way to perform the complex tasks involved without distributing the responsibility for leadership and creating a common culture that makes this distributed leadership coherent. It is the "glue" of a common task or goal—improvement of instruction—and a common set of values for how to approach that task that keep distributed leadership from becoming another version of loose coupling. (p. 5)

Recognizing that teacher leadership, as part of a shared leadership model, is critical in the school-improvement process, administrators and teachers must coalesce and begin to determine the direction of the school together. Elmore (2000) provides clarity on the why and purpose of a shared leadership model, and we believe it is critical to ensure that everyone who is part of the team clearly understands the following five key components.

1. The purpose of leadership is to improve practice and performance.
2. Improvement requires continuous learning, both by individuals and groups.
3. Leaders lead by exemplifying the values and behavior they want others to adopt.
4. People cooperate with one another in achieving their goals when they recognize other people's expertise.
5. Leaders are responsible for helping to make possible what they are requiring others to do.

We believe that the *powerful force* Kotter (2000) describes is a school's guiding coalition. The guiding coalition, the representative body of teachers and leaders from across the school, is the driver for the collaborative teams, the engine that drives the school. DuFour and his colleagues (2016) note that "no one person will have the energy, expertise, and influence to lead a complex change process" (p. 27). In fact, it is critical that change is a collective enterprise. In *Leading With Learning*, Wilhoit, Pittenger and Rickbaugh (2016) state, "Leadership is not the sole responsibility of a single individual. Leadership is the work of a team that possesses complementary knowledge, skills, dispositions, and contextual knowledge" (p. 9). The guiding coalition is this team.

The development of the guiding coalition is very important. There must be a high level of trust, which will develop over time, so it is critical that the right people are part of this team. There are different ways that schools have gone about determining the makeup of their guiding coalition, with some school leaders choosing to hold interviews, others going directly to key teachers, and others allowing teams to decide. (This last way might be reserved for schools that are further along in the PLC process.) Regardless of how membership is determined, Kotter (2012) identifies four key considerations when identifying potential members of the guiding coalition. Do potential members possess the following characteristics?

1. **Positional power:** These teachers are considered the movers or key players on their team or within the school.

2. **Expertise:** These teachers will be able to make intelligent decisions based on their content knowledge and experience.

3. **Credibility:** These teachers' reputations within the building allow for their decisions to be taken seriously by others.

4. **Leadership:** These teachers have the potential to drive the change process.

Teachers who participate in the guiding coalition then become collaborative team leaders who are able to lead their teams with a clear (or clearer) understanding of the why, what, and how because they have been an integral part of moving the school forward via their leadership role on the guiding coalition. These structures for teacher collaboration and ownership are aligned with what Hattie (Visible Learning, n.d.) considers the greatest effect size (1.57) on student learning: collective teacher efficacy. Teachers see themselves as part of something bigger, something that when they work together, they can affect change for the students they serve.

The role of the guiding coalition is cemented early on in the PLC process through engaging in developing, implementing, and refining the key structures of PLCs.

This begins with clarifying priorities, providing direction, determining (and adhering to) specific behaviors, and identifying common focus priorities, the work of the four pillars.

A Strong Foundation

DuFour and colleagues (2016) describe the four pillars of a PLC—the mission, vision, values (collective commitments), and goals—as the foundation schools need to ensure all students have pathways to success to achieve high levels of learning.

All too often, changes are implemented without stakeholders having an understanding (or very little understanding) of the why of the work. It is critical that teachers and other staff understand and commit to the reasons for transforming their educational system. Outlining the mission, vision, values, and goals of the organization collaboratively helps build a common understanding and commitment to the work. From there, collaborative teams in PLCs will work collaboratively to define the specifics at each grade level.

Mission: Why Do We Exist?

The first pillar of a PLC is the *mission*. The mission answers the question, Why do we exist (DuFour et al., 2016)? It is too common in schools for a committee to be thrown together to develop a mission as part of a strategic plan, accreditation, or some other external factor. Unfortunately, an inordinate amount of time is spent wordsmithing a statement that no one knows, remembers, or lives by. In schools that have developed a true mission, this process is internal. As we describe in *Breaking With Tradition* (Stack & Vander Els, 2018), those within a school must be clear on their fundamental purpose and engage in sometimes difficult conversations to begin the process of not only clarifying and understanding the mission, but truly living it. Having conversations as a staff about why the school exists can be incredibly empowering, and simultaneously, it provides collective understanding and collective responsibility.

Equity is a driving force behind this question related to mission building. The sixth design principle of competency-based learning states, "Strategies to ensure equity for ALL students are embedded in the culture, structure, and pedagogy of schools and education systems" (Truong, 2019). Equity starts with tough conversations among staff. Do we believe that *all* students can learn at high levels? And are we willing to confront those who stand in the way of ensuring that all students' voices, cultures, and experiences are honored? And are we willing to do whatever we can to make equity a reality in our school? Hattie's research (Visible learning, n.d.) finds that *teacher estimates of achievement*, the *belief* that students could be successful, had an effect size of 1.29 (among the top three). It is imperative that we have conversations as a staff to develop our collective and shared understanding of why we exist and then make that belief a reality within our school culture, how we structure support, and ultimately, what happens in our classrooms.

A teacher's role in this process cannot be overstated. For Jada, as a member of the guiding coalition, her engagement as part of this process is critical. Jada and her fellow guiding coalition members began to think about why they existed together as a team, but they also participated with key stakeholders within the school community, including community members, business leaders, parents, and students.

> Equity starts with tough conversations among staff. Do we believe that *all* students can learn at high levels? And are we willing to confront those who stand in the way of ensuring that *all* students' voices, cultures, and experiences are honored? And are we willing to do whatever we can to make equity a reality in our school?

Vision: What Must We Become to Accomplish Our Purpose?

The *vision* question (DuFour et al., 2016) specifically asks teachers to focus on what needs to change. Again, the school can determine the answer only through honest and open dialogue. The outcome of that dialogue provides inspiration not only to educators within the school but also the greater community. And engaging in this type of process allows stakeholders across the spectrum to own and take personal responsibility within the process.

> In many schools going through this reflective process, adults come to the realization that in the school their focus has been on *adult-centered issues* instead of what they should be expending their energy on—the *student-centered issues* that truly matter within their school.

In many schools going through this reflective process, adults come to the realization that in the school their focus has been on *adult-centered issues* instead of what they should be expending their energy on—the *student-centered issues* that truly matter within their school. Once a staff makes that distinction, it becomes much easier to focus their collective energy. Teachers will start to look at how the school can truly commit to learning for all and put students first. This shift in mindset is shown in table 2.1.

Table 2.1: Mindset shift from adult focused to student focused.

Adult-Focused Mindset	Student-Focused Mindset
"This student isn't in my homeroom or class, so he's not my responsibility."	"The student needs support. The adult is available and will contribute to supporting the student."
"When am I supposed to prep for another period for intervention?"	"The team has identified specific needs of students in a grade level or content area. We will prioritize time to plan how to best support these students."
"But I'm not a reading teacher."	"Our students need additional, focused support. All available adults will support these students to the best of their ability with available resources."
"We've always done it this way and it's worked just fine. Why change now?"	"The way we've been doing things has not worked for all students. What do we need to change to meet all students' needs?"

In many successful competency-based learning districts in the United States, educators have made a concerted effort to deeply involve their communities in the systems change process. One way in which we've seen many competency-based systems successfully engage in this process is through the development of a profile or portrait of a graduate, a step in helping a school or district develop its vision. In *Transforming Schools*, Bob Lenz (2015) defines a profile of a graduate as a "communitywide vision statement describing what a learner should know and be able to do before he or she graduates from the school" (p. 23). Battelle for Kids (n.d.) describes the profile as serving as a "North Star for system transformation [by] provid[ing] strategic direction for the redesign of the overall educational experience for students"; they go on to state that "this collective vision reinvigorates and re-engages students, teachers, and community stakeholders."

The profile of a graduate idea correlates to the seventh design principle (Levine & Patrick, 2019) of a competency-based system, which outlines the critical importance of identifying "rigorous common expectations for learning, which include academic content knowledge, and 21st century skills like communication, collaboration, creativity, and self-direction" (p. 3). Battelle for Kids (n.d.) identifies the types of questions that can frame the conversations for a team developing their portrait.

> What are the hopes, aspirations, and dreams that our community has for our young people?

> What are the skills and mindsets our children need for success in this rapidly changing and complex world?

> What are the implications for the design of the learning experiences—and equitable access to those experiences—we provide in our school systems?

James Neihof, former superintendent of schools from Shelby County, Kentucky, and his team began their transition to competency-based learning with the development of a portrait of a graduate. This has been their North Star for eight years of systems change.

> ### Practitioner Perspective
> ### James Neihof, Former Superintendent of Schools, Shelby County Schools, Kentucky
>
> By the time I became the superintendent in 2008, our public schools in Shelby County, Kentucky, had, like nearly all public schools across the United States, worked extremely hard for nearly two decades at achieving an overarching transactional goal: increasing test scores. Yet despite much effort on the part of teachers and students, achievement gaps remained in our district. By 2012, we were convinced that the federal government's well-intended transactional goals to achieve test scores akin to achieving factory production quotas was flawed. Although noble in intent, transactional goals alone had not and would not motivate our students, teachers, or community leaders. Furthermore, we believed there were more robust and meaningful ways to prove student mastery than standardized testing.
>
> We read and studied the overwhelmingly positive data supporting a transformational leadership model, leadership from the heart, and agreed to refocus our district on a transformational mission: to unapologetically lead from the heart of our community in order to create a lasting impact on human beings in our community.
>
> In July of 2012, we held a two-day retreat for the administrative team to study transformational leadership practices. Then in August, we began the school year with a transformational message for our staff to kick off a strategic planning year by publicly rejecting the idea that transactional goals—test scores alone—can ensure students are prepared for the robust challenges that await them as adults in the 21st century. With that admission on the table, we invited our community's parent leaders, business leaders, and student leaders to tell us why schools exist and what school and community leaders should do together to achieve objectives that matter to the community.
>
> Excitement levels were high that fall. Nearly one hundred people actively participated on the strategic leadership team. Through our reading and research we identified innovative schools and districts with clear transformational missions. Then, in November, the strategic leadership team members traveled to visit these schools in person.
>
> By December, the full strategic leadership team convened to establish a clear vision for a transformational mission for our district. The district leaders and I had developed a strategic planning process to guide the work. The first strategy, and the foundation upon which the others rest, was for all transformational school leaders to daily insist on reminding students and staff *why* they are there (Sinek, 2009). We believed that why the organization exists and why it plans strategically to achieve specific outcomes must be answered in the transformational mission and vision of an effective school or district. We realized that setting the mission and vision for the school district would require us to find a delicate

balance between what is audacious and what a majority might see as reachable. Having observed firsthand in our onsite visits how the most effective 21st century school leaders understand this balance and focus on simplicity and personalization of a transformational vision and mission that all can understand, we then went to work.

We asked our strategic leadership team to help us create a clear mission statement to guide our daily work. We wanted to strike a delicate balance between the value of test score attainment for all of our students and producing graduates of high character who would be productive citizens.

Four focal points emerged:

1. **Curricular wisdom:** We should teach students to practically apply knowledge.
2. **Mastery:** Students can demonstrate mastery of academic standards in many ways.
3. **Leadership:** We should foster leadership as a skill.
4. **Responsibility:** We should embed responsibility for and to others in the curriculum.

Our mission statement put them together: "To prepare wise students who master standards, lead by example, and embrace social responsibility."

That clear mission statement became the driving force behind the district's strategic planning for the next six years of my superintendency and continues to guide the district's ongoing shifts to student-centered learning. It became the answer to why we exist as an organization.

(J. Neihof, personal communication, February 8, 2021)

Values: How Must We Behave to Achieve Our Vision?

The values pillar in a PLC provides the structure for how staff will behave and what they will commit to do to achieve their mission and vision (DuFour et al., 2016). In many competency-based schools, these values evolve as the learning and understanding throughout the staff deepens. These collective commitments frame the behaviors that staff members, as members of a PLC, must commit to every single day to support student learning and each other.

A staff that truly understands their why and the school they need to become to achieve that why will need to determine what behaviors and commitments will guide them toward that end. Making decisions based upon what's best for students, allowing students ownership in learning, working collaboratively, and committing to change practices to better prepare students for the world they will enter are easy for team members to identify but not always as easy to adhere to. Collectively identifying these commitments together will help a staff hold itself accountable to what it strives to be.

Goals: How Will We Measure Progress?

This fourth pillar involves developing *shared goals* (DuFour et al., 2016), which leads to the attainment of a shared purpose. Goals provide a school and collaborative teams within the school a focal point for their collective work. Shared goals help guide and answer questions about where the school and teams currently are, and very importantly, where they want to be. The process of developing goals together allows educators in a school to confront their current reality together, and then make collective, informed decisions about how they can move forward as a system to better meet the needs of their students.

SMART goals (strategic and specific, measurable, attainable, results oriented, and time bound) provide a concrete and comprehensive way for schools and teams to monitor progress toward stated goals, and they can be used productively to track progress on a short-term or long-term basis (Conzemius & O'Neill, 2014).

It's important that teams organize their work around SMART goals throughout the year. This process must be facilitated, especially at the beginning stages. The guiding coalition can lead this charge, with team members looking at multiple data points together to determine progress toward reaching SMART goals. Each of these teacher leaders can then lead this process within their own collaborative teacher teams. We recommend that teams formally assess their SMART goals every quarter or trimester, but at a minimum, at least midyear and again at the end of the year. Ongoing data collection and analysis should happen throughout the year.

Teams often base their SMART goals solely on benchmark-type assessment data (annual or trimesterly/quarterly data). It is important to use this type of data, but it must be done so in a way that connects students' day-to-day learning. (We delve into this process in chapter 4, page 71.)

These four pillars provide the foundation of a PLC, and the three big ideas guide the work of schools.

The Three Big Ideas: Guiding the Work of Schools

As mentioned earlier, three big ideas guide the work of PLCs: (1) a focus on learning, (2) a collaborative culture and collective responsibility, and (3) a focus on results (DuFour et al., 2016).

A Focus on Learning

Members of PLCs accept learning as the fundamental purpose of the school and therefore are willing to examine all practices in light of their impact on learning (DuFour et al., 2016). This statement may resonate with all educators (we hope), but the reality in many schools is in direct contradiction to this statement. In traditional systems, educators most often view teaching as the fundamental purpose, rather than learning. Given the constant, long-standing pressures on schools, principals, and classroom teachers, we can see how that came to be. With programs viewed as the curriculum, rather than competencies and standards, there is significant pressure to get through all of the material. When faced with these pressures, teaching can become a cycle of ensuring you are on a specific lesson on a specific day, with a test given at the end before moving on to the next unit of study.

When teachers start to focus on what learning students are demonstrating, that conversation changes the day-to-day work of the school. When everyone agrees on this fundamental purpose, the shift to competency-based learning provides educators with even more data to support the benefits of this move (despite its many struggles); a traditional model of education will not make sense as it relates to individualized, personalized learning.

Making this transition to a focus on learning allows for innovation in the classroom and supports teacher autonomy, which is a hallmark of a competency-based learning environment because teachers rely on their own and each other's expertise. Teachers make instructional decisions based on experience and what teams feel will work best to support student growth.

A Collaborative Culture and Collective Responsibility

Members of a PLC are committed to working together to achieve a collective purpose. They cultivate a collaborative culture through the development of high-performing teams (DuFour et al., 2016). There is no more successful way to support a competency-based learning model than by doing so in collaborative teams. A team, as DuFour and his colleagues (2016) describe, is people working "together *interdependently* to achieve *common goals*" (p. 75) for which members are *mutually accountable* (see figure 2.1, page 38). The collaborative team may be the most critical component of a competency-based system, as much of what happens on a day-to-day basis to meet each student where they are occurs directly with teachers as part of a collaborative team. Teachers in the classroom have continued to be asked to do more with less. This can truly test the resolve of all, but the overarching calling to provide a better way for our students to prosper in their learning is too powerful to resist.

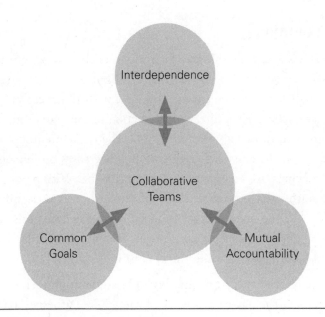

Figure 2.1: Collaborative teams in a PLC.

A Focus on Results

In a PLC, members assess their effectiveness on the basis of results rather than intentions (DuFour et al., 2016). There is a thirst for data, for information that will allow individuals, teams, and the school as a whole to gain insight into how their students are doing to seek relevant data and information and use that information to promote continuous improvement. In a competency-based learning system, teachers have more focused data and information about their students than ever before. Each assessment, whether formative or summative, provides a wealth of information about a student's progress. The goal is for *every* student to be college and career ready, think critically, solve problems, and understand what learning looks like, feels like, and consists of, so they can apply those skills to any problem. Because a competency-based learning system is geared to the individual learner, this all happens naturally.

Information is everywhere, but teams have to know what to do with the data they have in front of them. They must share with each other what they are learning. As Sturgis (2015) notes:

> The emphasis on sharing denotes that these approaches differ from those commonly used in traditional systems. These are collaborative approaches that generate respect and trust. They contribute to the formation of a different type of school culture—one that is student-centered rather than system-centered, empowering rather than compliance-oriented, cooperative rather than dependent on individual leadership, and motivated by learning rather than by carrots or sticks. (p. 11)

The collaborative processes inherent in a PLC provides the structure to analyze these data and put the information to good use. What may have once been a pile of numbers is now a piece of the puzzle that can help teachers dissect what is keeping a student from demonstrating growth and success. Staff members need encouragement to try various approaches when considering student learning needs. Teachers will develop their sense of autonomy based on the success of their action plans. At other times, these action plans may not work as predicted, but this is part of the learning process. In fact, teachers will often learn more from experiences that don't go as planned than those that do because they will carry the experiences forward, making changes based on their professional expertise.

Josh Ray and Faith Short are the principal and assistant principal of East Pointe Elementary in Greenwood, Arkansas. Josh and Faith have led the process of becoming a nationally recognized PLC at Work in their school. They share insight into how the collective understanding in their school of the three big ideas has evolved to the point that they live these ideas on a daily basis.

Practitioner Perspective

Josh Ray, Principal, and Faith Short, Assistant Principal, East Pointe Elementary, Greenwood, Arkansas

As we worked toward becoming a true PLC at East Pointe Elementary, we realized early on that our primary purpose was to ensure high levels of learning for every student. Initially, however, our staff-developed mission conveyed a much different belief and placed the burden of responsibility for learning on students. Recognizing this, we changed the wording of our mission from one that stated that we would *provide opportunities for learning for all students* to one that stated we would *ensure high levels of learning for all students*.

This evolution took time. It wasn't until we consistently utilized the four critical questions of a PLC at Work (DuFour et al., 2016) to drive our daily work that we truly began to understand, and, more importantly, began to believe that we could bring our mission to life and actually ensure that all students learned at high levels. The shift in focus to one that centered around student learning created a greater sense of commitment and collective responsibility for helping every single student learn. As a result of the continuous spotlight on student learning, teachers are learning from one another and growing in their instructional agility and practices more than ever before, strengthening their ability to provide instruction based upon the specific needs of each student.

Additionally, as we grew in our shared understanding of the process, our work became even more focused and more intentional. Beginning with the end in mind, our collaborative teams work through the four critical questions by coming to consensus around what we want students to learn and determining what students should be able to do and what they should know at the conclusion of instruction. We have deepened our assessment literacy and become more adept at creating common assessments that inform us of where students are in their learning so that we can provide targeted instruction and support based specifically on individual needs.

Our collaborative culture has grown as we develop the teams in our school. One of our first steps was to embed collaborative time into our master schedule, but refining our behaviors within that time is what is changing our school. Common goals for every team have become the way we consistently measure the effectiveness of our work. These goals specifically target student learning and are part of the larger goals of our building as a whole. Where before, students and teachers had victories and setbacks in isolation, we now hold ourselves mutually accountable for the success of every student. This belief was a significant step in the maturation of our culture, and it meant that every team member owned the success of each student and even the growth of the other members of their team. Collectively, we continue to work toward the high-water mark of highly effective teams—true interdependence.

As we began to demonstrate genuine vulnerability as adults, the influence we had on each other only intensified. Now, interdependence represents both the behaviors of the team and the effectiveness of their results. This reciprocal relationship is at the heart of our current growth as a PLC. The more students we reach, the more dependent we are on one another for the success of those who have not yet mastered their learning, and the more we rely on one another to help us reach the students we cannot seem to help on our own, the greater our level of success for every student across our team. As our behaviors change and more students succeed than ever before, we are realizing a level of success that we could have never achieved without one another.

At the onset of this journey, it was commonplace to hear teachers say things like, "I just know my kids." Although well-intentioned, such assumptions allowed us to misinterpret student learning, causing us to overlook areas of academic need and create gaps in learning for students. Now, all decisions are based on evidence and data, resulting in a greater impact on student learning. Despite this, our focus on results is still growing as a main component of the success of our school.

Initially, this meant that we were looking only at summative testing data trying to discern what did and did not work for our students. Gradually, we began to see the power of the results our students were producing daily causing us to invest significantly in our internal formative assessment practices. We now find ourselves with even more focus on exactly what we want our students to know, how we will define success, and how we can develop student agency in providing evidence of learning.

As our skill improves, the results we focus on become more targeted and therefore provide greater information on how we can continue to pursue high levels of learning for every student. One essential component of this is using results to spur adult growth. We are celebrating student success, analyzing class data, sharing best practices, and investing in one another as a means of striving to meet the needs for every student. Consequently, the goals for our entire school are shifting to reflect these ends. Mastery of essential standards has replaced state summative testing as the new standard for success. We are working to refine and refocus our staff collective commitments to further develop the behaviors we see as drivers for adult growth. And we are redefining our expectations and how we

> measure and ensure mastery for our students in ways that far exceed our level of understanding early in this process.
>
> The three big ideas have become something we not only understand at a deep level, but that we are living every day. Learning is the focus of our school, we help to achieve learning for our students through our collaborative efforts, and we monitor our progress through a balanced assessment system.
>
> (J. Ray and F. Short, personal communication, February 28, 2021)

The Four Critical Questions of a PLC and Competency-Based Learning

The four critical questions provide the roadmap for collaborative teams' focus in a PLC. These questions outline the curriculum considerations, the assessment considerations, and the instructional response necessary to meet each student where they are and ensure high levels of learning for all. The four critical questions (DuFour et al., 2016) are as follows:

1. What do students need to know and be able to do?
2. How will we know when they have learned it?
3. What will we do when they haven't learned it?
4. What will we do when they already know it? (p. 251)

What Do Students Need to Know and Be Able to Do?

This question is a curriculum question. The answer defines the competencies, essential standards, and learning targets that students will be able to demonstrate as a result of their learning experiences. Teachers must be clear on the intended learning in any unit, but also in each lesson students are engaging in. Determining what students need to know and be able to do takes time, but teachers' collective understanding of competencies and their underlying standards and learning targets ensures a guaranteed and viable curriculum—a curriculum that (1) gives students access to the same essential learning regardless of who is teaching the class and (2) can be taught in the time allotted (Marzano, 2017).

The four critical questions provide the roadmap for collaborative teams' focus in a PLC. These questions outline the curriculum considerations, the assessment considerations, and the instructional response necessary to meet each student where they are and ensure high levels of learning for all.

How Will We Know When They Have Learned It?

Question two is an assessment question. Teachers can answer this question confidently through aligned, deliberate, and balanced assessment practices. This includes daily formative practices, team-designed and administered common formative assessments, and finally, team-designed and commonly administered summative performance assessments. Teams must have designated time to sit down with their data and analyze what it's telling them. This critical work is the basis for critical questions three and four.

Sara Casassa is a middle school English language arts teacher in South Hampton, New Hampshire, at the Barnard School. Sara has been engaged in deepening her competency-based practices, and describes how her practices have evolved to where they are today. In particular, Sara explains how the first and second critical questions of a PLC guided her work. Sara also shares insight into the role of student ownership in learning; what students would like to demonstrate is considered and initiated in addition to the competencies that Sara has identified. This represents co-constructed learning.

Practitioner Perspective
Sara Casassa, South Hampton School District, New Hampshire

This year, our school made the shift to competency-based units of study: rubrics and grading shifted from a traditional base to a competency-based system. While I had had previous training and our school had gone through a two-year process of creating quality performance assessments, competencies were not something we were comfortable with. Sure, I knew the standards, and I understood the concept of authentic (real world) and transferable (applicable) learning experiences, but I could not yet see how all the pieces fit together. A new online grading system and a shift toward competency-based grading forced me to figure out how to put all the pieces together. I started creating units with the competencies in the forefront. I began by asking two questions: (1) What do I want my students to know? and (2) How will I know they know it? I created assessments and rubrics designed to answer those questions.

This intentionality, grounded in competencies, gave me a new focus, and I believe improved my units of study and the way students and I view assessment. I created a social justice unit anchored by the novel *Just Mercy* by Bryan Stevenson (2014). Throughout the unit, I designed check-ins, collecting evidence for essential standards. The students' formative work is closely intertwined in the summative assessments. Since students had a chance to provide evidence of learning for the power standards I identified at the beginning of the unit—they already wrote an informational essay on a research topic, a persuasive piece on criminal justice—their final project could be more flexible and less traditional. Tasked with finding a way to be a change agent of a social justice issue they were passionate about, students created their own final project. They submitted a proposal to me, and once we

> met and it was approved, we codesigned their rubric. I identified the two competencies (presentation and writing) that the projects would most likely fall under, and together we discussed and determined what a score of proficient would look like for the project. For a student who was writing a letter to a state legislator, I was able to pull up the competency for argument writing, and we used that to create her rubric. She chose the standards by which she felt she should be assessed. With another student, who was creating a TED Talk, we discussed what an effective talk would include and wrote a proficient descriptor for his rubric. While the students have never created a rubric before, they have been self-assessing themselves with competency-based rubrics all year, and each was able to tell me what the work would look like at a proficient level. The students approached this work very seriously, and their work more closely reflected what they identified as a proficient level.
>
> This has been an exciting process for me. By using competency-based assessments during the unit, students have had more freedom and creativity at the end to create meaningful, authentic responses to their research, learning, and thinking. They have been tasked with the charge to take their work outside our classroom walls, and they have had to change their projects and rethink their audiences in order to achieve that goal. These students have transferred their learning and skills to an authentic task. They have learned that their ideas, their convictions, and their work can make a difference. While they have had ownership over the entire process, what I believe they will remember most is that their voice and ideas matter and that they have the power to change the world!
>
> (S. Casassa, personal communication, March 20, 2021)

What Will We Do When They Haven't Learned It?

Once teacher teams have examined the assessment data they've collected, they must consider what they will do to provide support for students who have not learned. The following questions guide the work of teams.

- Who hasn't demonstrated their understanding of the learning target standard yet?
- What does the work tell us? Where is the skill deficit?
- Are there others who have similar needs?
- How can we provide them with more time? (This topic is addressed in more detail in chapter 5, page 101.)
- Who is most skilled at providing this support?
- When will it happen?

The third design principle (Levine & Patrick, 2019) states that "students receive timely, differentiated support based upon their individual learning needs." Critical question three and design principle three are aligned as they both focus on providing needed support for any student who requires it. The collaborative team is instrumental in identifying students in a timely manner who need support, then determining what that support will entail, when it will happen, and how it will be monitored.

What Will We Do When They Already Know It?

The following questions guide the work of teams in a competency-based system to answer this fourth question.

- Who is already demonstrating mastery of the learning target or standard?
- What is our body of evidence to make this determination?
- Are there others who also have demonstrated mastery and the need for extension?
- How can we provide them with more time to go deeper? (This idea is explored in depth in chapter 5, page 101.)
- Who is most skilled at providing this level of extension?
- When will students receive the extension?

Figure 2.2 shows each of the four critical questions and the actions teams in a competency-based system take to answer each question or in response to each question.

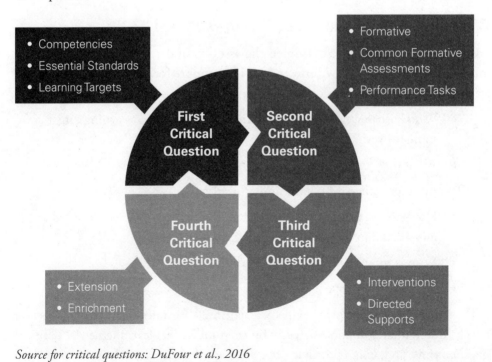

Source for critical questions: DuFour et al., 2016

Figure 2.2: The four critical questions as the framework for collaborative teamwork in a competency-based system.

As Jada and her team focus on the structures of the four pillars, the three big ideas, and focus their collaborative team work on the four critical questions, their team time becomes more intentional, and subsequently, more productive. The time they meet becomes something they want to do and look forward to, rather than something they have to do that has been mandated. Their collective focus on learning results in a better understanding of their role in learning, their students being more engaged, and subsequently, greater success.

The PLC process provides the structural support necessary to meet each student's needs within a competency-based system. The three big ideas, four pillars, and four critical questions that drive the work of collaborative teams in a PLC provide the framework and distributed leadership for schools to undertake the difficult work that lies ahead.

Reflection Questions

Consider the following reflection questions with your team.

1. It is impossible for teachers to implement a change process of this magnitude alone. How is leadership distributed in your school? Based on what you read in this chapter, what is missing?

2. In a PLC, the four pillars provide the foundation to engage in systems change. Has your district or school worked together to develop a profile or portrait of a graduate? Have you developed collective commitments and SMART goals to guide your day-to-day efforts?

3. There are three big ideas in a PLC. Has your school made the commitment to focus on learning rather than on teaching? Do you have a collaborative culture? Do you seek results to allow you to determine your progress?

4. Collaborative teams are the engines of a PLC. Can you identify examples of interdependence within your teaming processes? Do you have mutual accountability to common goals?

5. The four critical questions of a PLC guide the work of teams. Which of these questions do you and your teammates need to spend more time focusing on to help your students? How will you ensure that these questions remain a focus?

CHAPTER 3

Competencies, Essential Standards, Learning Targets, and Learning Progressions

One of the more unique challenges Jada and her team will face as they embark on their first year using competency-based learning in a school that has not yet fully adopted the competency-based learning philosophy will be how to identify the competencies, essential standards, and learning targets they will use with their students. This is the work collaborative teams in a PLC tackle when answering the first critical question: What do students need to know and be able to do? (DuFour et al., 2016). Answering this first critical question provides clarity of focus for not just Jada but her entire collaborative team. Jada's challenge is to kick-start some of the work and conversations that ultimately will need to happen across disciplines in not just her building, but in all grades in the K–12 system that she works in if her PLC is to shift to competency-based learning.

This chapter explores how in an effective competency-based system, competencies are completely aligned with national, state or provincial, or local frameworks and include skills that are transferable across content areas. They are mapped from K–12 as a continuum of learning progressions based on the standards. Competencies are applicable to real-life situations and require an understanding of relationships between and among theories, principles, and concepts. The cognitive demand is high; they require students to have a deep understanding of content as well as application of knowledge to a variety of settings by promoting complex connections through creating, analyzing, designing, proving, developing, and formulating. This chapter also explores how students can be empowered through curriculum in a competency-based system.

Often, it is the role of educators like Jada who work with their collaborative teams to unpack and make sense of the curriculum frameworks provided to them in order to develop the competencies, essential standards, and learning targets that they will use with their students. To help readers understand how this chapter will unfold and what the work will look like, consider the experiences from Shannon Schinkel, a humanities and drama educator from Prince George, British Columbia, who developed her competency-based classroom from the redesign efforts that British Columbia underwent in 2016.

> **Practitioner Perspective**
> **Shannon Schinkel, Humanities and Drama Educator and Cofounder of the Assessment Consortium of British Columbia, Canada**
>
> I embraced competency-based learning and grading following the implementation of our redesigned British Columbia curriculum in 2016. Our curriculum is special because its standards include competencies (what students are expected to do) and content (what students are expected to know). At its core, the British Columbia curriculum was designed to encourage competency-based learning and discourage the traditional exclusive focus on content.
>
> This doesn't mean that content isn't important. When I give presentations about assessment and the redesigned curriculum, I highlight how curricular competencies and content can be viewed symbolically as a house; in order to do the curricular competencies, students need content to apply the competencies to. There is more flexibility in lesson and unit design now, with a competency-based approach, because teachers can choose any content when teaching the competencies. I can use literary devices and elements, for example, to help students respond to text in personal, creative, and critical ways, but I could also, if I desired, use writing processes for the same competency.
>
> What does this mean for teaching and learning in my classroom? By focusing on competencies, I provide more student-centered learning opportunities like project-based learning and 20%Time, collaborative group work, and voice and choice learning opportunities. The competencies are skills, strategies, and processes that can't be assessed as absolutely as one might assess content through a test or handout. For example, for the curricular competency "Using oral, written, and digital texts, students are expected individually and collaboratively to be able to comprehend and connect (reading, listening, viewing)." Students can respond to texts like a novel, film, poem, or play through drawing, play building, scriptwriting, filmmaking, or story writing. Students can also choose the text they want to respond to and how they want to respond to it.
>
> For each competency, I've recommended and worked with teams of teachers around the province to create proficiency sequences that outline the criteria and the target. By explicitly teaching each level, students receive the opportunity to advance to their goal level and

> in subsequent learning opportunities, advance even further. The possibilities are endless. Students are loaded with ideas of how they can provide evidence of learning when the criteria are clear, and the focus is less on grading and more on personal learning goals. Where am I now? What are my next steps?
>
> I believe that through a competency-centered approach, I am effectively building important 21st century skills and preparing them for the future that needs effective communicators, responsible citizens, and critical and creative thinkers.
>
> (S. Schinkel, personal communication, December 2, 2021)

Refining the Curriculum

Jada's goal is to enable her students to develop the skills and confidence to become highly effective independent learners, taking ownership of all aspects of their own learning. She wants her students to feel comfortable taking risks in the learning process because she knows when they can do this, there is the potential for a huge reward. Ultimately, she wants to create a classroom experience for all of her students and for herself that supports creativity, flexible and varied thinking, and the sharing of knowledge, ideas, and applied thinking. To achieve this, she needs to raise the level of student engagement in ways that her students have never experienced before. She needs to become a co-constructor of learning experiences, sharing this role with her students as they work together in the classroom. It is for all of these reasons that classroom teachers must refine the curriculum to identify and articulate the connection between competencies, standards, and learning targets.

What Are Competency Statements?

Design principle seven in competency-based learning states that "rigorous, common expectations for learning (knowledge, skills, and dispositions) are explicit, transparent, measurable, and transferable" (Levine & Patrick, 2019, p. 3). This encompasses both academic competencies (content and grade level) and nonacademic skills and dispositions (critical thinking, problem solving, communication, collaboration, creative or innovative thinking, and self-direction).

At the top of the hierarchy are competencies, which represent the why of learning. In *Breaking With Tradition* (Stack & Vander Els, 2018), we define a *competency* as:

> Specific to the higher order skill or transfer of knowledge that is required within a specific content area or within skills and dispositions. At the secondary level, a course may be made up of several course-specific or grade-level specific competencies, or a subject area may contain multiple competencies, but they are the bigger ideas that students must be proficient in within that course or subject. (p. 46)

To give the reader a better understanding of what an effective competency statement looks like, consider these examples from the State of New Hampshire, a leader in competency-based learning, as shown in figure 3.1. New Hampshire has developed model competencies for all core content areas and grade levels.

Foundational Reading Grades K–2	Students will read to make meaning while flexibly using a variety of strategies, demonstrating foundational literacy skills.
Informational Writing Grades 3–4	Students will compose informative text to examine a topic and clearly convey ideas and information with a specific focus.
Nature of Science Grades 6–8	Students will work collaboratively and individually to generate testable questions or define problems in terms of given constraints and criteria; plan and conduct investigations or apply engineering design practices to analyze and interpret data; and construct and communicate evidence-based explanations or possible optimal solutions.
Mathematics Grades 9–12	Students will reason abstractly and manipulate symbolic expressions and models to represent relationships and interpret expressions, equations, and inequalities in terms of a given context (including real-world phenomena) for determining unknown values.

Sources: *New Hampshire Department of Education, 2016a; New Hampshire Department of Education, 2016c; New Hampshire Department of Education, 2017.*

Figure 3.1: Examples of academic competencies in the United States.

As another example for comparison, consider these examples from New Zealand (figure 3.2), another global leader in competency-based learning.

Listening, Reading, and Viewing Level 2	Students will select and use sources of information, processes, and strategies with some confidence to identify, form, and express ideas.
Speaking, Writing, and Presenting Level 4	Students will integrate sources of information, processes, and strategies confidently to identify, form, and express ideas.
Nature of Science Level 6	Students will understand that scientists' investigations are informed by current scientific theories and aim to collect evidence that will be interpreted through processes of logical argument.
Mathematics and Statistics Level 8	In a range of meaningful contexts, students will be engaged in thinking mathematically and statistically. They will solve problems and model situations.

Source: *New Zealand Ministry of Education, n.d.*

Figure 3.2: Examples of academic competencies in New Zealand.

The examples in figures 3.1 and 3.2 cover a variety of subjects and grade levels, and yet they have some commonalities despite having been adopted on opposite sides of the globe. We explore these in the following sections.

Content Relevance

An effective competency statement informs students how their learning aligns with national, state, or local standards. In the case of the New Hampshire examples in figure 3.1 and the New Zealand examples in figure 3.2, New Hampshire uses the Common Core as guidance for a foundation for both English language arts and mathematics. Science frameworks in this state are informed by Next Generation Science Standards (www.nextgenscience.org). New Zealand competencies are already articulated at a national level and bear strong resemblances to the statements from the United States.

Some states and provinces, and as a result some districts and schools, have a prescribed set of nationally aligned standards and frameworks they must adhere to for curriculum development. If this is the case, the teacher's job is much easier as it is equally as likely nowadays that model competency statements may be available from other states or schools for that particular grade level or content area that teachers can adapt to meet their classroom needs. If this is not the case, the teacher may have to research further what curriculum guiding documents and frameworks are needed to satisfy any local school needs. When doing that, teachers should keep this in mind. Effective competency statements draw connections for students to high concepts not only in the content area but across many content areas.

Lasting Knowledge

Effective competency statements promote lasting knowledge and enduring concepts that require students to transfer their knowledge and skills in and across content areas and in authentic, real-world tasks. To do this, students must have command of the ideas and relationships that connect the various concepts. A common mistake of novice competency-based learning teachers is to use textbook chapter titles as the competency statements for a course. This is not a dig against textbook and publishing companies; rather, chapter titles are simply not designed for this purpose. They are often limited in scope and sequence, or they are too content specific. As an example, consider two ways to write competencies for a ninth-grade physical science course, as shown in figure 3.3 (page 52).

> **Effective competency statements draw connections for students to high concepts not only in the content area but across many content areas.**

Ineffective Competency Statements	Effective Competency Statements
Physical Sciences: What physics and chemistry are all about and science and measurement	**Patterns:** Students will demonstrate the ability to observe and describe patterns in natural and human-designed phenomena and use those patterns to support claims about the observed or predicted relationships among phenomena.
Motion and Force: Motion and forces	**Cause and Effect:** Students will demonstrate the ability to investigate, explain, and evaluate potential causal relationships by using evidence to support claims and predictions about the mechanisms that drive those relationships.
Laws of Motion and Energy: Newton's Laws of Motion, energy and machines, and gravity and space	**Scale, Proportion, and Quantity:** Students will demonstrate the ability to describe and represent the significance of changes in observable and nonobservable phenomena in terms of relative scale, proportion, and quantity.
Electricity, Sound, and Light: Electricity and magnetism, waves and sound, and light and color	**Systems and System Models:** Students will demonstrate the ability to investigate and analyze a natural or human-designed system in terms of its boundaries, inputs, outputs, interactions, and behaviors and use this information to develop a system model that can be used to understand and empirically evaluate the accuracy of models in terms of representing the underlying system.
Matter: Temperature, heat, and the phases of matter; and the physical properties of matter	**Energy and Matter in Systems:** Students will demonstrate the ability to analyze evidence from a variety of sources (investigations, models) to predict, connect, or evaluate the cycling of matter and flow of energy within and between systems in order to understand, describe, or predict possibilities and limitations of systems.
Atoms, Elements, and Compounds: The atom, elements, and the periodic table; and molecules and compounds	**Structure and Function:** Students will demonstrate the ability to use evidence to support claims about the relationship among structure and function of natural and human-designed objects.
Changes in Matter: Acids, bases, and solutions; chemical reactions; the chemistry of living systems	**Stability and Change of Systems:** Students will demonstrate the ability to investigate and analyze static and dynamic conditions of natural and human-designed systems in order to explain and predict changes over time.
	Nature of Science: Students will demonstrate the ability to work collaboratively and individually to generate testable questions or define problems, plan and conduct investigations using a variety of research methods in a various settings, analyze and interpret data, reason with evidence to construct explanations in light of existing theory and previous research, and effectively communicate the research processes and conclusions.

Source: CPO Science, 2007; New Hampshire Department of Education, 2014.

Figure 3.3: Examples of ninth-grade physical science competencies.

The statements in the left column of figure 3.3 come directly from a popular physical science textbook (CPO Science, 2007). They do a great job explaining what knowledge is to be obtained, but they are simply too content-specific to serve as competency statements for the course. The column on the right, from the New Hampshire Department of Education (2014), articulates how students will need to apply and transfer knowledge in the course. They are informed by the content, knowledge, and skills that will be outlined in the standards for the course.

Rigor

Effective competency statements have a high degree of cognitive demand. Students are challenged to engage in deeper learning by way of creating, analyzing, designing, proving, developing, or formulating. In *Breaking With Tradition* (Stack & Vander Els, 2018) we introduce readers to Hess's (2012) rigor matrices: tools that assist teachers in the understanding and quantification of cognitive demand. Hess's matrices combine Norman Webb's (2002) four levels of Depth of Knowledge (DOK) with Bloom's taxonomy (Bloom, 1956) by helping teachers discover where these two models intersect. We delve deeper into the rigor matrix tools and how teachers can use them to support cognitive demand and deeper learning at the assessment level in a later chapter.

Colby (2017) writes:

> Learning at DOK levels 1 and 2 represents low-level thinking involving factual content and skills acquisition. Generally, the students' answers are either right or wrong; either they know the answer or they don't. Because DOK levels 3 and 4 require that a student apply strategic and extended thinking; a student may be searching for the best answer, not just any answer. The higher level of complex thinking and reasoning leads to deeper learning that students can then take into future learning situations, where low-level information is often forgotten. (p. 71)

It is for these reasons that teachers must consider cognitive demand when developing competency statements for grade levels or courses. The statements must be crafted in such a way so that collaborative teams can then develop assessments that will measure this deeper level of learning.

Connections to Assessment

Effective competency statements clearly and concisely identify what it is students must know and be able to do, and they provide multiple and varied pathways for students to demonstrate evidence of their learning. There is a strong correlation between competency statements and, ultimately, the assessments and grades that teachers will use to determine the degree to which a student has reached mastery. Colby (2017) writes, "When you are designing competency statements, it is important to think of the overall architecture. Make sure they are strong statements, and know how you are going to use them in your assessment and grading systems" (p. 39). We will take a deeper dive into competency-based assessments in a later chapter of this book.

In New Hampshire, in addition to having a set of common model competencies for core subjects, districts and schools are also able to develop their own competencies by utilizing a competency validation rubric tool, shown in figure 3.4, to guide them and to assess the quality of the competencies they will create. This tool outlines the four major areas to consider while developing competencies as noted in the previous list—content area relevance, enduring concepts, cognitive demand, and connection to assessment—and helps teachers determine what is necessary to refine to develop stronger competency statements. This is particularly helpful at the secondary level, where teachers must develop competencies for elective courses that don't necessarily have national or state standards to draw from.

Non-Academic Competencies

The need for students to possess nonacademic competencies, commonly referred to as 21st century skills, or skills and dispositions, has become abundantly clear. In chapter 1 (page 5), we provide research that supports the various skills and competencies related to what employers and colleges are seeking in potential employees. The need for learners to develop these skills is of paramount importance in a competency-based learning system.

The COVID-19 pandemic amplified the importance of 21st century skills. The need to not just deliberately include, but also to amplify social and emotional skills acquisition in school, focusing on relationships and the whole child, became increasingly evident.

The Collaborative for Academic, Social, and Emotional Learning (CASEL; n.d.b) defines social and emotional learning (SEL) as the following:

> SEL is the process through which all young people and adults acquire and apply the knowledge, skills, and attitudes to develop healthy identities, manage emotions and achieve personal and collective goals, feel and show empathy for others, establish and maintain supportive relationships, and make responsible and caring decisions.
>
> SEL advances educational equity and excellence through authentic school-family-community partnerships to establish learning environments and experiences that feature trusting and collaborative relationships, rigorous and meaningful curriculum and instruction, and ongoing evaluation. SEL can help address various forms of inequity and empower young people and adults to co-create thriving schools and contribute to safe, healthy, and just communities.

Competencies, Essential Standards, Learning Targets, and Learning Progressions

Competency Validation Rubric

	4	3	2	1
	◄ Strong Competency Statements		Weaker Competency Statements ►	
	The competency statement . . .			
Relevance to Content Area To what extent does this competency statement align with standards, leading students to conceptual understanding of content?	• Aligns with national, state, or local standards or frameworks; areas may be combined or clustered for learning • Articulates, in a clear and descriptive way, what is important in understanding the content area • Connects the content to higher concepts across content areas	• Aligns with national, state, and local standards or frameworks; areas may be combined or clustered for learning • States what is important in understanding the content area • Addresses conceptual content	• Has beginning alignment with national, state, and local standards or frameworks • Is either too abstract or too specific in its content-area focus • Is so detailed in language that it obscures the connection to higher concepts	• Has little evidence of alignment with standards or frameworks • Focus on content is factual in nature without connection to concepts
Enduring Concepts To what extent does this competency statement reflect enduring concepts?	• Includes skills that are transferable across content areas and applicable to real-life situations • Requires an understanding of relationships between and among theories, principles, or concepts	• Includes skills that are transferable across content areas with real-life connections • Is based on concepts supported by topics and facts	• Is a statement specific to the program or resource used • Is based on topics applicable to the course	• Is limited to scope and sequence of a textbook, program, or resource • Is very specific to facts in content

continued →

Figure 3.4: The New Hampshire competency validation rubric.

Cognitive Demand What depth of knowledge does this competency statement promote?	• Requires deep understanding of content as well as application of knowledge to a variety of settings • Asks students to create conceptual connections and exhibit a level of understanding that is beyond the stated facts or literal interpretation and defend their position or point of view through application of content • Promotes complex connections through creating, analyzing, designing, proving, developing, or formulating	• Reflects academic rigor and implies opportunities for students to apply knowledge in a variety of ways • Asks students to create conceptual connections and exhibit a level of understanding that is beyond the stated facts or literal interpretation • Promotes deep knowledge using reasoning, planning, interpreting, hypothesizing, investigating, or explaining	• Is limited in academic rigor and opportunities to apply knowledge • Asks students to show what they know in ways that limit their ability to build conceptual knowledge • Requires engagement of mental practices such as identifying, defining, constructing, summarizing, displaying, listing, or recognizing	• Asks for routine or rote thinking or basic recall, and lacks opportunities to apply knowledge • Asks students to show what they know in simplistic ways • Requires recall of information, facts, definitions, and terms such as reciting, stating, recognizing, listing, reproducing, memorizing or performing simple tasks or procedures
Relative to Assessment To what extent does the competency statement promote opportunities for students to demonstrate evidence of learning?	• Defines what is to be measured in clear and descriptive language • Promotes multiple and varied opportunities to demonstrate evidence of learning in interdisciplinary fashion	• Defines what is to be measured • Promotes either multiple or varied opportunities to demonstrate evidence of learning	• Is disconnected from the product of learning • Implies limited opportunities to demonstrate evidence of learning	• Lacks description of what is to be measured • Limits evidence of learning to recall

Source: New Hampshire Department of Education, 2010. Adapted with permission.

CASEL's focus, through their framework, is on five specific, interrelated areas of competence—(1) self-awareness, (2) self-management, (3) responsible decision making, (4) relationship skills, and (5) social awareness—across key settings: in classrooms, in schools, with families and caregivers, and in communities. There is a strong focus on equity, and CASEL (n.d.a) identifies five specific benefits of promoting SEL:

1. Leads to academic outcomes and improved behaviors
2. Has a long-term and global impact
3. Has an 11:1 return (for every dollar invested in SEL, there will be an $11 return)
4. Helps reduce poverty and improve economic mobility
5. Improves lifetime outcomes

One of the key considerations for educators when determining how to move forward with supporting students' growth with skills and dispositions is how to developmentally support each student where he or she is on a progression. Traditionally, educators have not provided helpful feedback in these areas, although they grade students, which is often done subjectively based on criteria that is not always clear. If we assess, we must instruct, and most importantly, we must help each student understand how to grow, and we must support them in doing so in a meaningful way.

Recognizing the need to support educators with developmental resources in the area of skills and dispositions, Sarah Collins Lench, Erin Fukuda, and Ross Anderson (2015) created developmental frameworks for the nonacademic skills of communication, collaboration, creativity, and self-direction. These frameworks provide schools with a research base to undertake the *process* of learning together about the role of skills and dispositions in classrooms, schools, and learning experiences—a process that, as Gene Wilhoit, the executive director of the Center for Innovation in Education, states in his foreword to the Essential Skills and Dispositions Framework, would "lead to further refinement and purposeful learning about what shapes a successful person in this dynamic and exciting world."

> **If we assess, we must instruct, and most importantly, we must help each student understand how to grow, and we must support them in doing so in a meaningful way.**

Lench and colleagues (2015) focus on four essential skills and dispositions: (1) communication, (2) collaboration, (3) creativity, and (4) self-direction. Figure 3.5 (page 58) shows an example of how self-direction is framed through five key components.

Self-Direction
Self-Awareness
Reflecting on past experiences to evaluate one's own strengths, limitations, motivations, interests, and aspirations within different learning contexts
Initiative and Ownership
Taking responsibility for learning, finding purposeful driving questions, shaping opportunities to fit personal interests and learning styles, and seeking input from others
Goal Setting and Planning
Developing long-term goals, establishing meaningful learning targets, identifying effective strategies and planning out steps
Engaging and Managing
Seeking out relevant resources and information to support learning goals and refining strategies; maintaining effective pace, reaching short-term benchmarks and long-term goals
Monitoring and Adapting
Evaluating progress, adapting strategies, seizing failure in order to grow from mistakes, and attributing success to effort and motivation

Source: Lench et al., 2015, p. 59.

Figure 3.5: The five components of self-direction.

These five components within self-direction frame focal points for how teachers and students, together, can begin the hard work of further developing these skills in students. Like any skill, there is a progression to development, and practice is key. We can't expect learners to get better at something if they are not given the opportunities to practice, and developing these skills is no different.

When beginning the move to integrating skills and dispositions like communication, collaboration, creativity, and self-direction into daily learning experiences, there is a tendency to start with assessment and oftentimes even grading. Remember, what we assess, we must also instruct.

What Are Essential Standards?

If competency statements are the why of learning, then essential standards represent the what. Content standards are often developed at a national or state or provincial level. In the case of New Hampshire, in the example from figure 3.1 (page 50), the Common Core State Standards are used for both mathematics and English language arts. As we note in *Breaking With Tradition* (Stack & Vander Els, 2018), the Common Core in the United States provides a great foundation for exploring standard-level learning goals in greater detail. The Common Core was first developed

Competencies, Essential Standards, Learning Targets, and Learning Progressions

in 2009 by educational leaders from across the United States with an emphasis on building a common set of rigorous, aligned learning goals that would prepare all students for their post-secondary lives in college, career, and life. The Common Core's learning goals outline what a student should know and be able to do at the end of each grade level. The standards were created to ensure that all students graduate from high school with the skills and knowledge necessary to succeed regardless of where they live in the United States.

Similarly, each provincial ministry in Canada has developed a curriculum structure that lends itself well to the advancement of a competency-based approach. In Quebec, the Ministry of Education (2001) identifies broad areas of learning that "encourage students to make connections between what they learn at school and in their everyday lives" and enable learners to "relate different areas of learning and to look critically at their personal, social and cultural environment." There are cross-curricular competencies grouped in the categories of intellectual, methodological, personal and social, and communication-related competencies. Finally, there are subject-specific competencies in the areas of languages; mathematics, science, and technology; social sciences; arts; and personal development. Under each of these the Ministry has identified essential standards and learning goals for each grade level.

It is important to note, the use of programs and standards alone (such as the Common Core State Standards or the Quebec Ministry of Education Approved Program) should *not* be mistaken for a curriculum. Rather, programs are resources and standards represent a set of shared goals and expectations for what students need to know and be able to do. It is up to the local teachers, educational leaders, and others to decide *how* the standards are to come alive in the classroom setting. Standards do not replace or eliminate the need for quality lesson plans and performance tasks that allow students multiple and varied pathways to demonstrate their learning and mastery of the standards. They are, quite simply, the building blocks of learning.

According to the Common Core State Standards Initiative (n.d.a), effective standards are:

1. Research and evidence based
2. Clear, understandable, and consistent
3. Aligned with college and career expectations

> **It is up to the local teachers, educational leaders, and others to decide *how* the standards are to come alive in the classroom setting. Standards do not replace or eliminate the need for quality lesson plans and performance tasks that allow students multiple and varied pathways to demonstrate their learning and mastery of the standards. They are, quite simply, the building blocks of learning.**

4. Based on rigorous content and application of knowledge through higher-order thinking skills
5. Built on the strengths and lessons of current state standards
6. Informed by other top-performing countries in order to prepare all students for success in our global economy and society

Essential standards, which are sometimes referred to as power, priority, or targeted standards, are a carefully selected subset of grade-level or course-specific standards within each content area that students must master by the end of each school year in order to be prepared to move on to the next grade, level, or course. In a PLC, collaborative teams usually identify essential standards. Douglas Reeves (2002) recommends teams consider these three questions when engaging in this process of identifying essential standards.

1. **Endurance:** Does the standard represent something that students will need to know long term?
2. **Leverage:** Does this standard integrate more than one content area?
3. **Readiness:** Does this standard serve as a prerequisite for future learning? (pp. 49–51)

Reeves (2002) explains how these questions have helped educators with whom he has worked to develop essential standards:

> I have done this exercise with several hundred teachers, and their responses are remarkable. Not once has a teacher ever said, "If your students are to enter my class next year with confidence and success, then this year you must cover every single state standard." Rather, the teachers create a list that is balanced and brief. (p. 52)

Learning goals are single standards, or an intermediate goal on the way to a standard or competency, or a combination of standards. Jay McTighe and Grant Wiggins (2004) break the definition down even further by comparing various types of learning goals by differentiating between acquisition, meaning-making, and transfer. All are important, but each is at a different depth of knowledge. *Acquisition* requires learners to acquire basic information and skills. *Meaning-making* requires learners to construct meaning of important ideas and processes. *Transfer* (which is the competency level) requires learners to transfer their learning autonomously and effectively in new situations.

How do students take these incremental steps to ensure they attain the building blocks they need to further their competency? This is achieved as students master the necessary skills and build on that mastery to move along to the next critical component or learning within that competency. This concept is known as a *learning progression*.

What Are Learning Targets?

According to Moss and Brookhart (2012), "the most effective teaching and the most meaningful student learning happen when teachers design the right learning target for today's lesson and use it along with their students to aim for and assess understanding" (p. 2). Bailey and Jakicic (2012) define these learning targets as the "smaller skills, strategies, and pieces of content information a student needs to know in order to be able to complete the standard" (p. 15).

To do this, teacher teams have to consider, in the pathway to meeting proficiency within a given standard, what the day-to-day lessons will encompass, how students can come to know and understand that deeply, and how it builds to the next day's target. In essence, these student-friendly, scaffolded building blocks help students develop the knowledge, skill, and stamina leading to successful demonstration of understanding.

Figure 3.6 provides a visual for the grain size of competencies, essential standards, and learning targets. Although there is some overlap, generally these different components can be thought of at these levels.

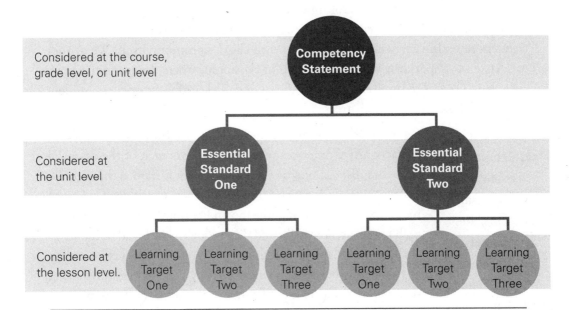

Figure 3.6: Visual for the grain size of competencies, essential standards, and learning targets.

What Are Learning Progressions?

As we note in *Breaking With Tradition* (Stack & Vander Els, 2018), "Learning progressions provide the pathways to learning that are crucial in a successful competency-based system" (p. 49).

Hess (2012) describes learning progressions as "research-based, descriptive continuums of how students develop and demonstrate deeper, broader, and more sophisticated understanding over time" (pp. 2–3). These progressions provide a road map for both a student and a teacher to follow how a student's understanding will progress and deepen over time. Heritage (2008) expands on this description by noting that learning progressions provide "clear connections between what comes before and after a particular point in the progression teachers can calibrate their teaching to any missing precursor understanding or skills revealed by assessment, and determine what the next steps are to move the student forward from that point" (p. 5). The progressions are made up of smaller, bite-size *learning targets*, which provide the day-to-day instructional focus.

What Is the Role of Metacognition?

There is a complementary relationship between assessment and instruction. Metacognition is at the heart of this relationship. *Metacognition*—thinking about thinking—plays a tremendous role in empowering students within the learning process and is a linchpin to learning and agency. Throughout this book, you will see this referenced within assessment, instruction, and the design rubric itself. We cannot overstate the importance of metacognition. In classrooms where metacognitive practices have become a consistent, embedded part of daily learning experiences, student agency and ownership have increased.

> **In classrooms where metacognitive practices have become a consistent, embedded part of daily learning experiences, student agency and ownership have increased.**

Lench, Fukuda, and Anderson's (2015) framework amplifies metacognitive practices within and across each of the essential skills and dispositions, as every component is framed through the "metacognitive sandwich." The components of self-awareness and monitoring and adapting (the top and bottom components within each of the essential skills and dispositions—the bread of the sandwich) provide the direction in the classroom for students to develop any skill, but they must be meaningfully included. Simply having students reflect at the end of a unit is not sufficient. In many cases it is too late for the student to change their behavior.

Embedded, meaningful reflection, with ongoing goal-setting and feedback (see figure 3.7), allows students to begin to own this process. In competency-based classrooms, these practices have had a profound effect.

Self-Direction
Self-Awareness
Reflecting on past experiences to evaluate one's own strengths, limitations, motivations, interests, and aspirations within different learning contexts
Initiation and Ownership
Taking responsibility for learning, finding purposeful driving questions, shaping opportunities to fit personal interests and learning styles, and seeking input from others
Goal Setting and Planning
Developing long-term goals, establishing meaningful learning targets, identifying effective strategies, and planning out steps
Engaging and Managing
Seeking out relevant resources and information to support learning goals and refining strategies; maintaining effective pace, and reaching short-term benchmarks and long-term goals
Monitoring and Adapting
Evaluating progress, adapting strategies, seizing failure in order to grow from mistakes, and attributing success to effort and motivation

Figure 3.7: Metacognitive skills framing self-direction.

Gail Bourn is the academic coordinator for teaching and learning for the Laconia School District in New Hampshire. Gail, as part of her district's committee to develop a plan for integrating work study practices, shares her journey to better understanding these competencies.

Practitioner Perspective
Gail Bourn, Academic Coordinator for Teaching and Learning, Laconia School District, Laconia, New Hampshire

Our district began its learning journey with work study practices (WSPs) as a way to measure students' behavior on our competency-based report card. The WSP team, which included administrators and teachers from the three elementary schools, began undertaking this professional learning with measuring students' behavior as the goal.

Very early on, our team members realized that WSPs were much more than just four skills to put on a report card. The team became a learning community with members working together to extend our collective knowledge and understanding of WSPs at a much deeper level. Through the course sessions, the team members entered into the reflective practice of learning, reflecting on new understandings, and revamping our original WSP goal for report cards. The team realized this was a learning experience for the administrators and teachers that was challenging the original reason for participating in the WSP course in the first place.

As the WSP team continued to learn and reflect on the WSPs, we added a second cohort of teachers to participate in the course the following year. Yes, our plans for adding the WSPs to the report card was pushed out for another year as we realized that our process importantly included building our collective understanding of the WSPs. The two WSP cohorts continued their learning, reflecting, and began planning on the process of bringing the WSPs to all the teachers and students across the three elementary schools. The teachers on the team began planning and implementing instruction for the four WSPs within their classrooms. The WSP team would reflect on the instruction and student learning to revise and rethink the entire learning process.

As we learned more, our team began to rethink their original goal of just putting the four WSPs on the report card and measuring them using a 4-point scoring rubric. We had many discussions on how to assess the WSPs. Our team continued to challenge each other's thinking on the WSPs, instruction, and assessment. The classroom teachers began having the students reflect on where they were with self-direction, communication, collaboration, or creativity within various learning experiences. This shifted the students' self-assessment beyond rote reflecting on the WSPs into an experience that included self-reflection, leading to true metacognition. The students were thinking and reflecting on where they were with a specific WSP. The WSPs were now taking on a new dimension for administrators, teachers, and students.

Digging into this work opened the door to many more questions. How do we assess the WSPs? Should we score them? What does this look like? Is it fair to put a score on WSPs? As our students grow, becoming more competent with WSPs, our thinking shifted. We thought of the WSPs as competencies. Then the "Aha!" moment came: we asked, Should the WSPs be on a continuum rather than a score or a rating? The students were moving toward being independent learners.

After this revelation by the team, the design for the continuum fell into place. The team developed descriptors for each WSP and continuum that went from "with support," to "minimal support," to "independent." The team created the WSP rollout plan for the following year that included professional development for all the teachers, resources for families, and templates for grade-level continuums.

When the COVID-19 pandemic hit in March 2020 and the school district switched to remote learning, the WSP team along with the teachers decided on the importance and relevance of the WSPs. With remote learning, self-direction, communication, collaboration, and creativity were raised to a new level of learning. During the weekly remote collaborative team meetings, the grade-level teams created WSP progress reports to share with students and parents rather than the traditional report card. The instruction included how to be self-directed when learning remotely, how to communicate through Zoom, how to collaborate with peers, and how to creatively share your learning remotely. We were leaning on the WSPs more and more during a very difficult time.

Our district's WSP journey continues as our portrait of a graduate now encompasses the four work study practices as well as two other skills: perseverance and problem solving. Through professional development, the PLC process, and the district WSP task

> force we are continuing to extend learning experiences for instructional strategies, reflection, and assessment tools to ensure that our students develop WSP competency as lifelong learners.
>
> (G. Bourn, personal communication, February 28, 2021)

Putting It All Together

Let's return to Jada's story and look at how she would organize the competencies, essential standards, and learning targets for her sixth-grade mathematics students in Kentucky. Jada and her team would use the Kentucky Academic Standards for Mathematics (Kentucky Department of Education, 2019, p. 116), as shown in figure 3.8. For sixth grade, Kentucky's mathematics standards are organized into five domains, as shown in the column headings in figure 3.8.

Ratios and Proportional Relationships (RP)	The Number System (NS)	Expressions and Equations (EE)	Geometry (G)	Statistics and Probability (SP)
• Understand ratio concepts and use ratio reasoning.	• Apply and extend previous understandings of multiplication and division to divide fractions by fractions. • Multiply and divide multi-digit numbers and find common factors and multiples. • Apply and extend previous understandings of numbers to the system of rational numbers.	• Apply and extend previous understandings of arithmetic to algebraic expressions. • Reason about and solve one-variable equations and inequalities. • Represent and analyze quantitative relationships between dependent and independent variables.	• Solve real-world and mathematical problems involving area, surface area and volume.	• Develop understanding of the process of statistical reasoning. • Develop understanding of statistical variability. • Summarize and describe distributions.

Source: Kentucky Department of Education, 2019, p. 116.

Figure 3.8: Kentucky academic standards for mathematics—Grade 6 overview.

Let's look deeper at the geometry domain. As it is written in figure 3.8 (page 65), the geometry competency for Jada's class could be written as follows: *Students will demonstrate the ability to solve real-world and mathematical problems involving area, surface area, and volume.* The Kentucky Academic Standards for Mathematics (Kentucky Department of Education, 2019, p. 130), shown in figure 3.9, breaks down this competency further into four academic standards, aligned with the National Council of Teachers of Mathematics (NCTM) mathematical practices and the Common Core.

Standards for Mathematical Practice	
MP.1. Make sense of problems and persevere in solving them.	MP.5. Use appropriate tools strategically.
MP.2. Reason abstractly and quantitatively.	MP.6. Attend to precision.
MP.3. Construct viable arguments and critique the reasoning of others.	MP.7. Look for and make use of structure.
MP.4. Model with mathematics.	MP.8. Look for and express regularity in repeated reasoning.
Standards (With Connections to Mathematical Practices)	
KY.6.G.1: Find the area of right triangles, other triangles, special quadrilaterals and polygons by composing into rectangles or decomposing into triangles and quadrilaterals; apply these techniques in the context of solving real-world and mathematical problems. **MP.1, MP.6, MP.8**	
KY.6.G.2: Find the volume of a right rectangular prism with rational number edge lengths. Apply the formulas $V = lwh$ and $V = Bh$ to find volumes of right rectangular prisms with rational number edge lengths in the context of solving real-world and mathematical problems. **MP.2, MP.5, MP.6**	
KY.6.G.3: Draw polygons in the coordinate plane given coordinates for the vertices; use coordinates to find the length of a side joining points with the same first coordinate or the same second coordinate. Apply these techniques in the context of solving real-world and mathematical problems. **MP.4, MP.5, MP.6**	
KY.6.G.4: Classify three-dimensional figures including cubes, prisms, pyramids, cones and spheres. **MP.2, MP.3**	

Source of standards: Kentucky Department of Education, 2019, p. 130.

Figure 3.9: Kentucky academic standards for mathematics—Grade 6 geometry standards.

Kentucky outlines the learning targets for the sixth-grade geometry domain as follows (Kentucky Department of Education, 2019):

> **Reason about relationships among shapes to determine area, surface area, and volume.** Students find areas of right triangles, other triangles and special quadrilaterals by decomposing these shapes, rearranging or removing pieces and relating the shapes to rectangles.

> **Discuss, develop, and justify formulas for areas of triangles and parallelograms.** Students find areas of polygons and surface areas of prisms and pyramids by decomposing them into pieces whose area they can determine. They reason about right rectangular prisms with fractional side lengths to extend formulas for the volume of a right rectangular prism to fractional side lengths. (p. 117)

It can be helpful to have learning targets written in student-friendly language. The State of New Hampshire, which offers a similar structure to that of Kentucky, does this with *I Can* statements (New Hampshire Department of Education, 2016):

> I can solve problems and justify solutions using geometric relationships, properties, and formulas (such as volume, surface area).

> I can decompose figures into new figures and construct figures with given conditions.

> I can represent authentic situations using coordinate graphing and diagrams. (p. 6)

These I can statements show what teachers can expect to see in student work on performance tasks when students apply their knowledge.

Educators in competency-based schools recognize the importance of examining their practices and prioritizing work that identifies and maps out a progression of competencies and standards and increases assessment literacy. Read more about this experience from Ellen Hume-Howard, currently the executive director of the New Hampshire Learning Initiative, and a former curriculum director who helped lead the transition to competency-based learning in her district. Ellen shares how her experience working with teachers across districts has allowed her to identify commonalities of teachers' questions in this process.

Practitioner Perspective
Ellen Hume-Howard, Executive Director, New Hampshire Learning Initiative

When supporting the transition to competency-based education, without fail, the first major hurdle teachers encounter is when they ask, "How are the standards and the competencies different? Do we get rid of standards once we adopt competencies? What are essential standards? What really matters?"

The truth is competencies are nothing without the standards. They belong together, and when districts have spent quality time helping teachers unpack their standards to understand what expectations are for students, it makes understanding competencies so much easier. However, part of that unpacking needs to include prioritizing. Not all standards are created equal; there are leveraging standards (essential standards) that support the skills that students need to demonstrate competency. Some standards take several years for students to master, while others are learned in a week. It is important teachers see the differences.

When I was a curriculum director in my own district, I started to really listen to what teachers said. I heard them express a desire to understand learners. How do they learn? What happens as they learn new concepts and ideas? What do they need to support them as learners? Teachers naturally want to personalize learning. They need assessment literacy to understand what evidence would best capture whether students are learning. They also need to see how students progress within the learning. Once their understanding of competencies and standards developed, they began to seek ways of collecting evidence of how students were demonstrating this learning.

I started to provide teachers with assessment training—not program training. We started by looking at the differences between formative and summative assessment. We trained teachers in performance assessment design and instructional planning, but it wasn't until we started to look at learning progressions that true assessment literacy started to take hold. We provided extensive training in the Ongoing Assessment Project (OGAP), a systematic, intentional, and iterative formative assessment system grounded in how students learn mathematics. This was a game changer. Then the teachers couldn't get enough. We found progressions for reading and writing and incorporated many other resources that supported the idea of learning as ongoing and part of multiple steps for becoming competent.

The next question I heard about competency-based education was, "Why are we doing another new thing?" This is a great question, and the answer is simply this: nothing in competency-based learning is new. The instructional practices and assessments where students demonstrate their learning and apply their knowledge and skills are part performance assessment, project-based learning, student capstones, student-led conferences with parents, learning simulations, science fairs, and other activities that students are often highly engaged in while actively applying what they know, understand, and can do. What is new is teachers' understanding of what should be the best evidence of learning. Most activities in classrooms are formative assessments that should be used to guide instruction, yet oftentimes they are used instead as the summative assessment of learning, actually stopping before students demonstrate the real learning.

Assessment literacy is by far the expertise most helpful to teachers. Combined with understanding the relationship between competencies and standards, using resources as a support for the learning, and looking at learning as a progression to guide learners, these strategies help teachers become competency educators.

(E. Hume-Howard, personal communication, February 22, 2021)

Ellen spends much of her time supporting schools and districts by working with teachers, allowing them time to calibrate their work around a common understanding of what students need to know and be able to do. Much of this work takes place through collaborative teaming, with teams taking ownership in the decisions related to competency and standard development, and the resulting assessment literacy work. Individuals on teams receive advanced professional development and training so that they can act as resident experts in these areas and support the work of teams in their school. It was with this approach that Ellen was able to help build a robust K–12 competency-based system in her own district, cocreated with teachers so that the system would be sustained and supported internally. It is this experience that influences her work with schools today.

Reflection Questions

Consider these questions with your team.

1. Curriculum conversations are a logical starting point for schools and teams. They should be framed to answer the first critical question of a PLC—What is it we want students to learn, know, and be able to do?—and also provide direction for design principle seven: rigorous, common expectations for learning are explicit, transparent, measurable, and transferable. How does your team calibrate their expectations for learning and understanding of mastery?

2. In a competency-based system, it is important to focus on not only the academic content knowledge, but also the skills and dispositions. How do you and your team support students by bringing these competencies to life for them through their learning experiences? How do you collect evidence of learning?

3. Understanding the relationships between and among competencies, essential standards, and learning targets is key in developing a cohesive framework to apply in the classroom. How would you describe these relationships to someone who is new to this work?

4. Teachers in collaborative teams must be part of the process for determining the what of learning, a critical component helping make up the trifecta of the why, what, and how. What role do teachers play in this process in your school now? What role would you like to see teachers play in the future?

CHAPTER 4

Meaningful, Balanced Assessment

What is the meaning of assessment? When most educators hear the word *assessment* they immediately think of testing. Our collective thinking about assessment and its role in learning must change. Instead of a narrow view of assessment as simply *assessment of learning*, it is imperative to move toward a more comprehensive view of assessment as *for learning* and even *as learning*.

As Jada and her team continued to work together, their collective understanding of the role of assessment changed dramatically. What started as an attempt to grade has transformed into a practice aimed at better understanding where their students are and what they collectively can learn from student work to determine what their next steps are to help each of their students continue to grow.

In a competency-based learning system, meaningful assessment is highlighted as the second design element (Levine & Patrick, 2019). In this chapter, we explore what meaningful assessment means in a competency-based classroom, asking questions such as, What can and should a classroom practicing meaningful assessment look like? and What is the role of the teacher and the student in this classroom? We also differentiate between formative and summative assessment practices, and the role of common formative assessments and common summative

> **Our collective thinking about assessment and its role in learning must change. Instead of a narrow view of assessment as simply *assessment of learning*, it is imperative to move toward a more comprehensive view of assessment as *for learning* and even *as learning*.**

assessments, as well as introduce the concepts of "ambitious teaching and learning" (Heritage & Wylie, 2020) in a competency-based classroom.

Additionally, we will explore the role of the collaborative team and how individual teachers within each team must work interdependently to answer the second critical question of a PLC, How will we know if students have learned it? (DuFour et al., 2016). In a competency-based system, balanced assessment is critical; understanding the various types of assessment and the role of the various assessment practices inherent in a competency-based system—including formative assessment and the role of performance assessments—strengthens teachers' ability to meet each student where they are. Collaborative teams, working together, can develop comprehensive assessment systems to support student learning. This work then leads to teams addressing critical questions three and four: How will we support students who haven't learned it? and How will we extend the learning for those who have? (DuFour et al., 2016).

First, we need to explore what assessment truly means. Assessment practices continue to evolve in competency-based classrooms. In fact, assessment has been a very powerful onramp to starting a competency-based journey for many schools and teachers. This really begins with a deepening understanding of what assessment truly means. As we noted at the start of the chapter, for many educators, the first thing we think of when we hear the word *assessment* is a test. But assessment and assessment practices are different. Ultimately, assessment strategies help to figure out where a learner is with their learning, or as Robert Marzano (2010) describes, to gather information about a student's knowledge regarding a specific topic with the goal of determining what additional supports and steps are needed for the student to be successful.

Components of a Balanced Assessment System

It is imperative to assess students on an ongoing basis. Kim Bailey and Chris Jakicic (2016) describe the needed components of a balanced assessment system. A balanced system includes classroom assessments, common formative assessments, interim benchmark assessments, and external summative assessments. These types of assessments are what teachers use to collect ongoing evidence of student learning.

- **Classroom assessments:** Classroom assessments include those day-to-day assessment opportunities that teachers engage in to gather quick feedback about where a student (or students) may be in their learning. They include observation, exit tickets, and quizzes.

- **Common formative assessments:** Common formative assessments (which we get into in more detail later in this chapter) are developed from the learning targets within an essential standard. These assessments occur as appropriate within a unit of study, but will trigger intervention and extension as appropriate.

- **Interim benchmark assessments:** Interim benchmark assessments (for example, NWEA MAP, iREADY, and Fountas and Pinnell Benchmark Assessments) are those assessments used in a district or school that provide staff information about growth over time. They are often administered around three times over the course of the year. These should be taken into consideration as specific student supports are considered.

- **External summative assessments:** These are typically state-level assessments used in accountability. These assessments also provide information related to growth over time.

Additionally, we must consider the role of the day-to-day collection of evidence that is happening in the classroom, as well as summative performance assessments, as important components. When we ask teachers how they know where their students are in their learning, the overwhelming response the teachers provide is that they know where students are in the learning based on more informal practices that occur in classrooms. Daily classroom practices such as observations, conversations, exit tickets, and other formative practices are the undergirding to supporting growth and must be highlighted because teachers rely on this information to determine their next steps in supporting and guiding students in progressing in their learning.

> **Daily classroom practices such as observations, conversations, exit tickets, and other formative practices are the undergirding to supporting growth and must be highlighted because teachers rely on this information to determine their next steps in supporting and guiding students in progressing in their learning.**

Formative Assessment as a Classroom Practice

Paul Black and Dylan Wiliam (1998) describe formative assessment as assessment that is "actually used to adapt the teaching to meet student needs" (p. 140). In classrooms dedicated to learning for all, this practice is of the utmost importance. Black and Wiliam identify three major criteria of effective formative assessment:

1. Teachers use assessment evidence to make adjustments to teaching and learning.

2. Students receive feedback during learning and are provided with advice on how they can improve.
3. Students are active participants in these processes through self-assessment.

Margaret Heritage (2010) highlights the FAST SCASS (Formative Assessment for Teachers and Students Standards from the Council of Chief State School Officers) definition of formative assessment as a "planned, ongoing process used by all students and teachers during learning and teaching to elicit and use evidence of student learning to improve student understanding of intended disciplinary learning outcomes and support students to become self-directed learners" (p. 14).

Of note, formative assessment practices are ongoing. Formative assessment as a practice is not actually a physical assessment (as opposed to common formative assessments). Formative assessment as a practice encompasses key components as outlined by Heritage and Wylie (2020):

> Clarifying learning goals and success criteria within a broader progression of learning
> Eliciting and analyzing evidence of student thinking
> Engaging in self-assessment and peer feedback
> Providing actionable feedback
> Using evidence and feedback to move learning forward by adjusting learning strategies, goals, or next instructional steps (p. 15)

Feedback is integral in learning and as Kay Burke (2010) puts it, "the heart and soul of formative assessment" (p. 21). It is also critical in increasing achievement. Hattie (2009) states that the "most powerful single influence enhancing achievement is feedback" (p. 12). Formative assessment includes timely opportunities for feedback, both for students, but also very importantly, for teachers. It is this symbiotic learning relationship and collaborative mindset between and among students and teachers that allows for assessment to be wholly meaningful.

It is this symbiotic learning relationship and collaborative mindset between and among students and teachers that allows for assessment to be wholly meaningful.

There are a number of critical factors that influence the ability for feedback to have its intended impact. Hattie (2009) cautions those who would just "provide more feedback" (p. 4) as a response to the strong correlation to student achievement seen with effective feedback strategies. Again, we must focus on the right type of feedback. This includes students providing each other with feedback in addition to teacher to student. And it is imperative that the culture in the classroom is one in which mistakes are welcomed as part of the learning process. Susan Brookhart notes that formative assessment is "as much about learning as it is about assessment" (as cited in Heritage, 2010). Likewise, James Popham (2008) notes that "assessments play a role in the process—they are not the process itself" (p. 7). It is critical that we do not look at assessment as the end but rather a critical component within the process itself.

Shifting the focus to formative assessment practices has had a significant impact in many schools and classrooms. Sunnyside Unified School District, in Tucson, Arizona began to shift its focus six years ago. Superintendent Steve Holmes, high school English teacher Kasie Betton, and fifth-grade teacher Samantha Fernandez share the impact on their teaching during this transition.

Practitioner Perspective
Superintendent Steve Holmes and Teachers Kasie Betton and Samantha Fernandez, Sunnyside Unified School District, Tucson, Arizona

Superintendent Steve Holmes: In communities of high poverty, school systems play a significant role in fostering inequalities that limit students' future opportunities for success. External accountability pressures coupled with systemic values of conformity, compliance, and completion result in enabling classroom environments where the expectations for student performance are low and the curriculum that students have access to is limited and narrow in scope.

In 2015, the Sunnyside Unified School District in Tucson, Arizona, a school system that had historically embraced a culture of low student achievement, decided to change its failed approach to teaching and learning. Through the vision of a new superintendent that was focused on building coherence around the fostering of student agency and identity in learning, the district embraced a strategy for providing deeper learning experiences to students through the process of formative assessment.

Using formative assessment to help teachers better notice and respond to student learning in the context of the learning process has helped create a learning culture in classrooms that supports learner agency. This shift in the classroom has had a profound impact on both students and teachers.

Samantha Fernandez: My formative assessment journey began in 2016 at my elementary school. This change began with a small cohort of lead teachers, focusing on what formative assessment really means in our district and what it had the potential to mean for our students. Our principal encouraged us to engage in this new work fully, believing that the more we delved into this new learning, the more we would buy into its impact for our students. While this was a large undertaking, and a complete shift in the way we thought about teaching and learning, the overall theme was the need for students to be at the center of the learning process and engaged in every aspect of their learning. We could not continue with our usual practice of delivering the learning for students to accept, practice, and then move on from. We were to become the facilitators while the students took ownership. Our role is now eliciting and collecting evidence of student learning.

My understanding of my role in the classroom was called into question, and throughout my professional learning, I saw that my role could not stay unchanged if my students were to become agents of their own learning. The uncomfortable process of looking closely at my own instruction and seeing the way I was unintentionally holding my students back had begun. This process, which in reality will never (and should never) end, is where I find myself today, reflecting on my teaching but mostly reflecting on my students. At this point, seeing the changes in my fifth graders tells me the most about the changes I have made in my practice, as well as the changes my colleagues have made as I inherit their students.

I have students who come to me as critical thinkers and problem solvers. My students do not expect me to hold knowledge and give it to them. I see students who look to their peers for help and support rather than just to me. I hear students ask for feedback and reflect on where they are in their learning and set next steps that could support their learning tomorrow. I watch students who previously felt disconnected from learning now feel a sense of accomplishment and success in their learning. This shift in student engagement allows me to focus on addressing misconceptions as they arise, give feedback to students throughout lessons instead of at the end of a unit, and support students in pushing their thinking. I do not need to rely on quizzes or tests to know where students are in their learning anymore. The change in control in my classroom has been a freeing experience and has changed the way students view themselves as learners and the impact they have on their own learning.

Kasie Betton: When I first started teaching, I didn't really understand what *learning* meant. I saw learning in a two-dimensional way: I had the information, and the students needed to take it from me. In my classroom, we would do many activities that relied on me to give them the "right" answer, a structure that inherently put me at the center of the learning. Even though the students did a variety of activities, even collaborated often with peers, I was the keeper of the knowledge. I did not trust my students to be partners with me in the learning process and this bred compliance rather than academic success.

Another problem I ran into was that I was only able to assess the students' growth after they had turned something in. This forced me to always play catch up in their learning. I was trapped in a cycle of reteaching and it was not allowing me to push my students to meet more rigorous expectations. Grade-level standards were getting harder and harder to meet or even approach because I was always looking backward.

Then, four years ago in 2017, I began my journey with formative assessment. Following WestEd's SAIL (2021) pedagogical approach about formative assessment, I was able to start to understand the nuances of learning. I gained the ability to critically reflect on my instructional practices and learned new methods to replace my flawed strategies.

I learned how to elicit evidence of student learning in a minute-by-minute way. I was able to see how students were struggling or succeeding during the activities, rather than waiting until I could grade them. Eliciting and responding to that evidence allowed me to consistently push my students forward rather than always looking beyond us. I could address misconceptions as they arose and could help my students move past them. Over time, my students were able to work with ease on many more higher-level tasks and grapple with much more rigorous concepts because I could support their needs in real-time.

More importantly, my work in formative assessment shifted how I saw my students as learners. I came to understand that they do not need to rely on me for information. In fact,

> they should not rely on me for information at all! I will not travel with them for the rest of their lives giving them the answers they need. Instead, my job is to teach them how to rely on themselves to learn successfully. My students became the active focus in the classroom. They have a choice in the way they approach learning, they have the ability to give and receive feedback from their peers, and they have a space to be curious rather than just being "right." This was the most important shift that I had in this process. Having my students be my partners rather than my subordinates makes my classroom a place where we truly celebrate the joys of true learning.
>
> (S. Holmes, S. Fernandez, & K. Betton, personal communication, March 16, 2021)

These personal reflections from educators in the Sunnyside Unified School District demonstrate how a district that held very strong perspectives on what learning was with little results, can actually make intentional shifts that provide more equitable learning opportunities for students that lead to great learner agency. These instructional shifts are not only better for students, but they also bring greater value to the role of the teacher as a professional who is dedicated to their own continued learning and development.

Ambitious Teaching and Formative Assessment

Teaching and learning in a competency-based environment look different than a traditional system. There are a number of factors that we can point to, but the learning relationship between students and teachers is a significant difference: the relationship is one where learning is shared. No longer is the teacher simply standing at the front of the classroom and sharing the information that is necessary for students to learn. Ultimately, students will take ownership of their learning, develop disciplinary knowledge, be able to apply this learning to unique situations and problems, and reflect, collaborate, and seek to understand others' perspectives. All of these educational objectives fall within the concept of *ambitious teaching*. Margaret Heritage (2020) identifies ambitious teaching as a "model for pedagogy that exemplifies the changes in teaching practices . . . to realize (these goals)" (p. 6).

Great teaching is always pushing students a bit out of their comfort zone. As such, ambitious teaching adapts to students' needs based on where they are. To do this, teachers must have information on hand to make these adaptations.

The first design principle states that "Students are empowered daily to make important decisions about their learning experiences, how they will create and apply knowledge, and how they will demonstrate their learning" (Levine & Patrick, 2019, p. 3). The practice of formative assessment, embedded into daily learning, allows for student agency and empowerment. This is the essence of assessment as learning.

The Role of Student Self-Assessment

The role of self-assessment in formative practices is critical. Olson (2003) as cited in Hattie (2009) states that "it is students themselves, in the end, not teachers, who decide what students will learn" (p. 241). Hattie's (2009) research indicates that student self-reporting has an effect size of 1.28, an incredibly powerful impact on overall learning. In 2018, when Hattie's research was updated, the effect size grew even more, landing at 1.33 (Visible Learning, n.d.).

However, to self-assess, students must understand a number of components in the process. As Black and Wiliam (1998) note in their incredibly influential piece *Inside the Black Box*, "When anyone is trying to learn, feedback about the effort has three elements: recognition of the *desired goal*, evidence about *present position*, and some understanding of *a way to close the gap* between the two" (p. 143). The learner must recognize all three of these components before true ownership of the learning process can happen.

A great example of student self-assessment in a competency-based system is the work done in skills and dispositions in schools and the correlation and impact on content areas. Teachers who facilitate students' reflection on where they are within a specific skill (self-direction, for example), who recognize where they would like to be within that skill (for example, successful in backward planning due dates for an upcoming project due in three weeks), and then monitor and adapt their next steps based on where they are (recognizing that they were unable to meet their goal at the end of week one, adjusting their goal to ensure completion by the end of week two), realize greater success in achieving their goals. They also begin to develop these skills through their ongoing practice, reflection, support from the teacher and peers, and ultimately the reward of finding success when they have been the ones to own the process.

Irene Stinson, a fifth-grade teacher in the Laconia School District in New Hampshire, along with her team, began to embed these processes for developing what New Hampshire refers to as the Work Study Practices (WSPs): communication, collaboration, creativity, and self-direction. Irene and her colleagues took a non-punitive approach, relying on developmental progressions, to provide students the opportunity to own the process, and students applied the skill of self-direction to what support they may individually need in mathematics. The result was students who knew where they were, where they wanted and needed to be, and what they needed to do to get there.

Practitioner Perspective
Irene Stinson, Fifth-Grade Teacher, Laconia School District, New Hampshire

Reflecting on my years of teaching, I can see that a desire for my students to be independent learners has always been a recurring theme. My first year in the classroom, I created a unit around teaching students how to be independent learners—one who initiates learning, perseveres through difficult tasks, and identifies their strengths and weaknesses. Little did I know, I was trying to teach students to become self-directed learners. However, I was missing a key component of the puzzle: metacognition. Much of this came into focus through our development of the WSPs and our implementation plan.

As our district team developed what WSPs meant for Laconia, a few of the teachers started implementing self-direction. As I looked at my classroom of learners, I saw that mathematics intervention was a small part of our day where I could take the time to explicitly teach self-direction and then, hopefully, students could transfer those skills into other areas. Mathematics intervention is a time where small-group instruction is delivered focusing on strengthening and extending skills for students. Group formation was teacher determined based on collected data. After many conversations about what it meant to be self-directed, developing an awareness of strengths and weaknesses, and setting obtainable goals, I allowed my students to choose which mathematics groups they would attend based on what they needed. There were some constraints and expectations; despite this, students thrived during this time, choosing groups they knew would support them on their learning journey. Students were able to articulate and reflect on their choices while student agency was evident, and growth was exponential.

The next school year was the complete implementation of the WSPs. Work done during the summer developed the plan for how students would be evaluated on the WSPs as well as our implementation plan. Each quarter, teachers would give direct instruction on a WSP and offer numerous opportunities to demonstrate and practice the skills. Quarter one focused on self-direction, and I implemented the plan for mathematics groups from the previous year. Again, students flourished and began understanding their strengths and weaknesses. Students used the data collected from informal assessments to look at different mathematics skills. Then, they created a list of skills they needed to improve or challenge themselves with. Through conferences, I helped provide feedback on the skills they identified. We also focused on setting action plans to achieve the goals set. This came with weekly student reflections in their reflection journal. Also, within this journal, I wanted students to think about their choices. For example, in my classroom, there are no assigned seats and many different seating options. This lends itself to be reflective of who you sit with and what type of seat you choose. I often had students reflect on their work completion based on their seating choice and peers around them. Students became quickly aware through reflection of themselves as learners and what supported their learning and what prohibited it.

As the year continued, our next focus was on communication where students focused on audience and purpose. Students continued to use reflection journals to capture evidence of learning and their thought processes. During quarter three, we pivoted to remote learning due to the COVID-19 pandemic. The students' way of learning completely changed; it turned upside down. The responsibility was now on students to access their assignments, reach out for help, and show their learning digitally. Due to the amount of work we put into

> self-direction and communication, as well as students knowing themselves as learners, students were successful during this remote time. They showed up to scheduled meetings, appropriately communicated their learning, and requested support as well as continued on their learning journey.
>
> During this time, I challenged my students to continue a project-based learning experience we started right before our transition to remote learning. Although we were not able to complete all the pieces originally planned, students were successful. Through the researcher's workshop, conferences, and goal setting, students were able to create a public presentation. Students presented their learning journey through a visual display over a Zoom meeting with members of our School Administrative Unit and our administrators. Having taught the skills of self-direction, communication, and metacognition, students were able to speak knowledgeably about their learning journey struggles and successes as well as the content they learned. It was truly a powerful moment. Without taking the time earlier in the year, I am truly unsure if the students would have been able to create what they did in the circumstances they faced. The power of metacognition and being able to think and reflect on your thought process supports student growth as well as allows the teacher to continue to offer appropriate learning opportunities.

(I. Stinson, personal communication, March 2, 2021)

Common Formative Assessment: Measuring Where Students Are

Whereas formative assessment practices such as observation, conversations, and exit tickets are the day-to-day ways in which teachers are collecting evidence about where students are, it is important to have a more formal measure that is specific to learning targets to determine not only where students are related to these targets but also as a means to trigger more formal intervention or extension. Common formative assessments are the best way to do this. Kim Bailey and Chris Jakicic (2012) describe common formative assessments as assessments that collaborative teams "develop and use to assure students are learning and to (help these teams) to know what to do next when (students) need additional time and support" (p. 21).

Common formative assessments will provide the timely, actionable feedback that teacher teams need to ensure that students are mastering the most essential learning, and provide the evidence needed to trigger the appropriate instructional response, based on students' needs.

> **Common formative assessments will provide the timely, actionable feedback that teacher teams need to ensure that students are mastering the most essential learning, and provide the evidence needed to trigger the appropriate instructional response, based on students' needs.**

Collaborative teacher teams in a school develop the common formative assessments. These are not ready-made quizzes as part of a program; it is critical that the questions in any type of assessment are deliberate, meaningful, and aligned to essential standards and learning targets. Oftentimes, less is more. Figure 4.1 is a tool teams can use to develop common formative assessments.

Team Members:	**Unit of Study:**
What is essential to learn (at the standard level)?	
What are the learning targets that lead to mastery?	
What are different ways students might demonstrate their understanding of these targets?	
What is the time needed for instruction and assessment of these targets?	
What will the evidence of learning include? Formatively—common formative assessments? Summatively—performance assessments?	
Which students will need additional support? How will this occur?	
How will we reassess? Who is responsible?	

Figure 4.1: Resource for common formative assessments.

Summative Assessment: Seeking Evidence of Transfer

Ultimately, students and teachers together are seeking evidence of students' ability to demonstrate their knowledge of content and skills through their application and transfer of the learned skills.

There are a number of ways to see this transfer occur, but ultimately, there will need to be application of some kind by the students. Performance tasks and performance assessments, in our experience, are the ideal way to allow students to demonstrate this application or transfer in a competency-based system.

Performance Assessment

The Center for Collaborative Education (CCE; 2012), in their publication *Quality Performance Assessment: A Guide for Schools and Districts*, defines performance assessments as "multistep assignments with clear criteria, expectations, and processes that measure how well a student transfers knowledge and applies complex skills to create or refine an original product" (p. 140). Performance assessments help students *apply* their knowledge in the context of new settings or problems and provide students with the opportunity to demonstrate their ability to *transfer* their learning in an authentic, real-world situation or task. This ability to apply and transfer are key components to a competency-based classroom.

Performance assessments, by nature, capture transfer of learning. When developed with this in mind, performance assessments allow students to demonstrate what they've learned. CCE (2012) identifies five major steps in building a performance assessment.

1. Design common tasks.
2. Craft clear criteria and a rubric.
3. Administer performance assessment and score student work.
4. Anchor assessments through exemplary work.
5. Refine and iterate performance assessment and rubric.

The process of engaging in developing, administering, reflecting, and refining is what makes performance assessments so incredibly powerful. Performance assessment is about teaching and learning, for both students and adults.

For many districts, performance assessment has been a successful entry point for deeper learning. It has provided an onramp for considering many of the other critical components of competency-based systems, to understanding the relationship between competencies and standards, student ownership in learning and agency, equity considerations, and what it means to transfer and apply knowledge. But this learning takes time.

Bill Dinkelmann, director of K–12 competency-based education and secondary curriculum for the Kenowa Hills Public Schools in Grand Rapids, Michigan, has been instrumental in planning a competency-based rollout within his district over the course of multiple years, with a specific emphasis on performance assessments.

> **Practitioner Perspective**
> **Bill Dinkelmann, Kenowa Hills Public Schools, Grand Rapids, Michigan**
>
> Kenowa Hills is located to the northwest of Grand Rapids, Michigan. The district includes forty-seven square miles with a blend of residential, retail business, industrial manufacturers, and fruit orchards. In 2020–2021, the school serves approximately 3,350 students within one early childhood building, three elementary schools, one middle school, and one high school.
>
> The district began focusing on increasing its capacity to develop, implement, and refine performance assessments during the 2018–2019 school year. This focus is a byproduct of a decision made in 2012 to implement a personalized, competency-based educational system. We organize and implement our personal-mastery efforts and initiatives (the name for our brand of personalized, competency-based education) within the five levels of Robert Marzano's high-reliability schools (HRS) model (Marzano et al., 2018). Unsurprisingly, performance assessments are identified as a critical area of growth that tightly align to several levels of the HRS model.
>
> As we explored how to move forward, we knew that we needed a deep, professional learning focus on performance assessments for our general and special education staff and building administrators. We saw this work as a natural next step to identifying essential standards that serve as the basis of our guaranteed and viable curriculum, as well as a complement to our continued and future work implementing standards-based grading and standards-referenced reporting systems. We also identified several strategic connections for this work to our social and emotional learning programs and the district's profile of a graduate.
>
> Our desire to elevate the collective capacity of our teachers to embed performance assessments within the natural flow of student learning experiences throughout the school year drove several critical elements of our plan to deliver this professional learning. As we dug deeper into planning efforts, we came to the following crucial agreements. We wanted to provide a high-quality learning experience for each of our 180 K–12 educators.
>
> - We wanted a professional learning series that unfolded over time as opposed to being compressed into an intensive one or two day event.
> - We wanted to embed this work into the flow of our teachers' semester planning efforts.
> - We wanted a challenging professional learning experience that provided multiple entry points to honor the differing experiences and capabilities of our K–12 educators.

> - We wanted KHPS educators to work with their peers in an intentional, structured design process that included feedback loops prior to and after the use of a performance assessment to model data analysis and reflection on how to improve.
>
> After identifying these design needs, we initiated a cohort model to provide a face-to-face professional learning series for all KHPS teachers grouped into five cohorts of thirty-three to forty K–12 educators across two-and-a-half school years.
>
> Each of our cohorts were scheduled to participate in three half days of professional learning. These sessions were scheduled to encourage teachers to administer the performance assessment and collect evidence of student learning prior to the last session to engage in a validation protocol to calibrate and develop inter-rater reliability. We started with our first cohort in the spring of 2019.
>
> Every educator understands that all good plans provide the basis for quick modifications when the realities of life hit you between the eyes. In this case, our detailed plan and commitment that all K–12 teachers engage in this professional learning allowed us to adjust after the arrival of the COVID-19 pandemic in March of 2020.
>
> Needing to adjust our plan to meet social distancing and group size limits called for by state and local health directives, we continued our cohort design, reengineering the series for the 2020–2021 school year. The new plan included a live, virtual professional learning series consisting of five ninety-minute Zoom sessions for our cohort three and four participants. We also needed to ensure that we could also bring our cohort two participants into the virtual series because their last cohort session had been cancelled in the initial chaos of COVID-19.
>
> As we wrap-up this two-and-a-half year professional learning journey, we are thankful for the growth that our teachers have experienced. We have received feedback that teachers are more confident in designing and facilitating performance assessments and that students are engaging with content at higher levels. Our future plans in this area include the development of a systematic process to collect, share, and refine performance assessments within our elementary grade-level and secondary department collaborative teams.
>
> (B. Dinkelmann, personal communication, March 29, 2021)

The Quality Performance Assessment Cycle

The five steps listed previously can be integrated into a cycle of three key components for collaborative teams to follow to structure their work. The Quality Performance Assessment cycle contains three major components. Figure 4.2 captures these three areas.

Meaningful, Balanced Assessment

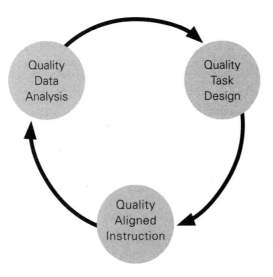

Source: *Center for Collaborative Education, 2012.*

Figure 4.2: Three components of the quality performance assessment cycle.

1. **Quality task design:** It is imperative to begin with the end in mind. Designing quality tasks allows teacher teams the clarity to collect the evidence they need to determine proficiency for their students on the "content and cognitive complexity" (CCE, 2012, p. 7) specific to their grade, unit, or course of study.

2. **Quality aligned instruction:** Working backward from the endpoint of where they want students to be, teacher teams must identify the learning targets and correlating instruction that will allow students to learn what they need to learn. Ultimately, teams intend to affect the instructional core through this work of aligning instruction, and the day-to-day learning that happens must be clearly aligned to the intended outcomes that teams have identified.

3. **Quality data analysis:** One of the most overlooked components of the process of performance assessment is collaboration. It is imperative that teacher teams maximize their collaborative team time to reflect on

> **Ultimately, teams intend to affect the instructional core through this work of aligning instruction, and the day-to-day learning that happens must be clearly aligned to the intended outcomes that teams have identified.**

student work, calibrate, and improve inter-rater reliability. Through these processes, not only will the learning experiences that students engage in improve, but also individual and collective teacher efficacy will increase.

Our "Student Work Calibration Protocol and Rubric Analysis Tool" (page 202) in the appendix can help guide these processes.

Reassessment

Reassessment is a crucial overall component of an effective assessment system in a competency-based learning model. Assessment is an ongoing process; it is not one and done. Teachers will continue to collect evidence of where students are in their learning. Likewise, the process of learning is ongoing. Assessment simply measures where a student is at that point in time. The results must be used to determine next steps. Bailey and Jakicic (2012; 2016) describe that this type of feedback is "intended to help students reflect on their own learning and adjust their strategies as needed in order to meet or exceed the expectation and achieve deeper understanding of the important concepts" (p. 21). A student's ability to understand where they are in their learning is a linchpin in a competency-based system. Teachers must scaffold this process for students until they can take on greater ownership in the process itself. We examine reassessment in greater detail in chapter 6, page 129.

Rigor, Complexity, and Cognitive Demand

In a competency-based learning system, high levels of rigor, complexity, and demand are embedded within a student's learning experiences. Daniel Joseph, Karin Hess, and Rose Colby (2020) define *cognitive rigor* as encompassing the "complexity of the content, the cognitive engagement with that content, and the scope of the planned learning activity" (p. 77).

Complexity reflects an increased depth of knowledge. Complexity is different than difficulty; something that is difficult might just be something unknown, but it could still be at a lower depth of knowledge. Hess and colleagues (2019) describe *cognitive demand* as the "potential range of mental processing required to complete a task within a given context" (p. 77).

Karin Hess developed rigor matrices (see page 205 in the appendix) that combine Webb's Depth of Knowledge (2002) and Bloom's Taxonomy (1954) that can help teachers in the development of both learning experiences (instructionally) and ways of collecting evidence (assessment). Remember that competency is about *transfer* of learning; learning experiences in a competency-based system ideally will get to a higher cognitive rigor, level of complexity, and require greater cognitive demand (Depth of Knowledge 3 or 4). Additionally, learning experiences should be engaging and connect to the students' world in some way.

Rubrics

Achieving clarity on and adequately articulating what we intend to assess, what success looks like for students, and the progression of levels specific to these indicators is an incredibly complex undertaking for collaborative teams. Task-specific rubrics developed at the standard level with learning targets in mind not only allow teachers the basis for which to plan their instruction, but also provide students with clear expectations for demonstrating their learning.

As Christina Brown and Amy Mednick (2012) explain, a "rubric describes the degree of quality, proficiency, and understanding along a continuum" (p. 65). Teachers should keep descriptors broad and general enough so as to allow multiple pathways to demonstrate proficiency, but detailed enough to allow others to understand what success will look like specific to a standard.

Figure 4.3 is a template for teacher teams to utilize as they develop a rubric to best capture student learning. The top portion—the competency statement—should reflect the overarching competency that the essential standards will flow into. If your school or district does not have competency statements (yet), you may also put the broader essential understanding here.

Competency Statement				
	Beginning 1	Developing 2	Proficient 3	Exemplary 4
Standard 1				
Standard 2				
Standard 3				
Skills and Dispositions				

Figure 4.3: Rubric template.

Notice the language used in the rubric template. It is consistent with growth. We all are *beginning* when we start learning a skill. *Developing* suggests growth and an almost-there mindset. *Proficient* is what we are aiming for and represents transfer and application, and through deeper, more complex experiences, we may be able to move students to *exemplary*.

Rubrics should be descriptive enough that they offer a progression of complexity, rather than just an amount of work. We would suggest staying away from numbers within the descriptors (3–5 facts, for example). As Susan Brookhart notes (2013), "Rubrics are not about the requirements for the assignment, nor are they about counting things" (p. 18). Keep the focus of the rubric on the learning, rather than just a checklist or outline for students to follow to earn points.

Teams need to determine which essential standards the assessment they are building will focus on. Teams should remember that less is more. We suggest no more than three standards be integrated into a performance assessment. This is not to say that teams cannot collect evidence of learning in other standards throughout the unit of instruction, but for the purposes of the performance assessment, teams should focus solely on no more than a few major areas. Otherwise, the performance assessment can become focused on too many discrete skills rather than the transfer of essential learning we know leads to competency.

Susan Brookhart (2013) describes the importance of writing performance-level indicators as "what one would observe in the work rather than the quality conclusions one would draw" (p. 26). Given this, teachers should begin developing their rubric at the 3 or proficient level by asking themselves what they should expect to see demonstrated in student work that provides evidence of the essential standard. From proficient, teachers should work backward to the 2 or developing stage, considering what the progression of steps leading to proficiency is and what a student who is developing (close to proficient, but just not there yet) may be providing for evidence of learning. Similarly, for a 1 or beginning level, teacher teams should try to capture that initial level of understanding.

The 4 or exemplary level offers an opportunity to consider those students who will be able to go deeper. Teams can use the Hess (2012) Rigor Matrices to consider how to go deeper.

The sample rubric in figure 4.4 provides a glimpse at an elementary teacher's early attempts at clarifying what she is intending to capture. (The rubric is adapted from Amanda Loder, a singleton third-grade teacher at Lincoln Akerman School in Hampton Falls, New Hampshire, who developed this with feedback from vertical-level colleagues). The second example, shown in figure 4.5 (page 90), provides an example of a secondary science rubric.

Please note the progression of complexity evident as the descriptors move from one to four.

	Beginning 1	Developing 2	Proficient 3	Exemplary 4
ELA.03.INF.01: Writes informative/explanatory texts to examine a topic and convey ideas and information clearly	Introduces a clear and focused topic. Organizes information by subtopic. Includes some facts. Uses minimal relevant text features to convey information.	Introduces a clear and focused topic and organizes information into multiple subheadings in meaningful ways. Includes facts and text features to convey information.	Introduces a clear and focused topic and organizes information into multiple subheadings in meaningful ways. Includes facts, ideas, and opinions about the topic that are supported by relevant text features to convey information.	Introduces a clear and focused topic and organizes information into multiple subheadings in meaningful ways. Includes facts as well as well-developed ideas and opinions, and meaningful connections to their community, the world, and personal experiences that are supported and enhanced by relevant text features to convey information.
ELA.03.INF.02: Edits and revises text for clarity	Uses a rubric to compare work to the standards against which it will be evaluated. Makes some revisions.	Uses a rubric to compare work to the standards against which it will be evaluated. Revises work to convey ideas with clarity.	Uses a rubric to compare work to the standards against which it will be evaluated. Considers the organization of information in the piece and revises work to convey ideas with clarity.	Uses a rubric to compare work to the standards against which it will be evaluated. Considers the reader's background knowledge as well as the organization of the information, and makes purposeful revisions to convey ideas with clarity.
SAU.CAR.R: Recognizes own responsibility for personal and community outcomes.	Sets personal goals for work completion. Sometimes meets goals. Adjusts behavior as necessary with many prompts and teacher redirection. Provides self-directed feedback to set relevant and timely goals with support.	Sets personal goals for work completion. Usually meets goals. Remains motivated to work toward meeting goals and adjusts behavior as necessary with prompts or teacher redirection. Provides self-directed feedback to set relevant and timely goals with support.	Sets and reaches personal goals for work completion. Remains motivated to work toward meeting goals and adjusts behavior, as necessary. Provides self-directed feedback to set relevant and timely goals.	Sets and reaches personal goals for work completion. Remains motivated to work toward meeting goals and adjusts behavior, as necessary. Independently reframes personal goals when they are reached to continue progressing. Applies metacognitive strategies to set relevant, timely, and thoughtful goals, and monitors and adapts these goals as appropriate.

Students will compose informative text to examine a topic and convey ideas and information with a specific focus.

Source: Amanda Loder, 2021, Lincoln Ackerman School, Hampton Falls, New Hampshire. Adapted with permission.

Figure 4.4: Elementary rubric example.

C1: Asking Questions and Defining Problems—Students will demonstrate the ability to ask and refine testable questions that lead to descriptions and explanations of the natural and designed world.				
	Beginning 1	**Developing 2**	**Proficient 3**	**Exemplary 4**
Standard 1	I can ask questions that are not testable or require evidence to answer.	I can ask testable questions but do not describe evidence that would answer the questions.	I can ask testable questions and describe sufficient and relevant evidence that would answer the questions.	I can ask precise, testable questions and describe sufficient and relevant evidence that would answer the questions. I can evaluate the testability of the questions.
Standard 2	I do not form a hypothesis or form a hypothesis that does not predict or explain relationships between independent and dependent variables and controls, if applicable.	I can attempt to form a hypothesis to discuss predicted relationships between the independent and dependent variables and controls, if applicable, and use scientific principles to explain the predicted relationships, but prediction is illogical or incomplete.	I can form a hypothesis to discuss predicted relationships between independent and dependent variables, and controls, if applicable, and use scientific principles to explain the predicted relationships.	I can form a hypothesis to discuss predicted relationships between independent and dependent variables, and controls, if applicable, and use scientific principles and prior knowledge to explain the predicted relationships.
Standard 3	I can partially define a problem but do not use scientific principles to explain how specific design elements are necessary to solve the problem.	I can define a problem and attempt to use scientific principles to explain how specific design elements are necessary to solve the problem, but explanation is inaccurate or incomplete.	I can define a problem and use scientific principles to explain how specific design elements are necessary to solve the problem.	I can define a problem precisely and use scientific principles and prior knowledge to thoroughly explain how specific design elements are necessary to solve the problem.
Skills and Dispositions: Reflection—The learner is self-aware, takes responsibility, openly receives feedback, and seeks improvement.	With modeling or direct support or explanation, I can perform the expectations.	I can inconsistently perform or need routine support in order to perform the expectations.	I can perform the expectations with occasional prompting or support.	I can independently and regularly perform the expectations.

Source: Erica Pappalardo, 2021, Inter-Lakes School District, Meredith, New Hampshire. Adapted with permission.

Figure 4.5: Rubric example 2.

When taking a first attempt at writing a rubric, teams should do their best to attempt to identify what student performance they expect to see for proficiency. However, they must also understand the need to go back to the rubric post-assessment to reflect and refine based upon what they have learned throughout the completed unit of instruction.

The data-analysis step that follows administration of the assessment is one of the most powerful activities teams can engage in together, looking at student work, developing consensus on how a specific example of student work rates in relation to the rubric, and then refining the rubric. Once a team has agreed that a specific piece of work is at a 3 or proficient, then they should ask themselves, "What specifically does this artifact contain within its evidence that makes it proficient?" When teams are able to clarify this, they will be able to adapt their descriptors to better match their expectations.

The Unit Planning Template

The resource in figure 4.6 (page 92) differentiates between three critical processes inherent in unit planning. These three parts correspond with the four critical questions of learning in a PLC.

1. Section one should be the first portion the teacher team completes. Beginning with the end in mind, teacher teams can determine together the competencies and underlying essential standards, 21st century skills, tasks, and rubrics. This section corresponds with the first critical question of a PLC: What do we want students to know and be able to do (competencies and essential standards)? as well as the second critical question of a PLC: How will we know if they've learned it (tasks and rubrics)? (DuFour et al., 2016).

2. Section two is the next part the teacher team completes. Section two outlines the instructional components of the unit, including essential questions to guide learning, the content and skills to be learned, the common formative assessment focus and schedule, the resulting intervention and extension plan, how to ensure all students can access the learning, and any applicable resources.

3. Section three is often skipped, but is critically important within the process. Teams must revisit the unit after the summative assessment and reflect together. This includes looking at student work, and ensuring that any refinements to the assessment, rubric, and instruction are made and noted for the future.

CBL Classroom Assessment Planning Template	
Section One	
Unit:	Grade Level, Content Area, Team Members:
Essential Outcome (Why is this learning experience important?):	
Competency Statement: **Essential Standards:** 21st Century Skills (Communication, Collaboration, Creativity, Self-Direction):	
Task Summary:	**Rubric:**
Section Two	
Essential Questions to Guide Learning:	
Students will know (content) and be able to demonstrate (skills); teacher driven:	Students would like to know (content) and demonstrate in their unique way (skills); student driven:
Assessment Schedule (to include CFA and CSA):	Plan for Ongoing Intervention and Extension:
Resources:	Considerations for Those Furthest From Accessing Learning:
Section Three	
Plan for Post-Intervention and Extension:	
Revisions to Task (after administration):	

Sources: Center for Collaborative Education, 2012; Hess, 2012; McTighe & Wiggins, 2004.

Figure 4.6: CBL classroom assessment-planning template.

Section One

The following list describes each step teams take in this first portion of the assessment-planning template.

- **Unit**: Indicate what unit of study the learning experiences will occur in.
- **Grade level, content area, and team members**: Identify this information for organizational purposes and for potential sharing with other teams and schools.
- **Essential outcome**: The essential outcome is critical because it helps both teachers and students understand the relevance within this learning experience as well as what key takeaways students should have from the learning experience. Ultimately, the essential outcome explains why this is important.
- **Competency statement, essential standards, and 21st century skills**: The competency statement is the specific competency the task will provide evidence for mastery of. The essential standards identify those that the competency focuses on. There is also space for teacher teams to consider which 21st century skills and dispositions the task may lend itself to. For example, does the performance task require collaboration? If so, being explicit about how students can collect their own evidence of growth and learning through the learning experience should be included.
- **Task summary:** The task summary should describe the task itself and answer the following questions.
    - What specifically are we asking students to do?
    - Where specifically will they be able to demonstrate transfer or application for the essential standard?
    - How specifically will this give us evidence of their learning?
- **Rubric:** Creating a rubric that concisely captures what student work will represent in a given task is one of the most difficult parts of the assessment process. This process captures the essence of a PLC's ongoing process of action research. Your rubrics will (and should) change constantly through the process of reflection and refinement.

    The following tips will help teams write rubrics.

    1. Remember that less is more. Be crystal clear on what is most important to assess. For every standard you choose as part of the assessment, you must also have an accompanying section within the rubric that identifies the levels of proficiency.

2. Begin with level 3 (proficient), and then work backward to level 2 and level 1 (the progression leading to proficiency). As a final step, focus on level 4 (beyond proficiency).

3. Use positive language. Identify what the student work will show, not what it won't.

4. Use student-friendly language. The expectations should be in words that students can understand.

5. Revisit the rubric once you have samples of student work. Remember that rubrics are always a work in progress.

6. Take the opportunity to consider how students can demonstrate critical 21st century skills and dispositions like communication, collaboration, creativity, and self-direction during the learning experience.

Notice that in the complete unit design template in figure 4.6 (page 92), the essential standard, the task summary, and the rubric, appear in bold. This is to remind teams as they are developing their tasks of what we refer to as the through line. There should be clear evidence of alignment between the indicated essential standard or standards, what the task describes (ask yourself, will this task give me as the teacher evidence of the standard?), and the rubric (the rubric should actually address what the teacher team is intending to collect evidence on). Again, this through line, shown in figure 4.7, must exist for the task to truly be aligned.

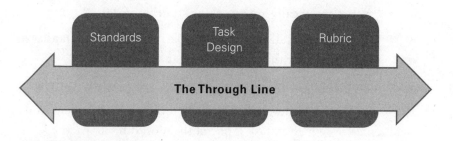

Figure 4.7: The through line.

Section Two

The following list describes each step teams take in the second portion of the assessment-planning template.

- **Essential questions to guide learning:** This portion of the template clarifies the big, overarching questions that "aim to stimulate thought, to provoke inquiry, and to spark more questions" (McTighe & Wiggins, 2013, p. 3). These questions help to guide students to uncover interesting aspects of the learning that may otherwise be left untouched.

- **Students will know (content) and be able to demonstrate (skills):** This portion of the planner clarifies the specific content knowledge that students should understand as a result of the unit of study as well as the specific skills they should be able to demonstrate. Teachers must be clear on the specific learning outcomes intended through this learning experience (while empowering students to also provide input).

- **Students would like to know (content) and students would like to demonstrate (skills):** Design principle one states that "Students are empowered daily to make important decisions about their learning experiences, how they will create and apply knowledge, and how they will demonstrate their learning." It is critical that we become more explicit about the ways in which we are empowering students in their learning. Students can and should be making decisions about what they are learning and how they are learning it. Teachers provide the structure, but they must allow students to make meaning of the why, what, and how of their learning experiences to realize true agency. When students are helping to make important decisions about their learning experiences (student-driven learning), including how they can demonstrate their understanding, they are truly empowered as agents of learning.

> **It is critical that we become more explicit about the ways in which we are empowering students in their learning. Students can and should be making decisions about what they are learning and how they are learning it. Teachers provide the structure, but they must allow students to make meaning of the why, what, and how of their learning experiences to realize true agency.**

- **Assessment schedule:** In a six-week unit that is focusing on one, two, or possibly three essential standards, teacher teams should consider, working backward, where they will collect evidence of learning throughout the unit. There are also learning targets that lead to mastery of each of these essential standards, so the team needs to break down (instructionally) the standards with clarity about what students will know and by when. Common formative assessments will drive the response during the course of the unit, so the assessments must be planned accordingly.

- **Plan for ongoing intervention and extension:** Based on the results of the common formative assessments, teachers should be providing both intervention and extension, as needed, during Tier 2 intervention, during the course of the unit. The collaborative team drives these decisions.

- **Resources:** Teams should be considering what resources, both human and otherwise, will best support the unit of study.

- **Considerations for those furthest from accessing learning:** Competency-based learning meets each student where they are in order to support them in mastering high standards. It is critical to consider ways in which *all* students can be successful in their learning experiences and open up the possibilities for what successful demonstration of learning might look like.

> Competency-based learning meets each student where they are in order to support them in mastering high standards. It is critical to consider ways in which *all* students can be successful in their learning experiences and open up the possibilities for what successful demonstration of learning might look like.

Universal Design for Learning (UDL) provides some guidelines as to what it could look like so that "students have what they need to flexibly meet learning goals" (Posey, n.d.).

- Providing multiple means of engagement (the *why* of learning)
- Providing multiple means of representation (the *what* of learning)
- Providing multiple means of action and expression (the *how* of learning)

Each of these actions has three levels of progression: accessing, building, and internalizing, with concrete considerations for each. Accessing is the initial level, allowing students to engage in some way with the learning. Building is a developing stage, allowing students to engage at a deeper level, while the internalizing stage ultimately allows students to manage their own learning.

Paul Butler, a former New Hampshire special education teacher at the middle school level, shares how competency-based learning and performance assessment allowed the students he worked with to thrive in ways that they hadn't been able to in a traditional system. Paul's practitioner perspective represents how, when done with fidelity, competency-based systems amplify equity, allowing *all* students the opportunity to learn and demonstrate their learning in meaningful ways.

> **Practitioner Perspective**
> **Paul Butler, Former Middle School Special Education Teacher, New Hampshire**
>
> Special education students, or as I prefer to call them, differently abled students, are uniquely positioned to benefit and thrive in a competency-based learning environment. In my thirty-seven years in special education, I have seen many approaches to student assessment. Competency-based assessment, when implemented with fidelity, is the best I have seen.
>
> For special education students, it is essential that their special education team be continually involved right from the very beginning of competency-based learning. It will not be effective for special educators to only jump in at assessment time to suggest accommodations and modifications. In fact, when the whole team is involved from the beginning of instruction, it is often the case that students need very few accommodations or modifications within the assessment.
>
> Rubrics that clearly spell out what is expected and how students will earn the grade they strive for present a road map for special education students to follow. This allows students and educators to set goals and monitor student progress along the learning path.
>
> One of the best aspects of competency-based education is its flexibility and the multiple pathways in which it allows students to demonstrate competence. They can show their competence in writing or oral expression, for example, in social studies, science, or other areas of interest. One exciting and important way to do so is through performance assessments.
>
> Performance assessments tap into different modes of learning and thinking, allowing students to use sometimes undiscovered skills and attributes. When done correctly, educators can learn a great deal about unique learners and continually improve their instruction.
>
> As a result of the competency-based approach, students often find that they need to advocate for their learning needs. Based on my personal experiences, those students who practice such self-advocacy skills have improved educational and life outcomes when compared to those who don't. Competency-based education helps special education students develop such skills that are essential for the adult world.

> We do need to balance our efforts so that we let students show their strengths but also work on their areas of weakness. This can be challenging, but when instruction is balanced, and thoughtfully diversified to meet all learners' needs, educators can develop both areas. Finding the right time and the right pathway to foster student's strengths and to encourage them to work on their weaknesses is the art of teaching. Teachers who know their students will find that balance as they work with them throughout the school year.
>
> Just because a student has a disability doesn't mean they don't have other abilities. Competency-based education allows students to show their skills, often in unexpected ways and places. Instead of underestimating differently abled students, we need to decrease emphasis on what they can't do and increase opportunities and expectations to see what they can do.
>
> (P. Butler, personal communication, March 8, 2021)

Section Three

The following list describes each step teams take in this third portion of the assessment-planning template.

- **Plan for intervention and extension:** Planning for intervention and extension during a unit is critically important. Teams must also determine which students still may not be where they need to be at the end of a unit. The summative assessment provides an opportunity for students to demonstrate their ability to take what they've learned and apply this learning in meaningful ways. If students still are not quite there yet, the team integrates intervention and support.

    Some schools do this by providing a week of intensive support post-summative assessment, while others integrate this within their typical tiered response.

- **Revisions to task (after administration):** This is an important but often overlooked component of the assessment process. Post-unit, teacher teams must revisit the objectives of the unit of study as well as the student work and refine the task, rubric, instructional components, and all of the other critical components of the unit of study. The best way to do this is together within collaborative teams.

A process of validation is the best way to approach the need for revisions. The last section of the unit planning tool (figure 4.6, page 92) provides the structure for teams to engage in reflecting on and refining their assessment, rubric, instructional activities, and other aspects of the unit. This includes developing interrater reliability through the analysis of student work, an important process for teams to engage in that will allow them to calibrate their assessment practices utilizing the developed rubric and individually and collectively scoring samples of student work.

Jada and her team, utilizing the CBL Classroom Assessment Planning Template, work through the process of reimagining one unit of study as an initial step in their work. Through this process, they gain greater clarity on what students should know and be able to do, the various assessment practices that they believe will provide them with the evidence they need to determine competency, the instructional techniques that will help students develop the skill needed to be successful, and the opportunity to reflect to determine what they can refine, and how to best support their students moving forward.

Reflection Questions

Consider these questions with your team.

1. Being clear on the purpose of assessment is critically important. What does *assessment* mean to you? What does it mean to your teammates? How can you better collect evidence of learning to allow you to better understand what to do next to support your learners?

2. Formative assessment is vital to changing the instructional core in competency-based classrooms. What practices do you currently employ to best understand where a student is in their learning? How does that correlate to what you will do next to support this student?

3. Feedback is a critical component of assessment, and students should be an integral part of the feedback process. What do opportunities for feedback look like in your classroom? Is it a mix of student and teacher, and peer to peer? We've created a tool ("Making Meaning of Assessment," page 219) that your team or school can utilize to better understand the true meaning of assessment.

4. Common formative assessments provide the information for teacher teams to enact timely, flexible supports for students based on what their unique needs may be. Do your teams develop common formative assessments together? How do you utilize these assessments to trigger intervention and extension?

5. Performance assessments are necessary to determine competency, as they require transfer and application of knowledge. What is a step your team can take to begin to embed a performance component into your summative assessment practices?

6. Rubrics should be utilized to assess student learning, and they should be based on essential standards. Does your team currently develop rubrics to align what is going to be assessed? Do you look at student work together and compare it to the rubric, developing inter-rater reliability?

CHAPTER 5

Structures and Systems to Support Instruction

One of the biggest questions for Jada and her colleagues as they embark on their competency-based learning journey is, how do they meet the needs of all learners in their classrooms, grade levels, and ultimately in their whole school? In traditional schools, this task has been unfairly left up to individual classroom teachers to figure out. Collaborative teams in schools and districts operating as PLCs, however, can implement practices and structures that allow teams to better meet the needs of individual learners through a rigorous, articulated, and responsive instructional system. For Jada and her colleagues, this collaboration will be key.

In a competency-based classroom, effectively meeting students where they are in their learning is highlighted in the third, fourth, and fifth design principles (Levine & Patrick, 2019); however, all design principles are evident in the competency-based classroom. As we've shared, meaningful assessment (design principle two) and effective instruction go hand in hand. Design principle six should frame the school's mindset, practices, and actions about equity, and design principle seven is the starting point for the planning of the unit, but ultimately, design principles one through five are the focal point.

In this chapter, we explore not only what effective classroom instruction in a competency-based classroom entails, but we also share schoolwide and classroom structures that best support student learning and teacher leading. We delve into the role of the teacher and the student in these types of classrooms and discuss how project-based learning and cocreated learning experiences (learning experiences that are created collaboratively by students and teachers) can enhance student empowerment, ownership, and ultimately, agency in learning.

We also clarify the role of the collaborative team in the planning, implementation, reflection, and refinement of learning experiences within schools. The collaborative team, whether at a specific grade level or in a content area, is the key structure in schools to engage deeply in this work.

The competency-based classroom is one in which teachers and students work collaboratively to ensure clarity on what students are to learn, how they will learn it, and how they will demonstrate the learning while simultaneously embracing the discomfort that may result within this shared approach to learning.

To frame this important point better, consider how instructional practice beliefs and priorities evolved over time with a move to a competency-based model as told by Vermont educators Stan Williams and Emily Rinkema in their work with the Champlain Valley School District.

Practitioner Perspective
Stan Williams and Emily Rinkema, Champlain Valley School District, Vermont

When we switched to standards-based learning in 2010, everything changed. Our job as educators was no longer to teach—it was to ensure that our students learned. That was not just a semantic difference; it was a fundamental shift in the what, why, and how of everything that went on in our classrooms.

There were two main tools that provided the structure for our standards-based classroom and supported the significant shifts we and our students were making: The K-U-D and Scales. Our course K-U-D articulated the nonnegotiables of learning in our class, laying out what our students would Know, Understand, and be able to Do at the end of the course. This was our collective destination, clearly and concisely communicated for all stakeholders. Our approach to standards-based learning keeps the system simple: our Ds from our K-U-D are our learning targets, the eight to ten most important, transferable skills our yearlong course will instruct, practice, assess, and report. Those learning targets are the third level of our four-level Scales, which are skill-based rubrics that increase in complexity as we move up the scale. Once we had our K-U-D and Scales in place, we had everything we needed for curriculum, instructional design, formative and summative assessment, feedback, differentiated instruction, and even reporting.

Having a simple foundation was essential because getting all students to or beyond our targets was so complex. We had been teaching in a transactional system for so long (and had both been taught in such systems as well), and breaking old habits took a level of intentionality and focus that was tough to sustain initially. But being able to fall back on the solid foundation helped us keep going as we shifted our instruction in two fundamental ways: from teaching to learning and from task-centered to differentiated instruction.

Shifting our focus from teaching to learning came when we realized that our success as teachers was a direct reflection of the success of our students. And because that success was now so clearly articulated in what we wanted them to know, understand, and be able to do, we had to know where they were in relation to that destination at all times. While this shift changed so much about the why of our classroom, the most tangible change came in how we viewed assessments. Assessment became a tool to measure the success of our instruction, not a judgement on the success of our learners. Our assessments became more efficient, more intentional, and more frequent; we needed to know where students were in relation to our targets so that we knew what to do next. For students, this shift in thinking and practice meant that assessments were much more transparent, much less judgmental, and directly connected to their subsequent instruction or practice. For us, this shift meant our assessments now drove our planning.

The shift to a standards-based classroom dramatically changed the amount of time we spent on grading and planning. Because our assessments were now much more efficient and targeted, and because we had the Scales as a feedback tool, the time it took to assess went way down, which was good, since the time it took to plan went way up. Each assessment gave us new information about what we needed to do next and for whom, and the majority of our time was now spent figuring out how to differentiate effectively.

Shifting our focus from task-driven instruction to differentiated instruction had the greatest effect on the efficiency of learning in our classroom and on the engagement of students in their own learning. We used to pride ourselves on creating engaging whole-class tasks and activities, and when we shifted to a much more intentional system of learning, we were afraid we would have to give up that engagement; what we found, however, was actually the opposite. When instruction and practice were targeted to our learners more intentionally and accurately, not only did they learn more quickly, but we tapped into their zones of proximal development in a way that increased engagement. Students began to expect flexible grouping almost daily, and always after assessments. They would come into the classroom and see their names (on playing cards) placed at different tables based on what they needed more or different practice in based on their assessments. Over time, we became better at management structures and systems, as did they, and pretty soon we had an environment where we smoothly moved in and out of whole-class activities, small-group instruction, and individual and group practice.

We can't express enough how significant the change was for us as classroom teachers. We became more intentional in our design and practice, and students became more invested in and in control of their learning. We saw engagement and confidence increase, and stress and grade-obsession decrease. And while the complexity still exists, the focus on student learning keeps us grounded and challenges us to continuously improve our practices.

(S. Williams and E. Rinkema, personal communication, December 20, 2020)

Shaping Structures to Support Personalized Learning

The structures to support timely, differentiated support in the classroom will not occur without deliberate consideration. This planning and forethought must ultimately result in structural changes within the school. Structurally, what must occur?

Austin Buffum, Mike Mattos, and Janet Malone (2017) describe response to intervention (RTI) as a practical tool that will help transform thinking into action. We will demonstrate how the RTI structure provides the blueprint for supporting competency-based learning. RTI is made up of three tiers: Tier 1, core instruction; Tier 2, additional support for students who have not learned it; and Tier 3, more intensive support and reteaching.

It would be nearly impossible for a lone teacher to effectively meet the needs of all the students in their classroom. RTI provides clarity regarding the role of collaborative teacher teams and schoolwide teams to determine "the responsibilities of these specific groups to ensure that all students succeed" (Buffum et al., 2012, p. 12). But these teams must work in a cohesive manner to provide the comprehensive system of support necessary to meet the needs of all learners in a competency-based system.

> **The four critical questions of a PLC, by design, encompass curriculum, assessment, and instruction, and allow teachers to move through each unit of study with a focus on *learning* rather than simply on *teaching*.**

This tiered system works closely in conjunction with the four critical questions of a PLC discussed in chapter 2 (page 27), which provide the framework for a collaborative team's work. The four critical questions of a PLC, by design, encompass curriculum, assessment, and instruction, and allow teachers to move through each unit of study with a focus on *learning* rather than simply on *teaching*.

As Thomas W. Many, Michael Maffoni, Susan Sparks, and Tesha Thomas (2020) write, "It is the combination of effectiveness and efficiency that creates higher levels of productivity on collaborative teams" (p. 18). A collaborative team can find itself spinning its wheels given the daunting task of meeting the needs of all of its learners. The four questions not only help the team to focus on the task at hand, but also provide the framework for moving through the processes of learning.

The Three Tiers of RTI

In our work in schools, we have seen the importance of creating and implementing a cohesive and seamless system for supporting and extending student learning that outlines the responsibilities for individual teachers, teacher teams, and the school as a whole. The three-tiered RTI model is a cohesive model for schools to ensure they are meeting the needs of all learners. RTI includes three tiers represented as an inverted pyramid (Buffum et al., 2017) as shown in figure 5.1.

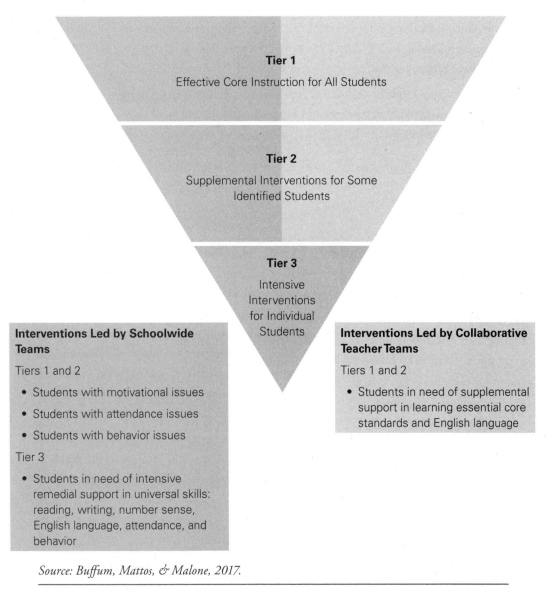

Source: Buffum, Mattos, & Malone, 2017.

Figure 5.1: Response to Intervention inverted pyramid.

Tier 1

All students have access to Tier 1 instruction, which consists of those grade-level and course-specific competencies and essential standards that are critical to the respective grade level, content area, or course. Instruction in Tier 1 begins with knowing the what: which competencies and standards we want students to demonstrate proficiency in.

Tier 1 is nonnegotiable. All students receive instruction in grade-level competencies and standards. Historically, many students with greater needs were pulled from class during vital learning opportunities, depriving them of learning they needed to continue to move forward, and creating an even wider gap. In a competency-based learning system, all students have access to Tier 1 core instruction.

Teacher teams should answer the first two critical questions prior to the unit beginning. The last two questions should be considered throughout the unit, as they are specific to the instruction that will result from the assessment data gathered.

Codesigning Learning

The first critical question of learning in a PLC is a curriculum question. As Jada and her team begin their planning for an upcoming unit, they identify, using a backward-design template (as shown in figure 5.2), the competencies, essential standards, and learning targets that students must show mastery of as a result of the unit.

> **Ultimately, students will be assessed at the essential standard level. Each essential standard should be broken into learning targets. These more granular levels of learning are what teachers focus on in the classroom. Mastery of these targets leads to mastery of the essential standard. Mastery of essential standards through application and transfer represents mastery of the competency.**

Ultimately, students will be assessed at the essential standard level. Each essential standard should be broken into learning targets. These more granular levels of learning are what teachers focus on in the classroom. Mastery of these targets leads to mastery of the essential standard. Mastery of essential standards through application and transfer represents mastery of the competency.

Traditionally, teachers have designed learning, but what does it look like when students and teachers begin to design learning experiences together? Student ownership, particularly in the development of learning targets, provides an opportunity to begin to create experiences for students that are truly codesigned.

If we are to truly empower students in their creation of learning experiences, doesn't it stand to reason that students have to become more responsible for what they learn, how they learn, and how they demonstrate their learning? Timothy S. Stuart, Sascha Heckmann, Mike Mattos, and Austin Buffum (2018) state that "in a co-constructed learning approach . . . teams and teachers ask and answer the four critical questions of a PLC, and they gradually release these questions to students as they develop agency" (p. 75).

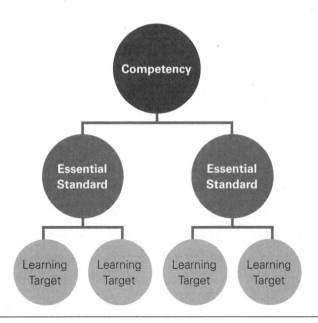

Figure 5.2: The relationship between competencies, essential standards, and learning targets.

Dylan Wiliam (2018) suggests structures within the classroom that allow students to "discuss and come to own the learning intentions and success criteria, making it more likely that they will be able to apply the learning intentions and success criteria" (p. 64).

Myron Dueck (2021) suggests that as teachers design their learning experiences, we need to include the student, and in our planning, always consider "elements that could be determined by the student collective" (p. 29).

Stuart and his colleagues (2018) offer the suggestion to begin to incorporate student-focused language within the four critical questions, specifically having students articulate, "What do I want to learn and be able to do?" It is important to note that the competency and essential standards are initially determined by the teacher and teacher teams, but the learning targets (as you'll see in the following section) can be co-constructed with students.

Co-Constructing Assessments

As Jada and her team plan, they first consider the summative performance assessment students will engage in. Jada and her team have initially approached their units first with the lessons, not with the assessment. But by utilizing backward design and understanding the importance of beginning with the end in mind, they begin with the competencies, standards, and what they will eventually be asking students to demonstrate related to the competencies and essential standards: the summative performance assessment. Together, they break the summative assessment apart by asking the following questions.

1. What will students need to know and be able to demonstrate to be successful on this assessment?

2. How do we ensure that any and all students can access the learning? (Are there any considerations for language, culture, and interest?)

3. What will we accept as sufficient evidence of learning?

4. Working backward, how will we scaffold our unit to ensure that students develop the knowledge and skills to be successful?

5. How do we ensure that our instruction matches our expectations for what students will be asked to demonstrate?

Jada, with her teammates, has developed common formative assessments to address the learning targets that lead to mastery of the essential standard for their unit of instruction. As a team, they will sit down together and look at the results of the common formative assessment to determine the type and level of support each student will need to ultimately demonstrate proficiency.

As they near the end of their unit, they will administer a performance assessment that allows teachers to assess their students' competence in both academic content knowledge and the skills and dispositions. Through this type of assessment, they will be able to provide evidence on whether or not a student is able to demonstrate their ability to transfer or apply their learned skills, ultimately demonstrating competency.

The answer to critical question two can be co-constructed with students. Stuart and colleagues (2018) note that by "empowering students to own their assessment, educators shift to an orientation that a student's demonstration of learning can take on a variety of forms and still remain valid" (p. 77). Providing students with the opportunity to determine how they might demonstrate their learning correlates strongly to design principles one, two, and six (Empowering learners in how they demonstrate knowledge, meaningful assessment, and equity).

Sarah Bond is an instructional coach at the University of New Hampshire and a former kindergarten and first-grade teacher. Sarah shares how intentionality in her classroom allowed her to truly codesign learning experiences with students.

Practitioner Perspective
Sarah Bond, Instructional Coach, University of New Hampshire; Former Kindergarten and First-Grade Teacher

Each moment of the school day serves as an opportunity for rich learning experiences in which students demonstrate individual growth and competency, yet these moments are often overlooked. A shift in pedagogical approach allows teachers to capture and expand on these organic moments, extending children's thinking and deepening their understanding.

A strong foundational understanding of child development coupled with sound knowledge of learning progressions—the building blocks of competency—allow teachers to personalize student learning experiences. However, traditional instructional methods and notions of what personalized learning looks like in practice often fall short of promoting true student agency. The pedagogical approach of codesign expands on the concept of personalized instruction by leveraging student agency and inquiry as mechanisms to achieve greater engagement, depth of knowledge, and equity.

Codesign centers on a foundation of mutual respect between teachers and students and is achieved by creating a strong sense of classroom community. Students in my classroom were not merely passive recipients of knowledge, and I was not a director. Instead, I served as a facilitator. Codesign encouraged me to learn alongside students and allowed students to take ownership of their learning. The collaborative dynamic between students and me resulted in learning experiences that were joyful, engaging, relevant, and meaningful for everyone.

My lens within the classroom integrated careful observations, varied documentation methods, and ongoing formative assessments to identify where each student was developmentally within a given learning progression. Photographs, work samples, video, anecdotal records, and the recording of students' quotes were meaningful tools to document evidence of student growth, learning, and competency. These methods aligned with the student-centered nature of codesign and allowed learning to become visible among all stakeholders. Most significantly, these methods send students the message that their words, ideas, actions, wonderings, and passions are not merely acknowledged but are respected and honored as valuable contributions.

At the heart of codesign lies intentionality. I viewed both planned and organic moments throughout the day as authentic opportunities to capture learning in action. I used documentation with intentionality and scaffolded students' learning across individual learning progressions and toward competency. The often cyclical and iterative nature of codesign allowed me to facilitate meaningful and relevant experiences with even the youngest learners in ways that are genuinely responsive to children's interests, inquiries, understandings, and misconceptions.

Ongoing reflection is a critical component of codesigned learning experiences. These opportunities for reflection are also co-constructed. Engaging students in reflective practices created a classroom community and environment where students celebrated success while taking risks and learning from challenges. Codesigned experiences not only resulted in increased content knowledge, skill acquisition, and application to other contexts but also fostered students' social and emotional learning. Teachers' ultimate goal is to prepare students to become independent, confident communicators, collaborators, problem-solvers, and contributors to society. Codesign serves as a vehicle to achieve this goal.

As a former classroom teacher at the primary level, my personal experiences codesigning learning and assessment opportunities in a public school setting served as evidence that our youngest learners are not only capable, but will excel when given opportunities to guide their own learning pathways. I noticed that many of our kindergarten and first-grade students who struggled in moments of didactic instruction became more engaged, curious, and confident learners as a result of engaging in codesign. Codesign blended seamlessly with our team's collective goal to provide increased process-oriented and project-based learning experiences within our classrooms. Regardless of the topic we were investigating, we were intentional in how we engaged alongside students in the cyclical processes of exploration, planning, implementation, and reflection. Our learners would surprise us daily, steering our journey down sometimes unexpected and always rewarding pathways. Students not only codesigned their learning experiences but were empowered to have choices about how they demonstrated their learning in terms of modality and materials. This sense of agency allowed students to capitalize on their individual strengths, which also increased equity.

At the end of a project-based learning experience, students prepared to demonstrate their knowledge and understanding to an authentic public audience. I remember reflecting with students on why they chose to represent their learning in a particular format. One first grader shared that she chose to create a poster. The student elaborated and reflected on a project-based learning experience during the previous school year when she learned how to create an effective poster as a means to communicate information. She thought that selecting this modality again would enable her to serve as an expert and help the new kindergarteners also interested in using this modality as a mode of communication. A kindergarten student loved to write and elected to transfer their understanding to practice by writing a persuasive letter to a community member. Another kindergartener engaged in the same project reflected on his choice. He used Book Creator on his iPad to express his ideas and understanding. He had never used the program and wanted to learn a new skill. The intent of this project was not to assess writing ability but to assess depth of content knowledge. As an educator, my research lens allowed me to see that incorporating technology for this student enhanced equity. It allowed him to record his voice while independently documenting and demonstrating his competency and in a way that was meaningful to him as a learner.

Codesigning learning and assessment opportunities is likely to involve some sense of uncertainty. It may be uncomfortable, and it may feel like a risk. It is a learning process for teachers, just as it is for students and one that is invariably evolving. However, as teachers take a step back and assume the lens of a researcher, they will find that their students will lead the way. They will likely discover that the benefits of codesigning learning experiences with students are limitless and will undoubtedly extend far beyond the classroom walls.

(S. Bond, personal communication, February 2021)

Tier 2

In a system focused on the needs of every student, educators create and define time for Tier 2 intervention (and extension) for every student within the school so that each receives instruction specific to his or her place along a learning continuum. During Tier 2, students who have not met the targets receive focused intervention. Once those students demonstrate mastery of the intended targets, the system should be fluid enough to allow them to begin to work on something else. In some cases, when a student is still not demonstrating expected mastery or progress, educators may need to intensify the intervention. This directly aligns with design principle three, "Students receive timely, differentiated support based on their individual needs."

At the same time, we must extend the learning of those students who have demonstrated their learning and can go deeper. This is an important distinction. Depth of knowledge, rigor, and complexity play a major role in extending learning. In a competency-based system, we not only want to provide timely intervention and support, but as design principle four outlines, also allow students to progress based upon mastery, not seat time.

DuFour and colleagues (2016) make an important distinction between enrichment and extension; enrichment is "students having access to subjects traditionally taught by specials or elective teachers (music, art, drama, applied technology, and physical education)," whereas extension is defined as students being "stretched beyond essential grade-level curriculum or levels of proficiency" (pp. 169–170).

Hess's (2010) Rigor Matrices, combining Webb's Depth of Knowledge with Bloom's Taxonomy provide a resource (see page 202 in the appendix) for teachers to not only consider rigor and complexity in assessment, but also, very importantly, within instruction.

Often, during the transition to a competency-based system, with assessment as a logical and powerful entry point, teacher teams create rigorous assessments that their students may not do as well on the first time they are exposed to having to transfer. This is typically due to the fact that instructional practices haven't changed, and that the students haven't had the opportunity to practice at that level of rigor. Once students are consistently engaging in more complex learning experiences, they will build the ability, stamina, and confidence to think critically, problem solve, and ultimately, successfully navigate more rigorous learning experiences.

> **Once students are consistently engaging in more complex learning experiences, they will build the ability, stamina, and confidence to think critically, problem solve, and ultimately, successfully navigate more rigorous learning experiences.**

All teachers are mutually accountable for student success and for working interdependently to meet the needs of all learners within the grade level or subject area. Each block of time for support is flooded with human resources to the best of a school's ability, allowing students to be organized into smaller groups for more focused support for the students who need it most.

Structurally, schools need to have timely progress monitoring within this system. This allows students to receive the support they need, when they need it, for as long as they need it.

Buffum and colleagues (2012) outline the following five characteristics of effective intervention.

1. **Intervention is research based:** It is proven to work, and allows collected data to demonstrate growth. We have found that as assessment literacy develops with teachers and within a school, teachers understand not only the specific, proven tools that are available, but also how each one may be able to support students better based on where they are.

2. **Intervention is directive:** It is not optional. Rather, collected data determines the need for interventions and remediation. Whether elementary or secondary, students who need support or extension should receive it. Over time, students will begin to seek out support on their own. This is precisely what a competency-based system seeks to do—to develop empowered learners.

3. **Intervention is correctly administered:** It is given by trained professionals deemed most effective to work with particular students and their needs. This requires schools to think outside of the box, as teachers often become accustomed to only working with certain students.

4. **Intervention is targeted:** It is precisely planned. If it is too broad, it is likely to be unsuccessful. Teams must work together to identify exactly where a student, or groups of students, may be struggling, and then plan specific interventions that will provide the remediation necessary for that student's success.

5. **Intervention is timely:** It promptly responds to student needs. Assessment should be ongoing and groupings flexible to allow opportunities for students to receive the support they need when they need it. Teams meeting on an ongoing basis can build regrouping into their weekly or biweekly meetings.

Tier 2 provides the structure in response to critical questions three and four: What do we do when students haven't learned it? and What do we do when they already know it? Ideally, students are moving seamlessly in between whatever tier they may need to address their specific needs. This, however, takes a high degree of monitoring, communication, and aligned intent between teachers, teams, and the available resources.

Figure 5.3 outlines how, through ongoing formative assessment practices, a team can collect appropriate evidence of learning and provide the appropriate support or extension based on what the evidence is telling them and also where students feel they need to be. Students should move into Tier 2 as needed based on timely assessment practices, with the goal of mastery of the grade level or content area competencies and essential standards.

> **Ideally, students are moving seamlessly in between whatever tier they may need to address their specific needs. This, however, takes a high degree of monitoring, communication, and aligned intent between teachers, teams, and the available resources.**

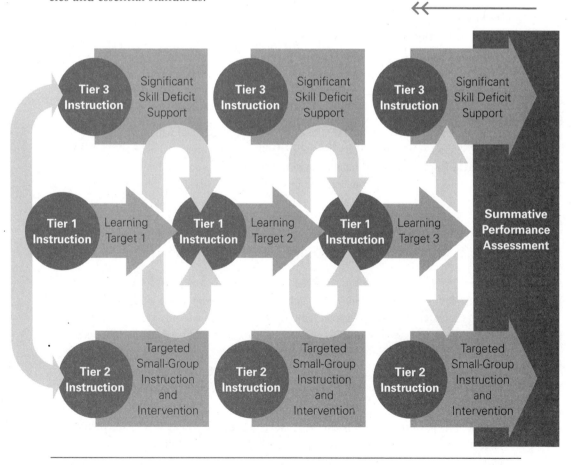

Figure 5.3: How flexible, tiered instruction supports student learning within a unit.

Feedback as an Integral Part of the Learning Process

Instruction, assessment, and feedback are inextricably linked. These components are often separated, which jeopardizes the connectedness of learning experiences. When teachers and students are engaging in formative practices together, the learning environment becomes one in which learning and the processes of learning are ever-evolving.

> **Instruction, assessment, and feedback are inextricably linked. These components are often separated, which jeopardizes the connectedness of learning experiences. When teachers and students are engaging in formative practices together, the learning environment becomes one in which learning and the processes of learning are ever-evolving.**

Feedback is constant within the learning process. As teachers are teaching concepts, students are practicing these concepts. Inherent to this process is reflection, with both students asking themselves where they are within the learning, and teachers providing feedback to students regarding what their next steps might be. Over time, scaffolds that may have existed are lessened when appropriate, to allow students to take more and more ownership in their learning. Rubrics help to guide this process.

Donald Conti, Elizabeth Szeliga, and Lisa Woodruff are middle school teachers at Lincoln Akerman School in Hampton Falls, New Hampshire. Since 2017, their school has been engaged in moving toward a competency-based system. Their individual and collective practices have evolved to the point that their classrooms are a constant cycle of feedback, iteration, and demonstration of learning.

Practitioner Perspective

Donald Conti, Elizabeth Szeliga, and Lisa Woodruff, Middle School Teachers, Lincoln Akerman School, Hampton Falls, New Hampshire

The shift to competency-based education not only transformed our teaching practice, but it also transformed our philosophy. This was not an overnight switch. We started by reviewing the competencies we teach and identifying the many skills that spiral throughout the two years we teach students. Skills like argumentative writing, reading comprehension, and informational writing are consistently taught, practiced, and assessed throughout the school year. Through ongoing and embedded formative practices, we provide constant, detailed feedback to the student. This feedback often feels like a form of coaching.

Prior to this approach, feedback was often at the end of the unit to defend the letter grade. And all of us have watched in horror as students glanced at all that work and feedback teachers put on a rubric before tossing it. Feedback teachers give throughout the learning process is so much different. Students engage with the feedback because they see it as a way to improve. Following are examples of our process from the subjects literature, science, and writing.

For literature, like for other subjects, learning occurs in a spiral fashion: concepts are taught, reinforced, and practiced throughout the year. In this spiraling model, formative assessments are frequent and most helpful. We view the competencies as transcending concepts and the specific literary work (novel, poem, short stories, and so on) and skills (theme, moral, character analysis, and so on) as the focus at that moment in time. The two nest easily. At the beginning of the year, scaffolds are put in place that teach the transcending concept, for example, writing about literature using evidence and analysis. Specific instructions and lessons focus on how to write claims or thesis statements, what is evidence, how to analyze evidence, how to connect ideas to the claim, and how to cite from the text. As the year progresses, students develop a habit, both verbally and in writing, of finding evidence to support their ideas and analyze the evidence. A deeper understanding of the competency happens through ongoing practice and feedback. Periodically there are formative assessments that offer students specific feedback on what to work on next, knowing that it will be continually reassessed throughout the year. Later, these supports can lessen but can also still be available for some students if needed. During this process formative assessments are key in determining what the student knows and how much support they may still need.

Assessment in science follows two pathways. First, students work all year to develop and refine the skills associated with competencies derived from the Science and Engineering Practices of the Next Generation Science Standards (NGSS; 2013). These competencies involve skills that students use across all units of study and so the opportunity to practice and improve them is continuous. Formative feedback is given frequently as students design and perform investigations in class throughout the year. Students are encouraged to reflect on feedback and to use it to identify areas of focus to carry into their next unit of study.

Second, domain-specific content follows a slightly different format. Formative assessment is done as students work toward demonstrating competency in specific Disciplinary Core Ideas (DCIs). Summative assessment occurs typically when instruction on DCI-specific content is completed. The instruction in these content areas is of a shorter duration, but approached with the same mindset that feedback is an opportunity for growth and deeper understanding.

Our practice of teaching writing was transformed by the concept of continued formative feedback. Direct instruction, feedback, and assessment—often in small-group or individual conferences—made learning authentic, individualized, and supportive. This was implemented through the use of a new rubric that put the emphasis on revision. Students would conference with the teacher and receive a bulleted list on their rubric of their strengths and where to revise before their next conference. This format allowed us to speak directly with kids about specific areas of focus for them. We meet multiple times with each student during the writing process. The benefit was clear: students were engaged and knew exactly how to improve. The final summative assessment was never a surprise to students because through conferences they could identify their score through self-assessment along the way. Beyond that, students now view the summative as the culmination of all their hard work.

(D. Conti, E. Szeliga, and L. Woodruff, personal communication, February 4, 2021)

Metacognition and Student Ownership in Learning

Metacognition is critically important within all tiers of a system. However, metacognition can serve to connect, in students' minds, the purpose and need of Tier 2 since the time is focused on providing students specifically what they need to progress in their learning. Students need to not only understand where they are in their learning but also where they would like to be, how they might get there, and how they will monitor their progress. These elements comprise the components of metacognition. Students must first be self-aware, then understand where they would like to eventually be, and finally recognize that they can monitor and adapt their behavior as necessary to progress.

Teachers in competency-based classrooms rely heavily on students developing metacognitive practices. Metacognition breeds agency. Students who are practicing reflection, goal-setting, and then monitoring and adapting their actions based on this ongoing process begin to take ownership in a way that exemplifies an empowered learner.

> **Metacognition breeds agency. Students who are practicing reflection, goal-setting, and then monitoring and adapting their actions based on this ongoing process begin to take ownership in a way that exemplifies an empowered learner.**

Embedding these practices in the classroom may appear to be too time-consuming. We would argue that these practices must be a common, ongoing occurrence in classrooms. Although we recognize that the practices have to be frontloaded and thus do take more time before the start of the unit, they will provide more time during instruction as students truly begin to self-manage consistently.

Anthony Doucet is a high school social studies teacher at Souhegan High School in Amherst, New Hampshire. Anthony shares how engaging in professional learning with his peers provided him with the opportunity to rethink the structure of his lessons and provide students with more ownership in understanding the intent of the lesson, as well as how real-world, worthy learning experiences increase engagement and student agency, and how these practices supported his shift to remote learning during the pandemic.

Practitioner Perspective

Anthony Doucet, Souhegan High School, Amherst, New Hampshire

It was roughly ten minutes into the professional development session when I realized my lessons were structured incorrectly.

I was sitting in a conference room with about fifty other teachers. We were attending a professional development session led by Margaret Heritage when she explained one of the first key principles of formative assessment: learning goals and success criteria.

See, until that point, I thought I was doing a lot right. Every day, my agenda was listed on the board with my essential questions for the unit. As Dr. Heritage continued to speak to the crowd of educators, I realized that students did not understand where our learning was headed without knowing the learning goals and success criteria. I knew what I wanted students to gain from the lesson, and I knew how I would know if they demonstrated understanding, but I was withholding these key pieces of success from them. How did they know if they understood the lesson? How did they know if they got what I wanted them to get from the lesson? They might have had an idea, but they couldn't say for sure.

I was upset with myself because it seemed so obvious. Once I got over that initial feeling, I got to work creating learning goals and success criteria for every future lesson, and the results were obvious and immediate. My learning goals and success criteria are now on the board alongside the agenda. When we shifted to remote learning during the COVID-19 pandemic, my colleague created an online agenda template that embeds the learning goals and success criteria into it. For example, during our Proposals to Improve Souhegan unit, where students choose something they would like to see changed about their school, one of the lessons is about how to write a proposal. Right at the start, we talk about our learning goal of "I understand how to write a proposal," with success criteria of "I can write an explanation of what I would like to see changed at Souhegan," and "I can explain my rationale with evidence to support my position." Throughout the lesson, we refer to them, and students are able to look to the success criteria as a way to see if they are able to understand the learning goal. Using learning goals and success criteria has the added benefit of helping me give better, more specific feedback.

Prior to implementing formative assessment practices, too often I'd ask the class if anyone had questions, only to move on when no one responded. This was an easy way to fool myself into thinking that everyone understood, and I was doing a great job with my instruction. Too often students sat in silence, irrationally fearing that asking for help would reveal an inner weakness. Now, I might use a program like Pear Deck, which allows for students to respond to questions on their computer, to allow me to check for student understanding, which helps me target which students to check in with first to provide support as students start working on their proposals. Because students have a greater understanding of what we are doing that day, they are better able to articulate where they are in their learning. They know if they are missing something, or not understanding it, and it allows us to frame our conversations better when they are struggling. I am sure to now ask open-ended questions to elicit evidence of their understanding. For example, "I've noticed you chose to write about shifting to a weighted grade point average. That's an interesting choice, but I'm noticing you are missing your rationale. Why do you think this is important?" This open-ended question allows me to see where students are in their understanding of the issue, and provide them guidance toward how to complete their success criteria.

The Proposals to Improve Souhegan project also leads to better educational outcomes because of student agency. Students have free choice in deciding what they would like to improve about their school. After brainstorming ideas, such as no homework policies, gender-neutral bathrooms, scheduling changes, and so on, students form groups and pursue their interests by connecting with community members, administrators, the superintendent, other schools across the country to get feedback on their proposals, with some eventually

> going to the school board for change. The structure is intentionally driven by student interest, and engagement is high.
>
> Ultimately, adopting formative assessment practices was the single most important and impactful change I have made to my own teaching, and as a result I have students who are better able to articulate their learning and take ownership of it.
>
> (A. Doucet, personal communication, March 14, 2021)

Tier 3

Buffum and colleagues (2012) identify RTI as the "best hope to provide every child with the additional time and support needed to learn at high levels" (p. xiii). In this vein, it is necessary for some students to receive an even greater degree of support—but not at the expense of their core learning. Tier 3 intervention should not replace the core Tier 1 curriculum. Tier 3 includes more intensive support in reading, for example, if the student is significantly below grade level in that subject. Whereas Tier 2 is very much aligned to what is occurring in Tier 1, the additional support provided in Tier 3 provides students with the individualized and focused intervention necessary for them to be successful. The goal is for no student to need Tier 3 intervention, but it must be available at any time for any student who needs it.

Schools must prioritize understanding the various tiers, how they are different, and how they work in unison. Tier 3 is not just a time for special education services to occur, as it is often misunderstood to be. There must be a clear focus for Tier 3 time to home in on the specific knowledge, content, and skills that a student needs to successfully engage with grade-level standards. Paula Rogers, W. Richard Smith, Austin Buffum, and Mike Mattos (2020) describe these as "focused acceleration" practices within Tier 3, noting these practices need to be "focused on accelerating the learning of critical prerequisite or foundational skills so students can be successful in mastering grade level essential standards and behaviors" (p. 120).

There are some key considerations for school teams and grade-level and content area teams to consider related to Tier 3. The following list of considerations can help guide teams in addressing some of these areas.

- Based on our various data points, which students need additional support with key prerequisite and foundational skills?
- Specifically which prerequisite and foundational skills do these students need support with?
- Who on our team is best suited to support this student or these students?

- When will this happen so that the student or students do not miss key learning opportunities within their classrooms?
- How will we monitor their progress?
- How will we communicate this progress within our team?

It is imperative that the three tiers of intervention work together as seamlessly as possible to support all learners. This requires a high level of communication, consideration (for each other's role in supporting learning), and commitment to ensuring that everyone is working together to support a student, or groups of students. These processes will evolve over time, ultimately allowing teams to efficiently and effectively provide all learners with needed support.

Planning Weekly Lessons That Empower Learners

In chapter 4 we provided a resource (figure 4.2, page 85) for a unit design template. The template in figure 5.4 (page 120) provides the framework for teams to thoughtfully and intentionally plan competency-based learning experiences for their students beginning with the end in mind.

There is a progression of learning that is necessary for students to experience on their way to mastery. Each week's lessons should scaffold students' learning as they navigate these learning experiences. Identifying the *lesson objectives* as well as how these objectives tie into the *learning targets* and ultimately lead to proficiency within the *essential standard* (which again feeds into the overall competency statement) is critical.

Teachers begin by considering the ways in which students will engage in learning, and should refer to the essential questions they've identified as part of their overall unit planning. Competency-based systems are about empowering *all* students, and beginning planning by considering how all students will be able to successfully access Tier 1 instruction ties directly into design principle five, "Students learn actively using different pathways and varied pacing." When we plan in advance for the unique strengths and needs of learners, every single student can find an entry point to learning, leaning into what may be difficult with the understanding that the process of learning is ongoing, and that they will have the supports necessary to ultimately be successful.

> **When we plan in advance for the unique strengths and needs of learners, every single student can find an entry point to learning, leaning into what may be difficult with the understanding that the process of learning is ongoing, and that they will have the supports necessary to ultimately be successful.**

CBL Weekly Lesson Planning Template	
Lesson and Unit:	
Lesson Objectives:	Essential Standard (the standard the learning target leads to mastery of):
	Learning Target (component of the essential standard that this lesson focuses on):
Essential Questions to Guide Learning:	
Considerations for Those Furthest From Accessing Learning:	Lesson Overview and Activities:
Assessment Opportunities (Where will students and adults collect evidence of learning?):	Metacognitive and Feedback Opportunities (Where will students engage in self-reflection, goal setting, monitoring, and adapting through meaningful feedback?):
Teacher Reflections (What worked well? What would you change?):	

Figure 5.4: Competency-based learning lesson plan template.

*Visit **go.SolutionTree.com/PLCbooks** to download the free reproducibles in this book.*

The daily lessons are at the learning target level. Ongoing *assessment opportunities*, for students and teachers, consist of both the ongoing formative practices, as well as the more formal common formative assessment opportunities that provide teachers and students with feedback on their understanding of the critical components of essential standards. These results should also be used to trigger additional support or extension, as appropriate. Students will eventually have to put it all together to demonstrate their competency. This transfer of learning will typically take place in a summative type of performance assessment.

As we discussed, metacognitive practices are a linchpin to learning and agency. It is necessary to explicitly consider how students will be metacognitively engaged within daily learning experiences, and to include opportunities for feedback through self-reflection, peer feedback, and student to teacher feedback.

Choosing School Experiences That Support a Competency-Based System

There are many current practices occurring in schools that correlate to the principles of a competency-based system. Great teaching (and learning) naturally incorporates teaming, collaboration, student agency, feedback, hands-on learning, meaningful assessment, and opportunities for students to demonstrate their learning in various ways, all components of competency-based systems. There are certain practices that tie these pieces together in ways that go beyond a typical learning experience.

Project-Based Learning

Competencies ensure that learners are acquiring the requisite skills as well as a deep understanding of content they can then transfer within learning experiences. Project-based learning (PBL) is a model that fits incredibly well with competency-based learning. PBL is an instructional method that allows learners the opportunity to develop their knowledge and skills through an extended project (Buck Institute for Education, n.d.). These projects are authentic, engaging, and typically challenge students to solve issues and problems directly connected to their world. Students develop the knowledge and then build the habits and skills through PBL necessary for success in today's world.

The Buck Institute for Education (n.d.) identifies a number of ways that PBL supports personalized and competency-based learning, all crucial components of a successful competency-based learning system.

- **Engaged hearts and minds:** In PBL, students are active, not passive; a project engages their hearts and minds, and it provides real-world relevance for learning.

- **Deeper learning:** Learning is about making connections. After completing a project, students understand content more deeply, remember what they learn, and retain it longer. Students who gain content knowledge through PBL are better able to apply what they know and can do to new situations.

- **Exposure to adults and careers:** Through mentorship and authentic audiences, students make connections to those in their community who can help them determine whether a specific career is of further interest to them.

- **Building success skills for college, career, and life:** In the 21st century workplace and in college, success requires more than basic knowledge and skills. In a project, students learn how to take initiative and responsibility, build their confidence, solve problems, work in teams, communicate ideas, and manage themselves more effectively.

- **A sense of purpose:** Meaningful learning can be a gamechanger for students. When students experience that what they have been engaged in makes a real difference and can impact their community, they will be more inspired to continue to engage in these types of learning experiences.

- **Success skills:** PBL, by design, amplifies the role of nonacademic competencies like communication, collaboration, self-direction, and creative thinking.

- **Rewarding relationships:** Through PBL, relationships with teachers, community members, business leaders, and peers will allow for a shared love of learning.

- **Creativity and technology:** The skills needed for success in our world have grown exponentially. Creative problem solving and the use of technology are vital for our future, and students have the opportunity to engage in direct application of these skills and tools through PBL.

Teachers embarking on providing project-based experiences for their students must plan for projects that will allow creativity to flourish, rather than inhibit it. So what does this type of learning entail?

Bob Lenz, Justin Wells, and Sally Kingston (2015) define a *project* as an act of creation over time. They note that the word itself gets at two critical elements: producing and complexity. Lenz and colleagues (2015) note that high-quality PBL includes the following components:

> An inquiry into a student-friendly essential question that will drive the learning

> A demonstration of key knowledge and skills

> Academic rigor and alignment with standards (remember, standards ultimately feed into a competency)

> Varying ranges of timelines to allow students to learn how to manage, backward plan, and apply self-direction skills

> An engaging launch—How can we "hook" students and get them excited about this learning experience?

> Applied learning. Remember, competency is the transfer and application of learning. PBL, by nature, allows for this.

> An authentic audience—Who in your school (or greater) community, can engage with students, provide feedback, mentor? Considering this will provide the "real world" experience that students crave and will benefit greatly from. (p. 68)

PBL amplifies teacher creativity. When teachers are thinking creatively, students can think creatively, and ultimately PBL provides many different ways for students to demonstrate their learning and growth. Design principle one states, "Students are empowered daily to make important decisions about their learning experiences, how they will create and apply knowledge, and how they will demonstrate their learning."

Learning is about growth, application, and ultimately the demonstration of evidence. PBL provides empowered learners various ways to engage in meaningful learning experiences that amplify the needed skills for success in today's world.

To see an example of how PBL can amplify student learning in a competency-based system, consider the work happening in Chilliwack's Imagine High in British Columbia, Canada. Kirk Savage, assistant superintendent, shares their story.

Practitioner Perspective
Kirk Savage, Assistant Superintendent, Chilliwack School District, British Columbia

The BC Curriculum was renovated in 2016 with a priority placed on competency-based learning. The prescribed learning outcomes (PLOs) for each grade and subject were replaced by Core and Curricular Competencies, paving the way for educators to approach learning in unique and personalized ways. This is exactly what Chilliwack's newest secondary school, Imagine High, did when it opened in September of 2021.

The curriculum design of the school is based on the integration of core subjects, meaning that students receive instruction for these subjects together. English, social studies, science, and mathematics are not taught in traditional silos; instead, they are taught together, connected to a larger inquiry learning umbrella. As students learn though experiential interdisciplinary projects, they build understandings of their strengths, develop interests, explore their thinking to build independence, and create powerful demonstrations of learning. The programming at Imagine High does not stop there. The school has taken CBE to even greater heights through their intensive Deep Drive Institutes.

Twice a year, the school shuts down the regular daily learning structure (timetable) for a three-week deep dive so that students can engage in an immersive learning journey of their choice. The deep dives offer opportunities for student to enhance their learning in an area of interest for them. During these intensive courses, students earn elective credits dependent on the focus of their learning. This personalized approach is powerfully engaging and presents almost unlimited possibilities for student choice and personalization.

> Imagine High is built on the foundations of the BC Curriculum, the First Peoples Principles of Learning, and current research on innovative learning environments. The school has visionary leadership provided by Principal Brooke Haller and Vice Principal Stacey Parsons.
>
> (K. Savage, personal communication, December 8, 2021)

Work-Based Learning and Extended or Expanded Learning Opportunities

Learning does not solely happen in the classroom. In fact, some of our greatest learning happens outside the school building. Competency-based learning schools work diligently to not only provide but offer competency credit for these types of experiences.

This can be done through work-based and extended or expanded learning opportunities. The New Hampshire Department of Education (n.d.) defines *extended learning opportunities* (ELOs) as opportunities that "allow for the primary acquisition of knowledge and skills through instruction or study outside of the traditional classroom including, but not limited to independent study, private instruction, performing groups, internships, community service, apprenticeships, and online courses."

Similarly the Wallace Foundation (n.d.) describes *expanded learning opportunities* as models that "provide educational supports as well as enrichment and recreational opportunities to young people and their families during nonschool hours."

These expanded or extended learning opportunities are unique to each learner and ideally are co-constructed with adults to support the student to the greatest degree possible while also empowering the student to follow their passion. Design principle five outlines that "Students learn using multiple pathways" and ELOs are a great example of what this can look like.

Donna Couture is the director of extended learning at Winnacunnet High School in Hampton, New Hampshire. Donna has transformed the ELO program within her school and has been influential within the State of New Hampshire, as well, having served as the president of the Extended Learning Opportunities Network there. Donna shares how her school program has evolved over the past eight years in moving toward a more cocreated program providing various and rich opportunities to engage in meaningful learning outside of school, but as an integral part of their overall school experience.

Practitioner Perspective
Donna Couture, Director of Extended Learning, Winnacunnet High School, Hampton, New Hampshire

In 2013, Winnacunnet High School began to dig deeper into what it means to personalize the educational experience for our students. We explored the increasingly complex picture of the path from student engagement to student achievement. We looked at relationships, teaching and learning, the role of the community, and the ways in which the various aspects of the school experience interact for students. Creating a robust and comprehensive ELO program provides an opportunity for students to earn credit toward graduation by engaging in learning experiences that are centered around their own interests, needs, and abilities. These learning experiences harness relationships with educators and community partners in order to extend learning outside of the classroom and into the real world. It rethinks traditional roles by putting the student in charge, having the teacher act as a facilitator, and bringing the community in as educators.

No matter the type of ELO experience, these experiences must be flexible enough to happen anytime, any place, and at any pace. That being said, there are hallmark components to every ELO experience that ensure the student is engaging in a high-quality experience. The New Hampshire Extended Learning Opportunities Network (New Hampshire Department of Education, n.d.) describes six of these critical components in their High Quality Framework (2019).

1. Establishing student goals and essential questions
2. Involving partners to help guide the student in their learning (such as an ELO coordinator, mentor teachers, community partners, school counselors, case managers, and parents)
3. Planning how and when the student will communicate with all ELO partners
4. Creating a specific list of timelines and benchmarks to monitor the progress of learning
5. Describing competencies that illustrate what a student should know and be able to do
6. Planning for assessment

The WHS administration, faculty, and community were on board with the philosophy of ELOs, but we struggled with how to systematize it. We conducted an assessment of what schoolwide needs the ELO program could fulfill. We considered many things, including how the ELO program could support alternative pathways to earning and recovering credit as well as opportunities to enrich our current curriculum. Our ELO program initially focused on providing elective options for students who wanted to explore careers and hobbies of interest. However, as the foundation of our program strengthened, we prioritized increasing access for students who are at risk for not meeting their graduation requirements. This meant developing individualized experiences for students who were struggling with traditional learning models. As more and more students struggled to engage in a remote learning environment during the COVID-19 pandemic, no idea was off the table. Our competency-based learning system gave us the flexibility to think outside the box and create unique ELO

> learning experiences. We put the student first and engaged all stakeholders in the process. Now, instead of struggling to find ways to help a student successfully fit into the expectations of a course, we are finding ways for the course to fit into the student's own interests, needs, and abilities. That shift in mindset is a game changer in the world of personalized learning. It requires everyone to reevaluate their traditional roles in a student's learning experience. Teachers no longer have to be the experts, students are put in charge of their own learning, and community members are creating real-world connections. Everyone has a role to play and everyone's input is necessary.
>
> After years of implementation, I am proud to say that our ELO program is full of unique and exciting opportunities for our students. We are seeing more ways for students to explore career interests and connect to the community through informational interviews, job shadows, and internships. More students are graduating with industry recognized credentials in areas like emergency medical systems and real estate. More students are meeting core graduation requirements through their own interests like engaging an interest in computer programming to complete English competencies. More students are earning graduation credit for interests we normally don't see in classroom curriculum, like gaming and building an airplane. Student engagement and achievement is guaranteed when the sky is the limit.
>
> (D. Couture, personal communication, March 14, 2021)

Instruction is at the core of learning. To engage students in the learning process is to provide every learner with the requisite skill set to tackle learning today and in the future. However, to do this effectively, we must have structures in place to meet each student where they are, and we must work collaboratively to meet the needs of the learners within a grade level, content area, and school.

Jada and her team, through their collaborative processes, recognize their collective role in supporting all learners within their grade level. Focusing their efforts on achieving clarity with Tier 1 essential standards allowed them to better determine which of their students need help. Additionally, this focus on essential standards provided the team with the information they need to implement the appropriate support or extension for their students in Tiers 2 and 3. The structures outlined in this chapter provide a pathway to achieving this end, as Jada and her team experienced.

Reflection Questions

Consider these questions with your team.

1. Instruction in a competency-based classroom is framed through a clearly articulated framework of competencies, essential standards, and learning targets. Reflect on this framework within your school, grade level, or content area. Is there a common understanding of what students should know and be able to do? Does your team

collaboratively determine what success will look like for students through the use of common rubrics? Do these competencies and essential standards drive instructional practices?

2. The three-tiered RTI model is ideal for supporting the individual student, the classroom, the individual classroom teacher, teacher teams, and the school as a system. Reflect on the system for supporting all learners in your school. Do all tiers work together seamlessly to provide students what they need? Are resources allocated to support this system of support?

3. Student empowerment and agency are necessary within a competency-based system. How do you provide opportunities in your classroom for students to codesign learning experiences? Are students able to demonstrate their understanding in multiple ways?

4. Metacognition is a key practice for students developing ownership of their learning. What opportunities exist in your classroom for students to reflect, set goals, and then monitor and adapt these goals? How do you make sure that their honest reflection isn't punitive?

5. What does personalized learning look like in your classroom—how do you meet the needs of all of your learners? How does the system in your classroom sync with the overall system of support in your school? What are the communication methods used to ensure continuity within the overall system of support?

CHAPTER 6

Structures for Feedback

As Jada prepares to start the new school year, her greatest challenge will be determining how she and her collaborative teammates will handle feedback for their students. This will be a particularly complicated task for them because they work in a school that is not yet ready for a schoolwide conversation on grading and reporting reform. Yet Jada and her team know they cannot wait. They will need to take the lead in this for now, forging ahead, because they know that how they report out on student learning is going to make or break their ability to be successful in their newly formed competency-based classrooms. The work will not be easy, and it will likely cause some of Jada's students and parents to question her processes. However, if she succeeds, her students will be the real winners.

This chapter focuses on structures for feedback, specifically the role of grading and reporting in a competency-based classroom. There are many considerations when it comes to grading and reporting, including what should be graded, how it should be recorded, and whether or not practices such as reassessment, ranking, and averaging belong in a grading system or not. These topics will all be explored in more detail.

Why Do We Grade?

When educators like Jada engage in conversations on grading and reporting, they often get to the heart of what are very deep-seeded core values and beliefs about learning. Sadly, many educators use grading practices and procedures simply because they are "the way things have always been done" without taking the time to think through whether or not those practices are best for students and the best way to report on student achievement. If you were to ask a group of educators why they grade, you would likely hear some of these common answers.

- "Grading provides students with an incentive to learn. Grades motivate them to do their work in the first place and work toward continuous improvement and mastery."

    While this is true, there are a couple potential pitfalls to this approach. First, understand that if grades are to be used to motivate students to do work, the act of *doing work* is not enough. The actual grade must be based on what work a student submitted, judging it against very specific criteria. Educators who assign grades for effort or work completion and include those grades in overall scoring are missing the point of grading entirely. A second pitfall is that educators can turn grading into punishment, thus counteracting the resulting motivation. For example, when students are late with assignments and teachers deduct a letter grade. In this instance, not only did the educators use grading as punishment, but they also watered down the grade by including nonacademic behaviors (not turning in work), which should be handled differently. We get into this later in this chapter.

- "Grades communicate student learning and achievement to students, parents, postsecondary institutions, and employers—everyone who needs it."

    Oftentimes, educators and schools fall short in determining what details they should communicate to students and parents. Grades need to tell the whole story. They need to show how a student has performed on the standards and competencies assigned to the grade level or course. They must be based on levels of proficiency, and not be an unrelated accumulation of points. There should be more emphasis placed on more recent work as it is a better indicator of where the student is at the current time. Grades must be about what students learn—not what they earn. All who look at grade reports should be able to quickly identify which skills and competencies are areas of strength, and which are areas of weakness. Students should be able to use grades as a self-reflection tool to set goals for continuous improvement.

- "Grades are used to help sort students for various reasons—for groups, levels, courses, or other special programs or interventions."

Sorting students has been a century-old practice. High schools have long been asked to move away from *tracking*, the idea that a student should be placed into a specific program or course level based on a perceived ability with little or no opportunity for movement or advancement to another track or level. Sorting for reasons such as this is not advisable, but sorting at the classroom level does and should happen regularly. In a heterogeneously grouped classroom, grades help educators sort students into ability groupings for the purposes of classroom-level reteaching, intervention, and enrichment. In some cases, they can help educators maintain mixed-ability groupings for particular learning tasks. Grades serve as important and relevant data points to help educators in these efforts.

▸ "Grades are an evaluation tool to help educators and schools determine the effectiveness of curriculum, instruction, and other programs."

Without relevant data points, how can one ever evaluate program effectiveness? When grades are tied directly to specific content standards, skills, competencies, and academic behaviors, and educators are able to drill down to examine grades at this level, they can provide powerful insight into the efforts to evaluate curriculum, instruction, and the overall effectiveness of other programs in the classroom or school. The data help educators identify trends as well as strengths and weaknesses in all of these areas. They allow collaborative teams to set goals and measure their success on achieving these goals on an ongoing basis.

> **When grades are tied directly to specific content standards, skills, competencies, and academic behaviors, and educators are able to drill down to examine grades at this level, they can provide powerful insight into the efforts to evaluate curriculum, instruction, and the overall effectiveness of other programs in the classroom or school.**

If these are the primary reasons to grade, then do classroom grading procedures and policies support these reasons? Are there contradictions? Jada's task, like other educators implementing a competency-based learning system, is to explore these questions in an effort to reach clarity about how to move forward with an effort to build an effective grading and reporting structure for a competency-based classroom. To start, there are frequently asked questions to consider.

What Should We Grade?

Determining what to grade is one of the first questions that educators like Jada must consider. Educators should be wary of falling into the trap of thinking that everything needs a grade. Many struggle with this because they believe that if they don't grade something, students won't do it in the first place. Yet grading everything is time consuming and it is likely to decrease the meaning of the grade. When teachers include too many types of work in a grade, students tend to attempt to artificially enhance their grade through shortcuts that allow them to avoid learning the material in the first place. This is especially prevalent with older students. Consider the example of Joey, a high school sophomore.

Joey's Mathematics Plan

Joey is a self-proclaimed "poor test taker." He is determined not to let that deter him from getting an A in his mathematics class. He devises the following plan, as outlined in figure 6.1, to get the grade he wants.

Weight	Category	Joey's Target	Points Earned
25%	Tests	60%	15 Points
20%	Quizzes	80%	16 Points
15%	Projects	100%	15 Points
15%	Classwork	100%	15 Points
15%	Homework	100%	15 Points
10%	Participation	100%	10 Points
5%	Extra Credit	100%	5 Points
			Total: 91 Points (A–)

Figure 6.1: Joey's plan to get an A in mathematics.

In this example, Joey estimates that he could still earn an A in his class with a test average that is no greater than 60 percent and a quiz average no greater than 80 percent. His logic is that he could do far better on a quiz, which is based on smaller amounts of materials, than a test. Joey set a goal to earn all of the points he could on what he describes as the "low-hanging fruit" of a mathematics grade—like projects, classwork, homework, participation, and extra credit. His logic is that projects are always given in advance, and so much of a project grade comes from things that he can control like a poster or a presentation slide show. Classwork grades, Joey argues, simply come from completing worksheets that are assigned each day in class. Homework is graded on a complete or not-complete scale, with no grades on the accuracy of the work. Participation is a very unknown, elusive grading category. What does it really represent? Joey's theory is that as long as he raises his hand at least once in every class, his teacher will remember that when it comes time to assign a grade. Lastly, there is the bonus extra-credit grade that Joey loves. He will be the first student to bring in a box of tissues or show up to support the basketball team (his teacher happens to be the coach). Joey's strategy, if he is successful, will earn him a final grade of a 91 percent, which equates to an A– at his school.

This example may seem like a bit of an exaggeration, but in fact it is not. Joey's example *did* happen, although the grade level and subject have been changed. Joey's example shows that significant flaws exist in a classroom where too many grades are included that distort the singular goal of grades: to be an accurate reflection of what a student knows and is able to do. After just one marking period, Joey had already accumulated several major gaps in his learning and understanding of the content, and this was going to create issues for him later in the class. To avoid such instances, grades should be limited to tasks that are used to provide evidence of learning.

In contrast, consider the following example from Anytown High School. At Anytown High School, all courses have an overall final course grade based on competency assessments through the year, with more weight given to more recent work. Academic grades are communicated separately from lifelong learning skills.

Anytown High School

Each course at Anytown High School has specific competency outcomes that students need to demonstrate to show their knowledge, skills, or abilities to earn credit for the course. Course competencies answer this question: What is it we want our students to know and be able to do? Each competency is broken down into a subset of specific skills and learning targets. Teachers give assessments throughout the year, linked to skills and learning targets that are then linked back to specific competencies. Students must receive a passing grade in each competency in order to receive credit for a course.

Throughout the year, teachers grade students on four major lifelong learning skills in all courses: (1) communication, (2) creativity, (3) collaboration, and (4) self-direction. These are communicated separately on report cards and the final transcript.

Diagnostic assessments generally happen at the beginning of a unit, serving as a way to tell both the student and the teacher how much the student already knows about an upcoming unit. This information helps the teacher plan their lesson and learning objectives, and plan how much time they will spend on various parts of the unit. Diagnostic assessments may or may not be recorded in the gradebook, but if they are, will carry no weight in the overall grade.

Formative assessments capture a student's progress and provide critical feedback to the student and the teacher on the extent to which learning is progressing. They are considered practice and can take on many forms. Formative assessments are recorded in the gradebook and must be completed before a student is able to attempt a summative assessment. Students who do not complete key formative assessments are not considered ready to provide evidence of their learning with a summative assessment.

Summative assessments are performance-based tasks that allow students to provide evidence of their learning at deeper levels. They include things such as research projects, presentations, labs, writing, tests, simulations, and inquiry tasks. They are linked to one or more of the competencies and are required to have a rubric to give students clear expectations.

What do you notice about the example from Anytown High School? First, it is apparent that at Anytown High School, only summative assessments carry weight in the grading system. Diagnostic and formative assessments can be reported on, but for informational purposes only. To ensure that students do not elect to skip these important feedback opportunities, the summative assessment cannot be started until the key formative work is complete and feedback has been given.

Second, assessments are directly linked to competencies, which are in turn linked to standards. For every piece of assessment data collected (formative or summative), that data point can be directly correlated to the skill being assessed. Finally, the lifelong learning skills, also known as the dispositions, are assessed regularly, but this data is reported separately. This concept is discussed in greater detail in the following section.

Should We Separate Academics From Skills and Dispositions?

Dispositions, or *lifelong learning skills* as they are called in the example from Anytown High School, are a critical set of skills that educators must develop in students. They must provide students with learning opportunities to grow these skills, with feedback along the way. These skills, some may argue, are more important than the development of academic content knowledge and skills. Let's be honest—when was the last time you heard of an employer who was looking for a new hire to be proficient at graphing polynomial and logarithmic functions (unless the job was that of a high school math teacher)? Will a student's ability to recite the Gettysburg Address be the deciding factor as to whether or not they will be selected over others for a job one day? We hope not.

The reality is that employers are looking for skills that go far deeper than content-specific knowledge. Schools need to think bigger when it comes to deciding what is important, and what matters for grading purposes.

As we mentioned early in this book, our global society is in the midst of a fourth Industrial Revolution led by innovations in fields such as robotics and artificial intelligence, genetics, bio and nanotechnology (World Economic Forum, 2016). We are starting to see the rise of smart systems in the residential, business, manufacturing, agricultural, and civic sectors. These systems are driving new ideas and a new outlook on how to share and integrate data and use it to operate more efficiently. All of this is bringing about tremendous changes in the workplace, and creating the need for schools to help students master these important dispositions.

Skills and dispositions are best assessed using an ongoing approach, with students actively tracking their own learning progressions. Students need ample opportunity for reflection and growth. Student self-reflection, goal setting, and monitoring are a regular part of the assessment process that an effective classroom teacher uses, with students taking active ownership in their growth related to these. Most importantly, however, teachers should track and report on these separately in the gradebook. Many educators and schools do this by creating a separate parallel scale for dispositions and tagging it to specific assessments throughout the year that collect evidence on these practices throughout the year.

What Grading Scale Should We Use?

To answer this question, schools and educators must first understand why a rubric-based scale is far superior to a percentage scale such as the one in figure 6.2.

0–9%	10%–19%	20%–29%	30%–39%	40%–49%	50%–59%	60%–69%	70%–79%	80%–89%	90%–100%
F						D	C	B	A
Failure						?	Passing		

Figure 6.2: A traditional percentage-based scale.

Guskey (2015) writes:

> From the perspective of simple logic, percentage grade scales make little sense. . . . Teachers who use percentage grades typically set the minimum grade for passing at 60 or 65. In other words, students must attain a grade of at least 60 in order to receive credit for a course or to meet the minimal level of performance judged as 'success.' Most

teachers consider percentage grades in the 60s to represent only modest success, while those in the 90s are regarded as representing high-level or excellent success. (p. 27)

Consider the intervals associated with passing and not passing in figure 6.2 (page 135). Assuming a passing grade is 70, why do we need such a wide range of values to represent failure? Wormeli (2006) suggests teachers who work in such a model should actually stop using the first 59 values in the percentage scale and instead record the lowest grade as a 60 instead of 0. Wormeli (2006) writes, "When we turn students' zeros into sixties in our gradebooks, we are not giving students something for nothing. We're adjusting the grade intervals so that any averaging we do is mathematically justified but, even more important, that any grade we determine from the pattern of grades is a valid indicator of mastery" (p. 137). Wormeli's strategy serves to help teachers overcome inequities in a percentage-based scale, making the range of possible values for each level of performance equal, and avoiding having such a lopsided scale with multiple levels of failure. Competency-based schools often use this strategy to get away from the percentage-based scale. In one such school that we worked with, in that first year, teachers started to refer to the practice of awarding a sixty as the lowest grade as a "fake sixty" because it just didn't feel right to students to get something for nothing. It took most of the year for teachers to start to shift their thinking and to recognize that grading wasn't simply an exercise in awarding points for work completion on a percentage scale, but rather an exercise in making a judgment on the depth to which a student has mastered a content or skill. By the end of that first year, teachers were asking when the school could move to a more logical 4-point rubric scale.

Educators in this school then convened a committee to develop appropriate language for a 4-point scale. Interestingly, they called on teachers from other grade levels in the system (grades K–8) to assist in this process. After a day of discussion and debate, they arrived at a version of a scale similar to the one shown in figure 6.3.

In this scale, failure is represented by just one level, titled *not yet proficient*. Although the will of the group when it was created was to set the passing grade at a 3, it was recognized that this may be too far of a stretch for a school that had historically set passing at 65 percent. As a result, it was determined that 2 would be designated as a basic level of proficiency. On individual assessments, however, teachers would emphasize to students that proficiency at a level 3 was the appropriate goal to aim for on each task.

	Level	Descriptor	Numerical Grade
Competent	Advanced	Consistently and independently extends and transfers content knowledge and skills beyond essential competencies	4
	Proficient	Essential content knowledge and skills are demonstrated consistently and independently with ability to apply and transfer to real-world situations or a new task	3
	Basic Proficient	Demonstrates the emerging application and transfer of essential content knowledge and skills in familiar tasks	2
Not Competent	Not Yet Proficient	Initiating the ability to demonstrate the essential content, knowledge, and skills	1

Figure 6.3: A typical 4-point scale.

Not apparent in the scale, but an important feature of competency-based grading scales, is the notion that there is an emphasis placed on more recent evidence. O'Connor (2018) lists this as an important point: "Use the most consistent level of achievement with special consideration for the more recent information" (p. 150). O'Connor (2018) goes on to write, "Teachers should base grades on the most consistent level of performance, not the whole range of performance" (p. 153). There are several ways to accomplish this, and many newer electronic grading systems offer a variety of alternatives. Two of the most popular, based on mathematical formulas, are power law and decaying average.

Power Law

The power law formula predicts a student's next score based on the scores that are already present, using a complex mathematical formula that few teachers are able to explain to students or parents (this is why gradebook systems handle the math). The important point is for teachers to be able to explain the theory behind why it is used, which is to answer the question: If we were to assess a student right now, what would be the likely performance level we would expect to see based on the previous performance?

To gain an understanding of how the power law works, let's look at sets of student scores and the power law calculation of each set compiled by JumpRope (2022; www.jumpro.pe), a standards-based grading system. In this example in figure 6.4 (page 138), there are four assessment scores and four students, and each earned the same scores of 1, 2, 3 and 4, but in a different order. A straight average would result in each student receiving a grade of 2.5, but the power law allows for more weight on recent assessments in different ways.

	Score 1	Score 2	Score 3	Score 4	Power Law Score	Interpretation
Student 1	1	2	3	4	4	The scores show continuous improvement. The student will likely demonstrate mastery on the next assessment.
Student 2	1	3	2	4	3.66	The scores show irregular improvement. The student will likely demonstrate high but not complete mastery on the next assessment.
Student 3	2	4	1	3	2.16	The scores show very uneven performance. The student will likely demonstrate a mid-level of achievement on the next assessment.
Student 4	4	3	2	1	1.28	The scores show continuous decline. The student will likely demonstrate a low level of achievement on the next assessment.

Source: Adapted from JumpRope, 2022. Used with permission.

Figure 6.4: JumpRope power law grade calculation examples.

The power law operates with a predictable (yet complicated) mathematical formula, which makes it a versatile option that many electronic gradebooks are able to offer to customers. It also does not penalize students for low scores early in the marking period. Rather, it looks for consistency as part of its trend calculations.

Decaying Average

When you learn anything new, ultimately it is your most recent work that is a better indicator of what you know and are able to do. For this reason, some schools use a decaying average for grade reporting. A decaying average is a type of grading calculation that puts more weight on the most recent score by assigning it a fixed percentage of weight as determined by the school district.

To see how it works, let's look at some examples. For these examples, let's assume the school district has determined the fixed decay percentage to be 50 percent.

Example 1: The Student With a Slow Start

A student receives the following five scores (in order): 2, 2, 2, 3, and 4. In this example (see figure 6.5), the student has a typical slow start, but then starts to demonstrate increased understanding with the final two assessment scores. The student is on an upward trend.

	Score	Calculation	Result	Interpretation
Traditional Average				
Score 1	2	2 / 1	2	The result after just one score.
Score 2	2	(2 + 2) / 2	2	The result after the second score is added.
Score 3	2	(2 + 2 + 2) / 3	2	The result after the third score is added.
Score 4	3	(2 + 2 + 2 + 3) / 4	2.25	The result after the fourth score is added.
Score 5	4	(2 + 2 + 2 + 3 + 4) / 5	2.6	The result after the fifth score is added.
Decaying Average (Using 50% as the weight for the most recent work)				
Score 1	2	2 × 100% = 2	2	The result after just one score.
Score 2	2	(2 × 50%) + (2 × 50%) = 2	2	The result after the second score is added.
Score 3	2	(2 × 50%) + (2 × 50%) = 2	2	The result after the third score is added.
Score 4	3	(2 × 50%) + (3 × 50%) = 2.5	2.5	The result after the fourth score is added.
Score 5	4	(2.5 × 50%) + (4 × 50%) = 3.25	3.25	The result after the fifth score is added.

Figure 6.5: Student with a slow start.

Example 2: The Student With Ups and Downs

A student receives the following five scores (in order): 3, 2, 3, 2, and 3. In this example (see figure 6.6, page 140), the student maintains a fairly consistent performance, earning 2s and 3s on their 5 assignments with no upward or downward trend apparent.

		Traditional Average		
	Score	Calculation	Result	Interpretation
Score 1	3	3 / 1	3	The result after just one score.
Score 2	2	(3 + 2) / 2	2.5	The result after the second score is added.
Score 3	3	(3 + 2 + 3) / 3	2.67	The result after the third score is added.
Score 4	2	(3 + 2 + 3 + 2) / 4	2.5	The result after the fourth score is added.
Score 5	3	(3 + 2 + 3 + 2 + 3) / 5	2.6	The result after the fifth score is added.
	Decaying Average (Using 50% as the weight for the most recent work)			
	Score	Calculation	Result	Interpretation
Score 1	3	3 x 100% = 3	3	The result after just one score.
Score 2	2	(3 x 50%) + (2 x 50%) = 2.5	2.5	The result after the second score is added.
Score 3	3	(2.5 x 50%) + (3 x 50%) = 2.75	2.75	The result after the third score is added.
Score 4	2	(2.75 x 50%) + (2 x 50%) = 2.38	2.38	The result after the fourth score is added.
Score 5	3	(2.38 x 50%) + (3 x 50%) = 2.69	2.69	The result after the fifth score is added.

Figure 6.6: Student with ups and downs.

Example 3: The Student With a Downward Trend

A student receives the following five scores (in order): 4, 2, 3, 2, and 2. In this example (see figure 6.7), the student has a strong start but then begins to struggle. Perhaps this is because the material has gotten more challenging, or perhaps it is due to something else. Regardless, it has led to a downward trend in scores and requires attention and intervention.

		Traditional Average		
	Score	Calculation	Result	Interpretation
Score 1	4	4 / 1	4	The result after just one score.
Score 2	2	(4 + 2) / 2	3	The result after the second score is added.
Score 3	3	(4 + 2 + 3) / 3	3	The result after the third score is added.
Score 4	2	(4 + 2 + 3 + 2) / 4	2.75	The result after the fourth score is added.
Score 5	2	(4 + 2 + 3 + 2 + 2) / 5	2.6	The result after the fifth score is added.

Decaying Average (Using 50% as the weight for the most recent work)				
	Score	Calculation	Result	Interpretation
Score 1	4	4 × 100% = 4	4	The result after just one score.
Score 2	2	(4 × 50%) + (2 × 50%) = 3	3	The result after the second score is added.
Score 3	3	(3 × 50%) + (3 × 50%) = 2.5	3	The result after the third score is added.
Score 4	2	(3 × 50%) + (2 × 50%) = 2.5	2.5	The result after the fourth score is added.
Score 5	2	(2.5 × 50%) + (2 × 50%) = 2.25	2.25	The result after the fifth score is added.

Figure 6.7: Student with a downward trend.

What Do You Notice?

In the first example, the student who is on an upward trend ends up with a higher result than they would have received using a traditional average calculation. In the second example with the student who has been getting fairly consistent scores all along, the result is still higher (slightly) because the last score was on a slight upward trend. In the third example, the student on a downward trend ends up with a lower result than they would have using a traditional average.

In all three cases, if you look at how the student has performed over time, the result based on the decaying average calculation is more representative of the most recent work. It is a better indicator of what the student knows and is able to do at the current time.

Had the traditional average calculation been used, then in all three examples the students would have earned the same result with no acknowledgement of the upward or downward trends in their learning.

Guskey (2015) offers two other alternatives to using most recent evidence. The first is to give priority to the most comprehensive evidence: "If certain sources of evidence represent cumulative summaries of the knowledge and skills students have acquired, then these should hold the greatest weight in determining students' grades" (p. 91). A second alternative, Guskey (2015) suggests, is to give priority to evidence related to the most important learning goals or standards.

> Those sources of evidence that relate to the most important or most crucial goals or standards should then be given more priority. Teachers might, for example, attach greater importance to students' scores on

a project that required them to synthesize and apply what they learned than they might give to the scores students attained on assessments designed to tap basic knowledge and comprehension of course content. (p. 91)

Decisions of whether to use any of these grading alternatives should be made with careful thought given to the impact these practices may have overall. They must also be considered within the context of other policies, procedures, and practices that must be changed. Curriculum coordinator Erica Pappalardo talks about how this was considered in her New Hampshire School District.

> **Practitioner Perspective**
> **Erica Pappalardo, Curriculum Coordinator, Inter-Lakes School District, Meredith, New Hampshire**
>
> Of all the shifts required to build a competency-based learning system, grading and reporting practices tend to generate the greatest amount of interest and excitement among all stakeholders. Some fully embrace the idea of having a coherent structure that aligns back to the developed competency framework, the very blueprint that guides all instruction and assessment; others are reluctant to adopt such practices. It's important to have an awareness of where stakeholders fall along this continuum as well as the key components they may not fully comprehend or embrace. This awareness presents opportunities!
>
> We tend to invest a great amount of time and support with school district staff to develop the understanding and skills needed to activate shifts in our practices. In this work, it is as important to provide opportunities for all stakeholders to engage in the work. The question then follows, how do we build relevant, meaningful experiences for our stakeholders?
>
> The Inter-Lakes School District's work truly began to flourish under the leadership of Mary Moriarty who took on the role of superintendent of schools during the fall of 2016. Mary understands how critical it is to support all stakeholders through the change cycle; her leadership exemplifies this understanding while simultaneously providing some inspiration to school leaders looking for ways to expand this work beyond the school district staff.
>
> The district teachers had been engaged in a great deal of work prior to Mary's arrival, primarily focusing energy on the creation of academic competency documents. With the change in leadership, this was an opportunity to refresh and reset understanding across the community. During the summer of 2017, the district hosted a competency-based learning retreat. In addition to the administrative team, community invitees included the school board members, parents, students, and teachers. This four-day event provided an opportunity for these stakeholders to dig deeper into the pillars of competency-based education and to voice hopes, wishes, and fears. Professional leaders in the field of competency-based education were invited as outside facilitators to provide state and national perspectives that the local team was unable to provide. This included a panel of college admissions representatives who spoke specifically to the concern many community members share—whether

the competency-based education model creates disadvantages for learners as they move from secondary schools to post-secondary institutions. There is power in hearing directly from external experts; these professionals can be the voice of information with no ulterior motive or bias toward district efforts.

There are other components of a competency-based model that cannot truly exist without providing a venue for a range of stakeholders to contribute to. In assuring that the district's competency framework is reflective of the community's vision of its graduates, many districts engaged in this work find intentional ways for stakeholders to contribute. Without these opportunities, schools will continue to work in isolation of the demands and needs of its community members. Lacking connections between school and community only perpetuates the disconnect some feel about this work. When making intentional connections and community-based learning experiences, it is critical that the profile of a graduate reflect the knowledge and skills deemed relevant and critical by these stakeholders. Leveraging the impact of experts from the field, Rose Colby, a nationally recognized native New Hampshire educational consultant on competency-based learning, facilitated community events during which she continued to build exposure to and understanding of the tenets of competency-based educational models. With her partnership, stakeholders had a voice in the process of refining the district's profile of a graduate.

Leading the work internally, the Inter-Lakes School District was evolving its design principles, practices, and procedures for learning, expectations for assessing learner progress, and its procedures for using grades to report learner progress. This district-created document outlines philosophical beliefs, expectations, and procedures K–12. Staff feedback fueled the revision process. With the anticipation of presenting the document for school board approval, the 2019–2020 school year integrated a School Board Learning Series. This five-session experience, facilitated by Brian Stack, provided the district an opportunity to focus on key elements of the document. Each session was designed as an interactive way for community members to make meaning of shifts in philosophy. Being able to showcase artifacts as evidence of how these philosophies translated into day-to-day work was impactful. Having teachers and students speak to their experiences was incredibly informative for the community. The culminating session focused on putting all of the pieces together and ultimately resulted in the school board's unanimous approval of the district's design principles.

Through this journey, I personally have sat in the seat of both consultant as well as the district's curriculum coordinator. We are now in our third year of successfully implementing a phased-in shift to our grading and reporting practices. I can attribute this success to the dedication Mary Moriarty has had to reaching out to the various stakeholders in our community and in taking the time to build understanding, garner feedback, and iterate all along the way, responding to and integrating the voices of all.

(E. Pappalardo, personal communication, December 15, 2020)

How Will We Handle Missing Work?

Both Guskey (2015) and O'Connor (2018) argue against the use of the common approach to handling missing work: assigning zeros. The reasons for this are clear and are based on the assumption that in a typical percentage-based scale, the zero artificially lowers a student grade by a significant amount since the range for failure is so great in that scale. Many teachers argue that the zero motivates students to complete the assignment at a later date. We argue that this is not true, and there are better ways to motivate students. Consider this alternative approach instead as an example.

Students are expected to complete all major summative assessments in a timely manner and will be given an expected completion date. Students who do not complete an assessment in a timely manner will be referred to a school administrator for additional support. For formative assessments, the grades will be recorded as *not submitted*. For summative assessments, the grade will be recorded as *insufficient evidence shown* (IES), with a comment entered to signify that the student has not yet completed the work. The teacher will work with the student and their parents to resolve the issue as soon as possible. The teacher will also involve other supports and staff (school counselors, case managers, and school administrators) as needed.

In this example, it is clear to students that not submitting work is not an option. If the teacher is unable to resolve the matter on their own, the school has outlined others who can be called in to support. Ultimately, the school holds students accountable for the submission of evidence that is used to make a judgment on learning.

To see how this practice plays out in a high school classroom where it can be notoriously difficult to get teens to submit work in a timely manner, consider the following example from Crystal Bonin, an English teacher in a New Hampshire high school.

Practitioner Perspective
Crystal Bonin, English Language Arts Teacher, Winnisquam Regional High School, Winnisquam, New Hampshire

In competency-based learning, our job as educators is to coach and support students as they work toward competency. This makes assessment tough. We know that some students work slower than others. Some work faster. Some don't work at all because they have no idea how to start. Despite this, the school year does eventually end. So we set goals and deadlines for summative assessments. Many secondary educators academically penalize students for late assessments, or assessments not passed in at all, because: "In the real world, students will have deadlines and they need to know that deadlines are important."

Let's be honest. How many of us here, in the real world, have missed a deadline or negotiated an extension? While I sit and type this, my car is 2,500 miles overdue for an oil change. My car will forgive me, and it probably won't die before I can schedule one soon. A few weeks ago, a furniture delivery I was expecting had to reschedule, due to icy roads leading to my home. I forgave the furniture guys because we rescheduled and they delivered the next week. Many years ago, I worked at an academic publishing company. Lightning hit our print shop, our schedule fell behind, and all of our books would be late. The schools forgave our company, because we gave them our best work, even though it arrived a few days late. They even ordered again the following year.

In many schools, it's common to give zeros for missing work, and it's expected that students should lose points for late work. I'm ashamed to say that I've caved to these expectations in the past. It made me feel rotten. Because of that rotten feeling, I don't academically penalize students for late work anymore. Honestly, it doesn't even make sense to me to do so. I don't give zeros on summative assessments. I bother students until they complete them.

Now, I consistently tell my students that if they're not turning in their best work on the due date, I'd rather take it the next day. Or the day after that. I tell them that if they're not finished with their assigned book, they shouldn't even start the assessment until they do. We make new plans. This makes me controversial.

The week I wrote this, my students had a summative project due on their 1930s book club books. In the days before the due date, I told students that if they felt like they couldn't meet this due date, for whatever reason, all I asked was that they communicate. By the night before the due date, I'd received thirty-five emails from students telling me that they wouldn't have it done on time.

Now, while you might think I'd be screaming inside, I felt a weird sense of peace. I was elated. My students understood that "best work" and competency took precedent over producing a rushed project, just to meet an arbitrary deadline. More than that, I was happy that they'd learned to take responsibility for procrastination, to be proactive, and to communicate, and to make a new plan for completion. That's a life skill.

On the original due date, only a small percentage of completed projects came in, and they all represented great work. A larger amount came in a few days later, and they also showed great work. I'm still waiting for some projects as I write this, and I'm confident that they'll also represent great work.

In the end, what's more important: meeting a due date with junk that will probably need to be reassessed, or communicating your struggles, making a plan, and showing your best work a little late? I vote for the latter, even if I'm still taking late work in June.

(C. Bonin, personal communication, February 27, 2021)

Will We Allow for Reassessment?

We allow people to retake their driver's license exam as many times as they need to in order to demonstrate competency. The same is true of professionals such as teachers, lawyers, doctors, and electricians who are required to pass a certification or licensure exam. Reassessment is a part of our real world. As such, it should also be part of the real world for students. We find it ironic that the question of whether or not to allow for reassessment is still debated in schools. The better question is, how should one handle reassessment in the classroom?

In competency-based systems, reassessments are a necessary part of the learning process. Making reassessments a schoolwide practice changes the learning culture for students from one where they are trying to earn enough points to pass to one in which they are held accountable for everything they need to know and be able to do. O'Connor (2018) writes:

> Teachers should focus on reteaching and reassessing proficiency on learning goals as a normal classroom practice. However, when appropriate, students should be given second (or more) chances to demonstrate what they know, understand, and can do on varied methods of assessment. (p. 166)

Here are some tried-and-true strategies that we have observed educators successfully use to manage reassessments:

- Students are encouraged to practice continuous improvement in their learning through reassessment. Students who demonstrate continued effort in their learning are eligible to reassess to demonstrate competency after meeting with the teacher and developing a reassessment plan. The plan would indicate a specific deadline that is strictly enforced and requires the student to have completed key formative assessments prior to reassessment.

- A reassessment targets the specific skill or standard that needs remediation, which may not mean retaking an entire summative assessment. The reassessment focuses on an assignment that demonstrates the student's competency and focuses on the lagging skills identified in the competency assessment. This, in theory, should mean the reassessment grade should never be lower than the original grade on the assignment.

- ▸ The teacher records the new grade in the grade book because the new assessment score is a better indicator of their competency knowledge. The old grade is either replaced, or the weighting of the old grade is changed to zero (so that the record shows growth in the skill over time).

- ▸ A teacher may assign a reasonable timeline for a reassessment opportunity.

When asked this question of whether or not to allow reassessment in your classroom, consider this: competency-based grading and reporting systems hold students accountable for their learning. They hold teachers accountable for ensuring that all students gain the ability to transfer content and skills in and across content areas. That learning happens at different rates for different students. Reassessment is a necessary part of the learning process for all.

How Will We Handle Class Rank and Grade Point Average?

In competency-based learning systems, a student's evidence of learning is compared to clearly defined performance criteria in order to determine student achievement. There is no place for the archaic, irrelevant practice of comparing student performance to that of their peers through a class rank calculation. Despite this, educators continue to use this flawed logic inappropriately. Guskey (2015) explains that this happens when educators choose to *select* talent instead of *develop* it: "In order to select the most talented students in any academic area, you must teach and assess learning in ways that allow you to distinguish those students with greater talent from the others with lesser talent" (p. 59). A teacher could put forth a minimal effort to support students with structured learning opportunities, and only a few would be able to rise above this to learn on their own and achieve at a high level. This creates wide variability among students and is apparent in a class rank computation. In contrast, in a system where educators develop talent, the work looks different. The starting point is to identify what students are to know and be able to do. Guskey (2015) continues:

> In competency-based learning systems, a student's evidence of learning is compared to clearly defined performance criteria in order to determine student achievement. There is no place for the archaic, irrelevant practice of comparing student performance to that of their peers through a class rank calculation.

> After clarifying those learning standards or goals, you then do everything possible to ensure that *all* students learn those things well. If

you succeed, there should be little or no variation in measures of student achievement. If your teaching is optimally effective, then *all* should attain high scores on assessments of their learning, and *all* should receive high grades. (p. 61)

This, Guskey (2015) argues, is what happens when a teacher chooses to develop talent instead of select it.

The practice of reporting class rank simply does not fit the philosophy of a competency-based learning. However, many schools fear that removing such a calculation will put their students at a disadvantage. While this may have some truth to it, the reality is that the process is quickly fading into the past, playing a lesser and lesser role by college admissions offices in their efforts to select students for acceptance into their programs.

Consider the work by the New England Secondary School Consortium (n.d.), which has historically tracked the number of colleges and universities that openly accept students who come from competency-based or proficiency-based diploma programs at the high school level. On their website, they take this position with regards to grade point average and class rank:

> As long as the school profile is comprehensive and understandable, and it clearly explains the rigor of the academic program, the technicalities of the school's assessment and grading system, and the characteristics of the graduating class, the admissions office will be able to understand the transcript and properly evaluate the strength of a student's academic record and accomplishments. Schools use so many different systems for grading, ranking, and tracking students that a school's system can only be properly understood when a transcript is accompanied by a comprehensive school profile. A class rank or GPA, for example, doesn't mean much unless the admissions office also has the "key" (the school profile) that it needs to understand the applicant's academic accomplishments and abilities in context.

This assertion is supported by the work of Blauth and Hadjian (2016) who learned from interviews with colleges admissions officers that they:

> Emphasized how clear, transparent transcripts and school profiles continue to help them understand necessary aspects of the proficiency-based learning model so they can review applications as accurately and efficiently as possible. This efficiency is especially important given the high volume of applications these selective institutions receive every year. (p. 3)

If schools are not yet ready to end their class-rank practices, they can at the very least minimize their role. Many competency-based schools have adopted a Latin honor system as described by Guskey (2015). In such a system, students earn the distinctions of, for example, *cum laude, magna cum laude,* or *summa cum laude* based on their final, unweighted grade point average at the end of senior year. The titles of valedictorian, salutatorian, and class essayist can still be awarded at the graduation ceremony, but it does not mean that these recipients have to be the automatic speakers at graduation. As an alternative, students could be invited to apply to be speakers for graduation events, submitting a speech several months prior to graduation for consideration. Speeches are then judged blindly by a jury of educators who determine the winning speeches.

We have seen with schools that have adopted this kind of a graduation model that students have still been accepted to great colleges and universities, and have not been at a disadvantage to their peers from other schools in the college admission process. Perhaps most importantly, students who otherwise wouldn't have had the opportunity to shine delivered some of the most memorable and impactful graduation remarks, simply because they had an inspiring story to tell. The world did not stop when the role of class rank was minimized.

Grading What Is Learned, Not Earned

One of the best ways to think about effective grading and reporting in a competency-based learning system is to explore an example that isn't even connected to the schools, but one that many of us have experienced in our lifetime: the act of obtaining a driver's license.

Government agencies worldwide have developed reliable systems to ensure that people are not issued a driver's license until they can prove that they are proficient in their driving ability, or at least proficient enough that the agency can be reasonably sure that they will not harm themselves or others from a lack of ability behind the wheel. In the United States, for example, the reliability of this system lies in how driver-education programs support the state's driver's license testing process, and ultimately, how states administer those tests to prospective drivers. What can we, as educators, learn from this system? Here are some parallels that can be drawn between the two systems to explain what meaningful and relevant assessments need to look like in an effective competency-based system.

In these systems, both formative and summative assessments serve important but distinct roles in the learning process: In competency-based systems, the summative assessment represents the demonstration of learning through performance. It is the basis for the final grade or grades for a course. Formative assessments are considered practice, and therefore not factored into final grades. Driver-education programs typically require students to spend a certain amount of time behind the wheel with an instructor to practice their skills and get feedback on their learning (formative assessment). The state asks students to demonstrate their learning through a performance task known as a road test where students show the evaluator that they have mastered each driving skill (summative, performance assessment).

In these systems, learning is individually paced, with opportunities for reassessment: the state will never penalize someone for how long it took them to prepare for the driver test, nor will they punish them if they need to take the test more than once. Once an individual has passed the test, they get their license, and they have validation that they are proficient with each driving competency. In competency-based school systems, learning happens along a continuum in a similar manner. Reassessment is a natural course of action when a student has not yet demonstrated their learning at a high enough level to move on to the next topic, skill, or course.

In these systems, final grades are rubric based, not calculated using averages and percentages. If you were to fail the highway driving competency but pass the others with a score high enough to give you a passing grade when all grades are averaged, should you get your driver's license? Should a pilot have a license to fly if they can't pass the landing competency? Of course not! In competency-based systems, students must demonstrate proficiency with each competency. Course credit is not awarded until the student is proficient with each competency. Driving a car cannot be measured with percentages. Would it make sense to suggest that one is proficient in a particular driving skill if they can perform it 80 percent of the time? What about 90 percent of the time? Of course not! Driver assessments are scored using criterion-referenced tools (rubrics), as shown in figure 6.8.

How competencies and standards create a blueprint for learning: the driver's education example

COMPETENCY (THE WHY)	STANDARDS (THE WHAT)	DEMONSTRATION OF LEARNING (THE HOW)
The driver can park a car safely, and legally, in a variety of settings.	The driver can park a car: • In a perpendicular spot (both forward and in reverse) • In a parallel spot • In reverse	The driver will complete a performance task where he or she will be asked to park a car in a variety of settings.

Figure 6.8: Driver's education as a blueprint for competency based learning.

So what does this all mean for Jada and her PLC teammates? Jada knows that educators in PLCs need to ensure that students are graded on what they learn, not what they earn. She needs to remember that school is not a game, yet so many of our students have learned to play the game of school very well when it comes to getting good grades. The problem is that many current grading systems promote compliance of learning behaviors equally to or even over the mastery of learning. This is true in Jada's school currently. As educators, we can all think of the students who earned an A by diligently looking for every way they could earn the easier points on the 100-point scale. How many of those students would have the top grade if it was a measure of the degree to which they had mastered a skill according to a well-defined rubric? We can do better. We *must* do better. Jada knows this and she and her team have committed to doing better.

> **The problem is that many current grading systems promote compliance of learning behaviors equally to or even over the mastery of learning.**

Reflection Questions

Consider these questions with your team.

1. Grading needs to be an exercise in judging student evidence against clearly defined criteria on well-defined rubrics. How do you use rubrics currently? To what extent do you and your team calibrate your rubric language?

2. Grades should represent to what extent and to what degree a student has learned something. To what extent does your grading practices follow this logic currently?

3. Grades cannot be time bound; students learn at different rates, and the amount of time it takes a student to learn something does not influence or impact a grade. How do you and your teammates provide students with flexibility to demonstrate their learning when they are ready to do so?

4. Grades should be based on what students learn, not what they earn. They are not based on points that can be "taken away" due to student misbehaviors (such as turning in an assignment late). How can you and your team hold students accountable for academic misbehaviors without lowering grades as punishment?

5. Achievement levels, and thus grading practices, must be fair, consistent, and calibrated across a school. Regardless of which educator is grading

an assignment, the grade assigned should be consistent from educator to educator. What can you and your team do to better calibrate your practices and understanding of achievement levels?

CHAPTER 7

The Design Rubric

Jada, our middle school mathematics teacher, may be one of the first in her school along with her team to start a shift to competency-based learning, but she certainly won't be the last. For now, however, she and her team face a reality similar to what other classroom teachers around the world may feel: she knows that a competency-based learning approach is better for her students, but she worries that she will struggle with many aspects of the implementation. Teachers who are going it alone and shifting to a competency-based system in their classrooms without the support of a team will likely have even more worries. We would argue that if teams and teachers plan their implementation correctly, they can slowly start to inspire others to join them over time, but they don't have to wait for that to happen to get started.

Every journey needs a roadmap. As you embark on your competency-based learning journey, use the design rubrics in this chapter as tools for both self-reflection and strategic planning to chart the next steps in the work to develop, refine, and implement the elements of a competency-based classroom.

As teachers like Jada think through what their first few years will look like, they can find solace and support in reading about what the journeys of others have looked like in those first three years. Consider the experience that veteran teacher Dawn Olson had over three years with competency-based learning as her middle school began the transition to a competency-based system.

Practitioner Perspective
Dawn Olson, Sixth-Grade Teacher, Seabrook Middle School, Seabrook, New Hampshire

Transitioning to competency-based learning after years of teaching a traditional way felt intimidating. It's a transition that calls for significant changes in practice as well as having to embrace a new way of assessing students' progress, moving away from the traditional letter grade. With some trepidation and unease, I embraced moving forward with this new model because the concept seemed very good for students: if it's good for our students, it's worth implementing.

At Seabrook Middle School, we began by engaging in the process of developing quality performance assessments (QPA). We knew we wanted to move away from all traditional tests where students solely define vocabulary words or are asked to recall dates or settings from literature. We moved forward with developing quality performance assessments after asking many questions, having many conversations with colleagues in our collaborative team, and making many mistakes and adjustments. After several revisions and a vetting process, we administered the assessments to students, made revisions based on data, and then administered the assessment a second time. At this point, I felt that the product was mediocre, and I had a nagging feeling that something was missing. On the other hand, I was pleased with the process and how it opened up lines of communication between teachers and students, teachers and their colleagues, and teachers and administrators. I felt supported and validated through the process and felt that other teachers and administrators appreciated my feedback as it pertained to the development of their own work. I felt that we were certainly moving in the right direction.

When we began the process of developing a second QPA and taking it through the vetting process, I really became excited. I had to force myself to step out of my comfort zone as a teacher. I have always hesitated to bring activities into the classroom that I, myself, wasn't comfortable with as a student, showing empathy for students' discomfort. As I considered an assessment for my second QPA, I knew that it needed to be real for students, applicable to their lives now, engaging, and something that would require students to take risks. The vetting process and talking to colleagues while creating assessments is crucial. You're asked the questions you hadn't considered, you refine, you revise, you tighten up, and make sure you're assessing what you think that you're assessing. It was during this process that my QPA met and exceeded my expectations. I began to see tremendous student engagement and growth. Students made community connections and engaged within the community in a way that was very real. Those that previously struggled to engage were the first to engage and show success. Furthermore, students no longer saw themselves on the fringe of their community, but, rather, completely immersed in it. I immediately saw that my previous misconceptions put a barrier up in my classroom. Competency-based learning opened up lines of communication with students enabling us to have conversations that we hadn't had together before as students engaged in scoring rubrics with me, multiple times, over a period of time. Those conversations extended to grading and growth in a way I hadn't anticipated. We, together, broke those barriers that had previously been present in the classroom.

Very soon after implementing our second QPA, we began the process of reporting out in a competency-based grading system while still reporting out in a traditional A–D grading system. It didn't take me very long to see the problem here; students and parents still strongly focused on the A–D traditional grading scale. If we were heading in the competency-based direction, and we were, then we needed to embrace competency-based learning one-hundred percent, including in the reporting out of progress. Under a traditional grading system, there are ways, other than actually showing the skill that a standard asks for, for a student to receive an A or B. Teachers, myself included, may add a few points here or there for consistently putting in great effort, and so on. On the flip side, we may dock points for late assignments. We grade not just on academic skills, but also on behavior; competency-based grading effectively eliminates that. If a traditional grading system is a behavior-based system, as it many times is, then it's not showing student growth accurately.

Though I was definitely extremely excited about competency-based learning at this point, the final puzzle piece that unequivocally convinced me is the conversations that students started having with me—conversations initiated by them! Students began to take real ownership of their learning. Not only did they ask how to advance through the levels of proficiency, but they also referenced specific notes that we had taken in class, and asked how they could implement the skills from those notes into our lessons and assignments so that they could take risks with their writing and learning to move from a 2 to a 3 or a 3 to a 4, for example. I was amazed and shocked the first time a conversation like this occurred.

Talking about moving to a competency-based learning system wasn't what sold me on it. Putting it into practice and seeing the results is what sold it. The depth and richness of the conversations that students were having with me initially shocked me. I hadn't expected it. Seeing the results and hearing the conversations after just a trimester of putting competency-based learning into action made me realize that after a year or so, I was going to see huge transformations in my students, in my classroom, and in my teaching.

Competency-based learning has been the missing puzzle piece in my practice. I can't wait to see students' growth, to have the rich conversations, to see my growth as an educator, and to see students own their learning. I'm excited to see them move from passive recipients to engaged, active creators of their own learning that they can mold to fit their strengths, passions, and weaknesses.

(D. Olson, personal communication, February 27, 2021)

Planning Your Transformation

In our 2018 book *Breaking With Tradition* (Stack & Vander Els, 2018), we introduce the first generation of a school design rubric to assist educators with the development of a plan for competency-based learning implementation in their schools and districts. The first rubric, based on a five-part definition for competency education developed by Sturgis (2015), unpacks each design principle into a series of two to three indicators, each with descriptors to help readers understand what the indicator should look like at the initiating, developing, and performing levels. This original tool has been used by educators globally for the purposes of self-reflection, development of a schoolwide implementation plan, and for progress monitoring of a competency-based learning system in their classrooms, schools, and school districts. Since publication of that book, the definition of competency-based learning has evolved from five to seven design principles. We revised the school-design rubric tool in 2019 and made it available as a free resource on the Solution Tree website (www.solutiontree.com/PLCbooks) with our 2018 book. The revised tool serves as the basis for our recommendations for classroom teachers in this chapter.

We introduced the revised definition for competency-based learning, developed by the Aurora Institute (Levine & Patrick, 2019), in the first chapter of this book. According to Levine and Patrick (2019), competency-based learning is based on these seven design principles:

1. Students are empowered daily to make important decisions about their learning experiences, how they will create and apply knowledge, and how they will demonstrate their learning.

2. Assessment is a meaningful, positive, and empowering learning experience for students that yields timely, relevant, and actionable evidence.

3. Students receive timely, differentiated support based upon their individual learning needs.

4. Students progress based on evidence of mastery, not seat time.

5. Students learn actively using different pathways and varied pacing.

6. Strategies to ensure equity for all students are embedded in the culture, structure, and pedagogy of schools and education systems.

7. Rigorous, common expectations for learning (knowledge, skills, and dispositions) are explicit, transparent, measurable, and transferable. (p. 3)

For classroom teachers and collaborative teams such as Jada's, trying to turn these principles into actionable steps at the classroom level can be a tall order. Which principle should she start with? Which principles can be used as leverage to produce the most gains? Are their certain principles that are best done at the school level instead of the classroom level? In an effort to help classroom teachers like Jada (and you), we will unpack each of the design principles in the context of how a classroom teacher should approach them to support their own competency-based learning journey.

Design Principle 1: Student-Centered Learning

One of the central themes for competency-based learning is that it actively promotes and supports student-centered learning, a model whereby students themselves are empowered daily to make important decisions about their learning experiences, how they will create and apply knowledge, and how they will demonstrate their learning. The model is supported by all teachers through inclusion of metacognitive practices, the promotion of a growth mindset, and finally the use of elements of learning that are cocreated by teachers and students alike.

In such a model, students are actively engaged in metacognition—an awareness and understanding of their own thought processes and learning needs—throughout the learning process, with ample opportunities for self-reflection and goal setting. In a classroom at the highest possible level, this means that students are authentically engaged in metacognitive practices within learning experiences. There are ongoing opportunities for reflection to increase a student's self-awareness and fluid, ongoing monitoring and adapting of goals that have been set. The classroom teacher provides feedback and support, as necessary, but students are the primary drivers for this work. This allows students to reflect on where they want to be and how to get there. Classroom teachers should take note that scaffolding is acceptable and critical, especially at the beginning of the work. Over time, students will take a more active role. Patience is a must here.

In competency-based classrooms, a culture of growth mindset in which innovative thinking and growth are honored and expected throughout all learning experiences is prevalent at all times. Growth mindset was made popular in the education field by Carol Dweck (2006), after decades of research on achievement and success, which resulted in the publication of *Mindset: The New Psychology of Success*. Here, Dweck first introduced the concepts of fixed and growth mindsets and started educators thinking about how a student's mindset would affect performance in a competency-based classroom. In an interview with Morehead (2012), Dweck explained the differences between a fixed and a growth mindset in this way.

> In a fixed mindset, students believe their basic abilities, their intelligence, their talents are just fixed traits. They have a certain amount, and that's that, and then their goal becomes to look smart all the time and never look dumb. In a growth mindset, students understand that their talents and abilities can be developed through effort, good teaching and persistence. They don't necessarily think everyone's the same or anyone can be Einstein, but they believe everyone can get smarter if they work at it.

In a high-performing competency-based classroom, a growth mindset environment represents one in which risk, innovative thinking, and growth are honored and expected throughout all learning experiences, in and out of the classroom setting. Structures for collaboration are deeply embedded within all aspects of learning, for both students and adults. To the extent possible, educators must acknowledge fixed mindsets but be careful not to use them as labels or excuses.

Lastly, in competency-based classrooms, student agency is promoted by way of learning experiences that are cocreated by teachers and students. By student agency, we mean a model whereby learning takes place through meaningful, authentic, and relevant activities that are organized around student interests, providing students the opportunity to become codesigners of their learning experiences. Teachers must recognize that what students come up with may be outside of what the teachers actually offer as options. Taking time to foster and deepen relationships between the classroom teacher and their students is perhaps the single best strategy to support student agency. At the highest level, a competency-based classroom fosters student agency through cocreated learning experiences that are reflected within curriculum (what it is students are demonstrating their learning in), instruction (how they are engaged in learning), and assessment (how they are demonstrating their learning). See figure 7.1.

Design Principle 1: Students are empowered daily to make important decisions about their learning experiences, how they will create and apply knowledge, and how they will demonstrate their learning.			
Big Ideas: • Students actively engage in metacognition throughout the learning process, with ample opportunities for self-reflection and goal setting. • A growth mindset culture, which honors and expects innovative thinking and growth throughout all learning experiences, is prevalent at all times. • Teachers and students co-create learning experiences that promote student agency.	**Notes:**		
Indicator	**SCALE**		
	Performing	**Developing**	**Initiating**
	School meets all characteristics in Developing and improves by . . .	School meets all characteristics in Initiating and improves by . . .	School characteristics include . . .

Metacognition	Students are authentically engaged in metacognitive practices within learning experiences. There are ongoing opportunities for reflection to increase a student's self-awareness, and fluid, ongoing monitoring and adapting of goals that have been set. Teachers provide feedback and support, as necessary, but students are the drivers for this.	Students' metacognitive skills are scaffolded by teachers, but reflection is beginning to become more ingrained throughout learning experiences. Goal-setting and monitoring and adapting are occurring, but it is still a product of teacher-led processes rather than students taking the initiative and ownership within learning experiences.	Students are provided opportunities to reflect on learning, but this typically happens at the end of a learning experience. Students may set goals, but do not have consistent opportunities to monitor and adapt these goals.
Growth Mindset	The environments within the school and classroom represent one in which risk, innovative thinking, and growth are honored and expected throughout all learning experiences, in and out of school. Structures for collaboration are deeply embedded within all aspects of learning, for both students and adults.	The environment within the school is beginning to shift toward one that is more student-centered. Decisions are beginning to be made based on what is best for the learners, rather than what is most comfortable for adults. Risk-taking and innovation are encouraged, and time is allocated for collaborative practices involving problem-solving and critical thinking within the school day for both adults and learners.	There is a recognition that the environment is one that has been adult-centered, and clear steps are being taken to shift that to a more student-centered approach to learning. School structures and classroom structures are beginning to include opportunities for collaborative problem-solving for students and adults.
Cocreated Elements of Learning	Learning experiences are cocreated by teachers and students. This is reflected within curriculum (what it is students are demonstrating their learning in), instruction (how they are engaged in learning), and assessment (how they are demonstrating their learning).	Students have choice in learning opportunities, but much is still very much teacher driven. Choice is often limited to learning experiences themselves (how learning happens) rather than what they learn and how teachers assess it.	Teachers are beginning to embed opportunities for students to make choices in their learning, but curriculum, instruction, and assessment are still very much teacher driven.

Figure 7.1: Rubric for competency-based learning school-design principle 1.

Design Principle 2: Meaningful Assessment

How will we know when students have learned it? High-quality and learning-focused assessment is the focus of the second of the four critical questions of a PLC (DuFour et al., 2016). The need for such a meaningful and balanced assessment system is critical in an effective competency-based classroom. To achieve this, classroom teachers must incorporate assessment practices that make extensive use of quality performance assessments that assess skills or concepts in a variety of ways. Grading practices that promote the ideal that grades are about what students learn, not what they earn, must be followed. Finally, teachers must work collaboratively with their peers by content area or grade level to calibrate their instruction, grading, and assessment practices in an effort to develop a common understanding of proficiency. Such calibration should also be conducted vertically (between multiple grade levels).

As we discussed in chapter 4 (page 71), a quality performance assessment model is preferred in competency-based classrooms. Performance assessments are, according to Brown and Mednick (2012), "multi-step assignments with clear criteria, expectations, and processes that measure how well a student transfers knowledge and applies complex skills to create or refine an original product" (p. 5). In a high-functioning competency-based classroom, quality performance assessments are the primary type of assessment used with students to demonstrate mastery. Just-in-time assessments indicate when students are proficient. Classroom teachers make use of project-based learning or other ways for students to demonstrate knowledge utilization at the highest level.

> **In a high-functioning competency-based classroom, quality performance assessments are the primary type of assessment used with students to demonstrate mastery. Just-in-time assessments indicate when students are proficient.**

It stands to reason that once a teacher refines how student learning will be measured through performance assessments, the next logical step to be considered is how that learning will be reported, using meaningful grading practices whereby grades are an accurate reflection of the degree to which a student has learned a concept or skill. This idea was our focus for chapter 6 (page 129), where we looked at the need for an overhaul to grading and reporting systems in traditional learning environments. We discussed what expectations are tight for such a system in a competency-based classroom are. In high-functioning competency-based classrooms, all assessments are graded against well-defined rubrics. Teachers make effective use of competency-friendly grading expectations that accurately report learning and student growth against each of the identified grade or course-level competencies. Teachers should consider the following questions when developing their grading practices:

- Will you use averages?
- Will you allow for reassessment?

- What scale will you use?
- What will you grade?
- Will you allow extra credit?
- Will you report with or without comments?
- How will you separate academic behaviors?
- How will you handle class rank and grade point average?

Grading and assessment, and how these practices are used to promote a deeper understanding of student learning, should have the same look and feel from teacher to teacher, classroom to classroom. While this may not be possible for a teacher who is starting out in a school as the only one engaged in competency-based work, it stands to reason that alignment and calibration of the work should still be considered to the extent possible, particularly as the competency-based approach grows in such a school. In effective competency-based schools, by way of the PLC process, teachers hold each other accountable as members of a collaborative team to calibrate both grading and reporting practices as well as assessments. With their teams, educators use the data from assessments to align instruction and make greater revisions of the curriculum as well as monitor the pace and progress of individual students. See figure 7.2.

Design Principle 2: Assessment is a meaningful, positive, and empowering learning experience for students that yields timely, relevant, and actionable evidence.

Big Ideas:	Notes:		
<ul><li>Balanced assessment practices make extensive use of both formative assessment practices and quality performance assessment and allow teachers to assess skills or concepts in a variety of ways.</li><li>Grades are about what students learn, not what they earn.</li><li>Teachers regularly calibrate their instruction, grading, and assessment practices to develop a common understanding of proficiency.</li></ul>			
Indicator	**SCALE**		
	Performing	Developing	Initiating
	School meets all characteristics in Developing and improves by . . .	School meets all characteristics in Initiating and improves by . . .	School characteristics include . . .

Figure 7.2: Rubric for competency-based learning-design principle 2.   continued →

Assessment Practices	The balanced use of formative assessment practices as well as summative quality performance assessments is widespread among all teachers. Performance assessments are the primary type of summative assessment they use with students to demonstrate mastery. Just-in-time assessments indicate when students are proficient. The school has developed the capacity for project-based learning or other ways for students to demonstrate knowledge utilization at the highest level.	In addition to traditional assessment measures, teachers in the school make extensive use of formative assessment *for* learning and some use of performance assessments: multistep assignments with clear criteria, expectations, and processes that measure how well a student transfers knowledge and applies complex skills to create or refine an original product. Students have choice about how to demonstrate their learning.	Although linked to specific competencies, assessment practices are still very traditional—predominantly paper-and-pencil tests and quizzes with no schoolwide systemic attempt to control the depth of knowledge level. Few assessments are graded against a well-defined rubric, and little to no common understanding exists between teachers on what proficiency means.
Grading Practices	All assessments are graded against well-defined rubrics. The school has established a system to hold all teachers accountable for the effective use of the common grading expectations. Teachers hold each other accountable as members of a collaborative team.	Most assessments are graded against a well-defined rubric. The school has established a common set of competency-friendly grading practices. Practices include separation of formative and summative assessments, use of a rubric scale, elimination of quarter averages, and promotion of reassessment without penalty.	Few assessments are graded against a well-defined rubric. Grading practices differ greatly teacher to teacher and grade level to grade level.
System of Calibration	Teachers collaborate regularly as to calibrate assessments and to use the data from them to align instruction and make greater revisions of the curriculum as well as monitor the pace and progress of individual students.	Teachers regularly collaborate to develop and calibrate these performance assessments against learning progressions by reviewing student work and monitoring the pace and progress of individual students. Teachers are beginning to align their instructional strategies with performance assessments.	Little to no common understanding exists among teachers of different grade levels and content areas on what proficiency means.

Design Principle 3: Differentiated Support for All

What will we do if a student hasn't learned it? What about a student who has already learned it? How educators provide differentiated support in competency-based classrooms is tied directly to the third and fourth of the four critical questions of a PLC, as defined by DuFour and colleagues (2016). In *Breaking With Tradition* (Stack & Vander Els, 2018), we stressed that it is inevitable that educators who are undertaking the shift to competency-based learning, which by its very nature is more personalized, begin to question and then ultimately identify new ways in which students can receive intervention and extension opportunities that are above and beyond what they could accomplish by providing instruction with the standard curriculum and instructional materials, over and over again, through whole-class instruction. Even if a teacher is the only one on a team or in a school planning to engage in a competency-based approach, the need for differentiated support for all is a necessary component a team or school must address. A competency-based system requires structures to exist to ensure all students have access to and receive regular, timely, differentiated support. There must also be systems to monitor the pace and progress of individual students throughout their learning.

> **Even if a teacher is the only one on a team or in a school planning to engage in a competency-based approach, the need for differentiated support for all is a necessary component a team or school must address.**

In highly effective competency-based classrooms, educators make use of a school's comprehensive support structure system to ensure that students who are not making progress receive regular timely, differentiated support based on their individual learning needs at the time of their learning. Consideration for schedules, and how time is used to promote individualized supports, must be made a priority. Building a schedule to truly support student learning requires educators to think critically about why their current schedule is set up the way that it is, and how they can maximize it in an effort to provide the support necessary for each student to progress. Professionals who share the same students including teachers, special educators, guidance counselors, administrators, and other specialists must collaborate regularly as teams on these personalized, differentiated support structures for students.

Collaborative teams in a high-functioning competency-based system monitor the individual pace and progress of students throughout their learning. Educators use the information collected on pace and progress to help develop personalized professional development plans to improve their instruction. Educators in such a system regularly align their thinking using questions such as the following.

- How will we determine the learning targets and progressions for each competency?
- How will we determine the support and extension each student will receive in our school?
- How will we monitor each student's growth and learning?
- How will we maximize existing human resources?

By working as an effective team, teachers achieve better results. See figure 7.3.

Design Principle 3: Students receive timely, differentiated support based on their individual learning needs.			
Big Ideas: • Structures exist to ensure that all students have access to and receive regular, timely, differentiated support. • There are systems to monitor the pace and progress of individual students throughout their learning.	**Notes:**		
Indicator	**SCALE**		
	Performing School meets all characteristics in Developing and improves by . . .	**Developing** School meets all characteristics in Initiating and improves by . . .	**Initiating** School characteristics include . . .
Support Structures	The school has a comprehensive support structure to ensure that students who are not making progress receive regular timely, differentiated support based on their individual learning needs at the time of their learning. Professionals who share the same students including teachers, special educators, guidance counselors, administrators, and other specialists collaborate regularly as teams on these personalized, differentiated support structures for students.	The school has some structures in place to ensure that all students receive regular timely, differentiated support based on their individual learning needs. These structures are offered regardless of whether or not the student is identified in some way and are scheduled in such a way so that all students can access them without conflicts in their schedule (such as a flexible learning period that all students can access).	The school has limited structures in place to ensure that all students receive regular timely, differentiated support based on their individual learning needs. Most of the structures are limited, either to identified students (IEP, EL, 504, as so on) who require them for an educational plan or to students who are available only at certain times of the day when these structures are made available in the schedule (such as lunch or after school).

Monitoring Structures	Collaborative teams monitor the individual pace and progress of students throughout their learning. School leaders use the information collected on pace and progress to help develop personalized professional development plans for teachers to improve instruction.	Teachers have a shared understanding of what the typical pace and progress of a student should be throughout their learning and use it to monitor individual students.	Teachers work individually to monitor the pace and progress of their students and make instructional adjustments, as necessary. Specialists are included as necessary.

Figure 7.3: Rubric for competency-based learning-design principle 3.

Design Principle 4: Mastery Based on Evidence (Not Seat Time)

Since its inception, one of the hallmarks of competency-based learning has always been to support a "move when ready" approach, where learning is not measured by seat time but rather by mastery of grade-level or course competencies. Imagine a learning model whereby students can move at their own pace, and the teacher acts more as a coach or learning facilitator and less as a provider of direct instruction. When students are ready to demonstrate what they know, they are provided the opportunity to do so and then can move onto the next phase of their learning. This type of model is radically different from the one used by most schools today, yet it represents the future of learning that we, as educators, must find ways to implement in our classrooms.

> **When students are ready to demonstrate what they know, they are provided the opportunity to do so and then can move onto the next phase of their learning. This type of model is radically different from the one used by most schools today, yet it represents the future of learning that we, as educators, must find ways to implement in our classrooms.**

Developing and supporting such a system, either at the classroom or the school level, requires a few key considerations. First, policy language must exist to support a model whereby students can advance academically upon demonstration of mastery, regardless of grade level. This policy language could be as simple as a classroom syllabus, or more formal such as a school procedure or a district policy. At the highest level, these policies provide students with multiple and varied opportunities to advance upon demonstrated mastery any time, any place, and at any pace, unbounded by a school calendar or clock. They allow students to advance beyond the school that they are in to the next level.

At the elementary level, policies support multiage groupings of students and at the secondary level, extensions to higher education when students are ready based on their own learning progression.

Second, educators must have a system to monitor the pace and progress of each student as they are challenged at their appropriate level. If teachers are engaged in this work as a team, the team can take responsibility for the management of such a system. In the most effective competency based systems, students are the primary drivers for success when they effectively monitor and self-assess their own pace and progress. A mechanism exists for the teacher or the school to track student pace and progress such as personalized learning plans.

Finally, students must produce sufficient evidence in order to be deemed proficient. How much is sufficient will depend on local policies, practices, and procedures. In the most optimal situation, it is the school or district that has an established quality-control system with clearly defined levels of mastery that teachers use to determine when students are ready to move on with teacher input. There exists several opportunities for students to advance along their own continuum of learning upon demonstrated mastery through blended and online learning. At the elementary level, this can happen through multiage classrooms and at the secondary level, through extended learning opportunities such as apprenticeships, community service, independent study, internships, performing groups, college courses, private instruction, and extended learning opportunities. See figure 7.4.

Design Principle 4: Students progress based on evidence of mastery, not seat time.			
Big Ideas: • Policy language supports a model whereby students can advance academically upon demonstration of mastery—regardless of grade level. • Teachers monitor the pace and progress of each student as they are challenged at their appropriate level. • Students must produce sufficient evidence in order to be deemed proficient.	**Notes:**		
Indicator	**SCALE**		
	Performing	**Developing**	**Initiating**
	School meets all characteristics in Developing and improves by . . .	School meets all characteristics in Initiating and improves by . . .	School characteristics include . . .

Policy Language	Policies provide students with multiple and varied opportunities to advance upon demonstrated mastery any time, any place, and at any pace, unbounded by a school calendar or clock. They allow students to advance beyond the school that they are in to the next level. At the elementary level, policies support multiage groupings of students and at the secondary level, extensions to higher education when students are ready based on their own learning progression.	Policies allow teachers to meet students where they are by allowing them to access the curriculum that is before or beyond grade level as needed.	Policies support standards-referenced grading and student advancement, which happens at the end of a grade level or course.
Monitoring of Pace and Progress	The student effectively monitors and self-assesses his or her own pace and progress. A mechanism exists for the school to track student pace and progress such as a personalized learning plan.	Teachers have the ability to manage personalized classrooms with clear academic levels. They can group and regroup students so that they can access units that are before or beyond the grade-level curriculum as needed.	The school calendar drives learning opportunities and monitoring and the start and end times of the school day in each grade level or course.
Evidence of Mastery	The school has an established quality-control system with clearly defined levels of mastery that teachers use to determine when students are ready to move on with teacher input.	Within the existing school calendar, the school has several opportunities for students to advance along their own continuum of learning upon demonstrated mastery through blended and online learning. At the elementary level, this happens through multiage classrooms and at the secondary level, through extended learning opportunities such as apprenticeships, community service, independent study, internships, performing groups, college courses, private instruction, and extended learning opportunities.	Students advance at the end of a grade level or course when they have produced sufficient evidence to be deemed proficient based on grade-level or course standards.

Figure 7.4: Rubric for competency-based learning design-principle 4.

Design Principle 5: Active Learning With Multiple Pathways and Varied Pacing

Student engagement increases dramatically when students are active learners. By this, we mean that students are engaged in activities where they participate or interact with the learning process, as opposed to passively taking in information. Key considerations for this design principle include these three ideas: learning outcome and disposition design, instructional strategies, and expanded learning opportunities.

Instruction and assessment of competencies, skills, and dispositions must be designed so that demonstration of mastery includes application of skills and knowledge with multiple and varied opportunities for assessment. Levine and Patrick (2019) explain this in more detail:

> In competency-based schools, student pathways are personalized, reflecting each student's unique needs, strengths, interests, goals, and pace. The order in which students master learning targets both within and across academic disciplines may vary. Rather than coupling the standards with specific ages or grade levels, they are based on learning progressions that provide guidance to students within their zone of proximal development. Personalized learning experiences may include formal and informal learning opportunities both within and outside schools. (p. 5)

At the highest level of implementation, instruction and assessment of competencies, skills, and dispositions are ongoing, with students actively tracking their own learning progression within these competencies. Students receive ample opportunities for reflection and growth. Student self-reflection, goal setting, and monitoring are a regular part of the assessment process, and students take active ownership in their growth related to these.

Instructional strategies in competency-based classrooms are learner-centered approaches that promote student agency and deeper engagement with pacing that is varied to meet the unique interests and needs of each student. Levine and Patrick (2019) provide a blueprint for how to accomplish the varied pacing piece.

> The primary goal is deeper learning, not faster learning. Varied pacing can mean that students who are proficient in certain standards are encouraged to engage in ways that lead to greater depth of knowledge and multiple ways of demonstrating competency. Varied pacing does not imply that there is a single learning pathway that students simply navigate at different speeds. Each student's pace of progress matters, with schools actively monitoring progress and providing more instruction and support if students are not on a trajectory to graduate by age 18 or soon after. (p. 5)

In the most effective of competency-based classrooms, learner-centered instructional strategies regularly place student interests and needs at the center. Examples include project-based learning, workshop instruction, and Universal Design for Learning. The strategies flexibly allow for pacing to be varied to meet the unique interests and needs of each student in an effort to increase student agency and engagement.

In competency-based classrooms and schools, expanded learning opportunities provide a way for students to personalize how they will demonstrate mastery of lifelong learning skills based on their needs and life experiences in order to help them be college and career ready. What does this look like? At the elementary level, students would be able to pursue areas of interest, demonstrating that they are personalizing competencies and have ownership in how they are going to show their mastery. At the secondary level, students are readily able to participate in robust, real-world projects or other inquiry-based learning opportunities where they have the opportunity to apply learning in a new context. These are offered outside of the classroom experience. At all levels, students can exhibit their learning. See figure 7.5.

Design Principle 5: Students learn actively using different pathways and varied pacing.	
Big Ideas:	**Notes:**
• Instruction and assessment of competencies, skills, and dispositions are designed so that demonstration of mastery includes application of skills and knowledge. Multiple and varied opportunities exist to assess these. • Instructional strategies are learner-centered approaches that promote student agency and deeper engagement with pacing that is varied to meet the unique interests and needs of each student. • Expanded learning opportunities provide a way for students to personalize how they will demonstrate mastery of lifelong learning skills based on their needs and life experiences in order to help them be college and career ready.	

Figure 7.5: Rubric for competency-based learning-design principle 5.

continued →

Indicator	SCALE		
	Performing School meets all characteristics in Developing and improves by . . .	**Developing** School meets all characteristics in Initiating and improves by . . .	**Initiating** School characteristics include . . .
Learning Outcome and Disposition Design	Instruction and assessment of competencies, skills, and dispositions are ongoing, with students actively tracking their own learning progression within these competencies. Students receive ample opportunities for reflection and growth. Student self-reflection, goal setting, and monitoring are a regular part of the assessment process and students take active ownership in their growth related to these.	Student expectations for competencies, skills, and dispositions are clearly defined by rubrics that provide more opportunity for growth. Teachers assess these on a regular and ongoing basis. Data collected is used by the school to determine a student's college and career readiness.	The school has established learning outcomes that measure application and creation of knowledge as well as the development of important skills and dispositions. One specific rubric does not define the dispositions, which teachers only assess at certain times during the year, limiting active student agency.
Instructional Strategies	Learner-centered instructional strategies that place student interests and needs at the center have widespread use at all levels of the system. Such models include project-based learning, workshop instruction, and Universal Design for Learning. The strategies flexibly allow for pacing to be varied to meet the unique interests and needs of each student in an effort to increase student agency and engagement.	Efforts have been made by teachers to shift from teacher-centered to learner-centered instructional strategies on a more frequent basis. Individual student interests and needs have been considered, and in some cases embedded into instruction in several ways.	The majority of instructional strategies prevalent in classrooms are teacher centered, meaning that the teacher is maintaining order and control over the what, when, and how of instruction.

Expanded Learning Opportunities	At the elementary level, students would be able to pursue areas of interest, demonstrating that they are personalizing competencies and have ownership in how they are going to show their mastery. At the secondary level, students are readily able to participate in robust, real-world projects or other inquiry-based learning opportunities where they have the opportunity to apply learning in a new context. These are offered outside of the classroom experience. At all levels, students can exhibit their learning.	The school has established many opportunities for students to engage in real-world projects and other inquiry-based learning opportunities as part of their regular programming.	The extent to which students have the opportunity to engage in real-world projects and other inquiry-based learning varies by grade level and teacher.

Design Principle 6: Strategies to Embed Equity Into the System

We believe that the idea of "learning for all, whatever it takes" needs to be more than a slogan painted on a school wall or a quote in the signature line of an email. "All means all" needs to be a core value that calls on all educators in a school to take meaningful and deliberate actions to eliminate equity issues in their school culture and climate. In chapter 1, we discussed a framework for equity developed by the National Equity Project (n.d.) which includes three action steps:

1. Ensuring equally high outcomes for all participants in our educational system; removing the predictability of success or failure that currently correlates with any social or cultural factor;
2. Interrupting inequitable practices, examining biases, and creating inclusive multicultural school environments for adults and children; and
3. Discovering and cultivating the unique gifts, talents, and interests that every human possesses.

> We believe that the idea of "learning for all, whatever it takes" needs to be more than a slogan painted on a school wall or a quote in the signature line of an email. "All means all" needs to be a core value that calls on all educators in a school to take meaningful and deliberate actions to eliminate equity issues in their school culture and climate.

This design principle is best achieved when educators work in a collaborative culture with a shared purpose of learning for all, whatever it takes. This strong culture for learning, inclusivity, and empowerment must be apparent in all aspects of the school. This is realized by all educators who nurture a strong culture of learning, inclusivity, and empowerment in all interactions and activities. In highly-functioning competency-based systems, the community itself has been involved in shaping new definitions of success and graduation outcomes. The school invests in both student and adult mindsets, knowledge, and skills.

In competency-based classrooms, learning outcomes must be completely transparent, and educators must work in collaborative teams through a continuous improvement process to monitor and respond to student progress, proficiency, pace, and need. In this model, teachers must regularly respond and adapt to student needs using continuous improvement processes. Equity is ultimately realized by all educators in the school through transparency about learning.

Competency-based educators must recognize that pedagogy promotes student agency because it is based on the most recent scientific research about learning which ensures that all students receive feedback and experiences resulting in powerful learning outcomes. Excuses such as "This is the way I have always done things" or "Colleges want to see pedagogy look this way" are simply not acceptable. In highly-functioning competency-based systems, educators work in collaborative teams to develop a shared understanding and practice of pedagogies that draw from the most recent scientific research about learning, ensuring all students receive feedback and experiences that result in powerful learning outcomes. This promotes all students to become active learners, fostering their ability for agency, self-direction, and empowerment. All students are held to the same high standards for rigor and excellence, including demonstration of mastery and fluency of foundational skills. See figure 7.6.

Design Principle 6: Strategies to ensure equity for all students are embedded in the culture, structure, and pedagogy of schools and education systems.			
Big Ideas: • There exists a collaborative culture with a shared purpose of learning for all, whatever it takes. This strong culture for learning, inclusivity, and empowerment is apparent in all aspects of the school. • Learning outcomes are completely transparent, and educators work in collaborative teams through a continuous improvement process to monitor and respond to student progress, proficiency, pace, and need. • Pedagogy promotes student agency because it is based on the most recent scientific research about learning which ensures that all students receive feedback and experiences resulting in powerful learning outcomes.	**Notes:**		
Indicator	**SCALE**		
	Performing School meets all characteristics in Developing and improves by . . .	**Developing** School meets all the characteristics in Initiating and improves by . . .	**Initiating** School characteristics include . . .
Purpose and Culture	District or school-based leadership have a deep commitment to learning for all, whatever it takes. All educators nurture a strong culture of learning, inclusivity, and empowerment in all interactions and activities. The community has been involved in shaping new definitions of success and graduation outcomes. The school invests in both student and adult mindsets, knowledge and skills.	The school has expanded upon its approach to equity by committing to a belief that high expectations are possible for all students. The school has started to identify and consider the unique set of experiences, strengths, needs, identities, and passions of each student, and use these to make decisions related to school improvement.	The school realizes equity by providing the same resources and educational experiences to all students, and emphasizes equity by holding different students to a shared set of school or district expectations.

Figure 7.6: Rubric for competency-based learning-design principle 6.

continued →

Structure	Equity is realized by all educators in the school through transparency about learning. Teachers work in collaborative teams to continually monitor and respond to student progress, proficiency, and pace, and regularly respond and adapt to student needs using continuous improvement processes.	Educators in the school are actively unpacking the curriculum and looking for ways to ensure that all students are growing at a meaningful pace. The school is developing processes and strategies to measure and monitor student growth based on student performance levels and uncover bias in an effort to provide better learning opportunities for historically underserved students.	The school curriculum is filled with examples of learning targets and rubrics that use language that makes them inaccessible to all students. There exists some scaffolding to provide access for students to the curriculum but it lacks the ability to help them develop proficiency in prerequisite skills. This leads to a strong emphasis by educators to "cover" the curriculum and pass students on at the end of the year to the next grade level without reaching proficiency.
Pedagogy	Educators work in collaborative teams to develop a shared understanding and practice of pedagogies that draw from the most recent scientific research about learning, ensuring all students receive feedback and experiences that result in powerful learning outcomes. This promotes all students to become active learners, fostering their ability for agency, self-direction, and empowerment. All students are held to the same high standards for rigor and excellence, including demonstration of mastery and fluency of foundational skills.	An effort has been made by educators to begin to make use of pedagogical strategies that use a growth mindset model, which recognizes that students start with different sets of academic skills, social and emotional skills, and life experiences in an effort to better meet the needs of diverse learners. These strategies have become more learner-centered and culturally responsive.	Teacher-centered pedagogical strategies that offer little opportunity for students to actively apply their learning are widespread in the school. While formal processes to provide feedback and communicate progress in lifelong learning skills necessary for student agency exist, educators lack support in how to coach or assess the skills in ways that guard against bias. Expectations of what it means to be proficient can look different across grade levels and schools in the system.

Design Principle 7: Rigorous, Common Expectations for Learning

What is it we want students to learn and be able to do? The notion of rigor and common expectations for learning pairs well with the first of the four critical questions of a PLC, as described by DuFour and colleagues (2016). We expand on this in much greater detail in chapter 3 (page 47). For classroom teachers and schools looking to deepen their competency-based work, there are three things to consider: (1) the development of a framework of standards, learning progressions, competencies, and dispositions, (2) consideration for rigor by way of cognitive demand, and (3) a system to calibrate efforts between teachers, grade levels, and schools in a system.

In competency-based systems, there exists a framework of standards, learning progressions, competencies, and dispositions aligned with national, state, or local frameworks. This framework is reviewed and revised regularly, as needs change. In highly effective competency-based models, these competencies, skills, and dispositions are applicable to real-life situations and require an understanding of relationships among theories, principles, and concepts. According to Levine and Patrick (2019):

> An essential purpose of schooling is to have students develop skills and deep understandings that they can apply or "transfer" to other academic content areas and interdisciplinary work, as well as to new and unfamiliar contexts beyond the classroom. In addition, there are "transferable" knowledge and skills that are used in learning within and across content areas. Transferable knowledge is a product of deeper learning. (p. 5)

Competencies must have a high level of cognitive demand and rigor. They must require students to have a deep understanding of content as well as application of knowledge to a variety of settings by promoting complex connections through creating, analyzing, designing, proving, developing, or formulating. Hess (2018) has developed a helpful series of tools to promote rigor and depth of knowledge known as cognitive rigor matrices. Hess's matrices apply Webb's Depth of Knowledge Levels to Bloom's Cognitive Process Dimensions in an easy-to-follow format for educators.

Finally, an effective competency-based model requires a system to calibrate the competencies and dispositions across grade levels and content areas to ensure a common understanding of proficiency. In the most effective models, this happens by way of collaborative teams, where teachers regularly engage in the calibration of the competencies and dispositions across grade levels and content areas to ensure a common understanding of proficiency by looking at student work. See figure 7.7 (page 176).

Design Principle 7: Rigorous, common expectations for learning (knowledge, skills, and dispositions) are explicit, transparent, measurable, and transferable.

Big Ideas:
- There is a framework of standards, learning progressions, competencies, and dispositions aligned with national, state, or local frameworks.
- Competencies have a high level of cognitive demand and rigor.
- There exists a system to calibrate the competencies and dispositions across grade levels and content areas to ensure a common understanding of proficiency.

Notes:

Indicator	SCALE		
	Performing School meets all characteristics in Developing and improves by . . .	**Developing** School meets all characteristics in Initiating and improves by . . .	**Initiating** School characteristics include . . .
Framework of Standards, Competencies, and Dispositions	Competencies, skills, and dispositions are applicable to real-life situations and require an understanding of relationships among theories, principles, and concepts.	The school has expanded the framework of standards to include competencies, skills, and dispositions with performance assessments and include both academic skills that are transferable across content areas as well as habits of learning behaviors. These are mapped K–12 as a continuum of learning progressions based on the standards so that students know exactly where they are and what they need to do next. The school district has established clear transitional and graduation competencies that articulate what it means to be ready for the next level.	The school has developed an academic framework of standards (knowledge and skills) that are aligned with national, state, and local frameworks in the school and are limited to scope and sequence of the textbook, program, or resource. Dispositions are identified by the school but are not easily measurable.

Cognitive Demand	The cognitive demand of the competencies, skills, and dispositions is high—they require students to have a deep understanding of content as well as application of knowledge to a variety of settings by promoting complex connections through creating, analyzing, designing, proving, developing, or formulating.	The cognitive demand of the competencies, skills, and dispositions is medium—they ask students to show what they know in limited ways through identifying, defining, constructing, summarizing, displaying, listing, or recognizing. Teachers occasionally ask students to create conceptual connections and exhibit a level of understanding that is beyond the stated facts or literal interpretation through reasoning, planning, interpreting, hypothesizing, investigating, or explaining.	The cognitive demand of the competencies, skills, and dispositions is low—they ask for routine or rote thinking and require basic recall of information, facts, definitions, and other similar simple tasks and procedures.
System of Calibration	In collaborative teams, teachers regularly engage in the calibration of the competencies and dispositions across grade levels and content areas to ensure a common understanding of proficiency by looking at student work.	Standards-referenced grading makes it clear what students know and how they are progressing. Teachers have a shared understanding of proficiency for both academic skills and dispositions by grade level and course by looking at student work.	The competencies are very specific to the facts in the content. The school has selected a taxonomy to have common language about depth of knowledge and has started a process to identify the competencies for each grade level, content area, and course. Dispositions are identified by the school, but a common process to collect evidence and report progress on dispositions does not exist in the school.

Figure 7.7: Rubric for competency-based learning-design principle 7.

How to Use the Rubric Tool

Throughout this chapter, we have introduced you to the seven parts of our Competency-Based Learning School-Design Rubric, a tool that correlates directly to the seven design principles for competency-based learning. This tool, which is collected in the appendix (page 184), can serve a variety of purposes for teachers like Jada, her collaborative team, her school leaders, and even her district office.

One of the primary uses for this tool is for the purposes of self-reflection. Educators are encouraged to complete a self-assessment against all seven design principles before starting the work and consider the following questions as they do so.

1. What elements of competency-based learning already exist to some degree in my classroom or school?

> **The work to transform your classroom or school into one that is competency based will not happen overnight. It involves some significant transformative work around school culture and beliefs about learning and assessment. Being true to yourself on your starting point is important.**

This initial self-assessment is considered your current reality and will serve to plot your course for future work and also serve as a benchmark to show growth in your plan development over time. Many who complete this first step tell us that they rated themselves in the initiating stage in most categories. Some even jokingly ask us if there is a category below initiating. This is perfectly acceptable, and even normal! The work to transform your classroom or school into one that is competency based will not happen overnight. It involves some significant transformative work around school culture and beliefs about learning and assessment. Being true to yourself on your starting point is important.

2. What needs to evolve in my classroom or school to advance the design principle to the next level?

By answering this question, you will recognize your next steps in your journey. Transforming a classroom or school into a competency-based model may take an average of three to five years, and perhaps even longer than that if you want the model to truly become part of the culture for your students and community. Knowing where to start is important, and self-reflecting on a regular basis (such as annually) will allow you to stay focused on appropriate next steps to continually advance your work.

3. Which design principle will be the easiest for me to implement and why?

   In this step, you will identify your future milestones that you will be able to celebrate. Transformational work is hard, and it takes time. Building in opportunities to celebrate small victories along the way is important to sustaining momentum and increasing buy-in amongst stakeholders. In Brian's school, one early victory when he went through this work was reaching a point where every teacher in the school felt comfortable developing one new quality performance assessment to implement with their PLC and their students. We as humans rally around victory, and it makes us thirsty for more of the same.

4. Which design principle will be the biggest challenge for me to implement and why?

   Early in the journey, it is important to think about where the challenges will be, and steps that can be taken to mitigate, or work around, those challenges. Do they involve people? If so, think about ways that you can bring those people into the work on some level. Often, people are less of a barrier when they have a stake in the outcome. Do they involve policies or procedures? If you are a classroom teacher worried that your classroom competency-based approach will be too radical for a conservative school policy, try talking to your principal openly and honestly about your concerns. Many principles will allow teachers in this position to operate under the banner of a pilot program, with increased flexibility and latitude to operate differently as needed to demonstrate that the model can be effective. Do they involve community perceptions about competency-based learning? Engage with your community to understand what their questions or concerns are with the model. Oftentimes, their lack of support really translates into a lack of understanding, and that can always be overcome through increased communication.

Transformational work is hard, and it takes time. Building in opportunities to celebrate small victories along the way is important to sustaining momentum and increasing buy-in amongst stakeholders.

5. On which design principle do I want to plant my flag?

   Your self-assessment should yield (at least) one design principle that you can use to leverage the rest of your work. It should be one that once implemented successfully, can drive the work to advance other principles more effectively. For teachers in Brian's school, assessment was the leverage point when they began their work. Working in teams, teachers realized that if they could commit to assessment practices that measured learning at a deeper level, other design principles (instruction, support structures, empowerment, and so on) would fall into place. Collaborative teams felt so strongly in this focus that the staff as a whole worked on the assessment design principle for two years, including an entire year with a deep dive into rubric development. Teachers committed to using the PLC process to look at commonly developed performance assessments and rubrics, including student work. This led to greater calibration of assessment practices on the team and deeper discussions on what was necessary to ensure that all students learn at high levels. Assessment acted as a leverage point that advanced competency-based learning in classrooms.

From self-assessment, educators can then use the tool to establish a classroom and schoolwide implementation plan for competency-based learning. Each design principle should have a goal established each year, with one to two actionable steps that can be taken to accomplish the goal. When building a plan, it is helpful to think both short term (one year at a time) as well as long term (three to five years out). In fact, it may even be easier to start with the long term vision and then work backward. To illustrate, let's look more closely at Jada's short-term plan, where she and her team self-assessed at the initiating level for each design principle in their classrooms and school. She and her team have built a plan to make some growth in each of the design principles, with more emphasis being placed on design principle five as their leverage point where they ultimately wants to plant their flag (see figure 7.8).

| \multicolumn{3}{c}{Jada's Collaborative Team's Short-Term Plan: Year 1} |||
Design Principle	Goal	Action Steps
1. Student-Centered Learning	We will incorporate elements of growth mindset into our classrooms.	• We will learn more about growth mindset. • We will increase opportunities for our students to self-assess and set goals for their learning.
2. Meaningful Assessment	We will work within our collaborative team to implement at least one quality performance assessment cycle with our students this year.	• We will work within our team to identify one competency that we can use as the basis for a performance task. • We will work with our team to review student work from the task and make adjustments.

3. Differentiated Support for All	We will work within our collaborative team to identify ways we can work collaboratively to provide just-in-time support to students.	• We will establish a mechanism to identify students who need support during a unit. • We will work to align our classroom schedules to allow for a common period of time that can be used for flexible grouping for RTI.
4. Mastery Based on Evidence (Not Seat Time)	We will pilot a self-paced unit this year.	• We will identify which unit to try this model with. • We will identify what technology tool (or tools) we will use to enhance the self-paced unit.
5. Active Learning With Multiple Pathways and Varied Pacing	We will increase opportunities for students to have choice and voice in both how they learn and how they demonstrate that learning.	• We will give students a choice each unit in how they learn. • We will embed opportunities for choice into all of our common assessments.
6. Equity	We will identify possible barriers to equity that currently exist in our classrooms as well as strategies that we can use to overcome them.	• We will survey students and parents. • We will ask our peers to observe our classroom practices to help us individually and collectively identify potential equity barriers.
7. Rigorous Expectations for Learning	We will work within our collaborative team to develop a common set of competencies for sixth-grade math that align with the district's curriculum frameworks.	• We will unpack our grade-level standards in order to develop power standards (competencies). • We will align our work with the grade levels above and below us.

Figure 7.8: Jada's short-term plan: Year 1.

Some may see Jada and her team's plan as too aggressive. Others may see it as not aggressive enough. When developing her plan, Jada and her team recognized that they are ready to move much further and faster with competency-based learning than their school is, and their plan reflects that. Notice that there are times in the plan that they talk about what they will do alone as a team. There are other times where the team references work they will do with other colleagues on other teams, such as seeking feedback. Even if the colleagues on other teams are not going to implement competency-based learning at this time in their classrooms, it does not mean that they can't be a part of the process. Many of the design principles can be taken as stand-alone projects with goals because they are best practice for students.

Final Thoughts

Our decision to start this book by referring to Jada and her team's decision to move to a competency-based model in their classrooms as a transformation was done with purpose. We believe that this describes perfectly what the shift to a competency-based model looks like in schools that successfully have made the transition. Such a shift calls into question every practice, procedure, and policy in the school. It causes a reevaluation of the values and priorities that a community holds regarding their mission and purpose as a school. Competency-based learning is a whole-scale philosophical shift and should be treated that way by all educators as they engage in the work.

As you work to implement competency-based learning in your classrooms, remember to keep student learning at the center. Strive for deeper learning. Above all else, don't settle for less. Your students deserve better, and they are relying on you to be there for them, every step of the way. You can do this!

APPENDIX

Competency-Based Learning School-Design Rubric: Principle 1

Design Principle 1: Students are empowered daily to make important decisions about their learning experiences, how they will create and apply knowledge, and how they will demonstrate their learning.			
Big Ideas: • Students actively engage in metacognition throughout the learning process, with ample opportunities for self-reflection and goal setting. • A growth mindset culture, which honors and expects innovative thinking and growth throughout all learning experiences, is prevalent at all times. • Teachers and students co-create learning experiences that promote student agency.	**Notes:**		
Indicator	**SCALE**		
	Performing School meets all characteristics in Developing and improves by . . .	**Developing** School meets all characteristics in Initiating and improves by . . .	**Initiating** School characteristics include . . .
Metacognition	Students are authentically engaged in metacognitive practices within learning experiences. There are ongoing opportunities for reflection to increase a student's self-awareness, and fluid, ongoing monitoring and adapting of goals that have been set. Teachers provide feedback and support, as necessary, but students are the drivers for this.	Students' metacognitive skills are scaffolded by teachers, but reflection is beginning to become more ingrained throughout learning experiences. Goal-setting and monitoring and adapting are occurring, but it is still a product of teacher-led processes rather than students taking the initiative and ownership within learning experiences.	Students are provided opportunities to reflect on learning, but this typically happens at the end of a learning experience. Students may set goals, but do not have consistent opportunities to monitor and adapt these goals.

page 1 of 2

Unpacking the Competency-Based Classroom © 2022 Solution Tree Press • SolutionTree.com
Visit **go.SolutionTree.com/PLCbooks** to download this free reproducible.

Indicator	SCALE		
	Performing School meets all characteristics in Developing and improves by . . .	**Developing** School meets all characteristics in Initiating and improves by . . .	**Initiating** School characteristics include . . .
Growth Mindset	The environments within the school and classroom represent one in which risk, innovative thinking, and growth are honored and expected throughout all learning experiences, in and out of school. Structures for collaboration are deeply embedded within all aspects of learning, for both students and adults.	The environment within the school is beginning to shift toward one that is more student-centered. Decisions are beginning to be made based on what is best for the learners, rather than what is most comfortable for adults. Risk-taking and innovation are encouraged, and time is allocated for collaborative practices involving problem-solving and critical thinking within the school day for both adults and learners.	There is a recognition that the environment is one that has been adult-centered, and clear steps are being taken to shift that to a more student-centered approach to learning. School structures and classroom structures are beginning to include opportunities for collaborative problem-solving for students and adults.
Cocreated Elements of Learning	Learning experiences are cocreated by teachers and students. This is reflected within curriculum (what it is students are demonstrating their learning in), instruction (how they are engaged in learning), and assessment (how they are demonstrating their learning).	Students have choice in learning opportunities, but much is still very much teacher driven. Choice is often limited to learning experiences themselves (how learning happens) rather than what they learn and how teachers assess it.	Teachers are beginning to embed opportunities for students to make choices in their learning, but curriculum, instruction, and assessment are still very much teacher driven.

Competency-Based Learning School-Design Rubric: Principle 2

Design Principle 2: Assessment is a meaningful, positive, and empowering learning experience for students that yields timely, relevant, and actionable evidence.

Big Ideas:	Notes:
• Balanced assessment practices make extensive use of both formative assessment practices and quality performance assessment and allow teachers to assess skills or concepts in a variety of ways. • Grades are about what students learn, not what they earn. • Teachers regularly calibrate their instruction, grading, and assessment practices to develop a common understanding of proficiency.	

Indicator	SCALE		
	Performing School meets all characteristics in Developing and improves by . . .	**Developing** School meets all characteristics in Initiating and improves by . . .	**Initiating** School characteristics include . . .
Assessment Practices	The balanced use of formative assessment practices as well as summative quality performance assessments is widespread among all teachers. Performance assessments are the primary type of summative assessment they use with students to demonstrate mastery. Just-in-time assessments indicate when students are proficient. The school has developed the capacity for project-based learning or other ways for students to demonstrate knowledge utilization at the highest level.	In addition to traditional assessment measures, teachers in the school make extensive use of formative assessment *for* learning and some use of performance assessments: multistep assignments with clear criteria, expectations, and processes that measure how well a student transfers knowledge and applies complex skills to create or refine an original product. Students have choice about how to demonstrate their learning.	Although linked to specific competencies, assessment practices are still very traditional—predominantly paper-and-pencil tests and quizzes with no schoolwide systemic attempt to control the depth of knowledge level. Few assessments are graded against a well-defined rubric, and little to no common understanding exists between teachers on what proficiency means.

page 1 of 2

Unpacking the Competency-Based Classroom © 2022 Solution Tree Press • SolutionTree.com
Visit **go.SolutionTree.com/PLCbooks** to download this free reproducible.

Indicator	SCALE		
	Performing School meets all characteristics in Developing and improves by . . .	**Developing** School meets all characteristics in Initiating and improves by . . .	**Initiating** School characteristics include . . .
Grading Practices	All assessments are graded against well-defined rubrics. The school has established a system to hold all teachers accountable for the effective use of the common grading expectations. Teachers hold each other accountable as members of a collaborative team.	Most assessments are graded against a well-defined rubric. The school has established a common set of competency-friendly grading practices. Practices include separation of formative and summative assessments, use of a rubric scale, elimination of quarter averages, and promotion of reassessment without penalty.	Few assessments are graded against a well-defined rubric. Grading practices differ greatly teacher to teacher and grade level to grade level.
System of Calibration	Teachers collaborate regularly as to calibrate assessments and to use the data from them to align instruction and make greater revisions of the curriculum as well as monitor the pace and progress of individual students.	Teachers regularly collaborate to develop and calibrate these performance assessments against learning progressions by reviewing student work and monitoring the pace and progress of individual students. Teachers are beginning to align their instructional strategies with performance assessments.	Little to no common understanding exists among teachers of different grade levels and content areas on what proficiency means.

Competency-Based Learning School-Design Rubric: Principle 3

Design Principle 3: Students receive timely, differentiated support based on their individual learning needs.

Big Ideas:	Notes:		
• Structures exist to ensure that all students have access to and receive regular, timely, differentiated support. • There are systems to monitor the pace and progress of individual students throughout their learning.			

Indicator	SCALE		
	Performing School meets all characteristics in Developing and improves by . . .	**Developing** School meets all characteristics in Initiating and improves by . . . :	**Initiating** School characteristics include . . .
Support Structures	The school has a comprehensive support structure to ensure that students who are not making progress receive regular timely, differentiated support based on their individual learning needs at the time of their learning. Professionals who share the same students including teachers, special educators, guidance counselors, administrators, and other specialists collaborate regularly as teams on these personalized, differentiated support structures for students.	The school has some structures in place to ensure that all students receive regular timely, differentiated support based on their individual learning needs. These structures are offered regardless of whether or not the student is identified in some way and are scheduled in such a way so that all students can access them without conflicts in their schedule (such as a flexible learning period that all students can access).	The school has limited structures in place to ensure that all students receive regular timely, differentiated support based on their individual learning needs. Most of the structures are limited, either to identified students (IEP, EL, 504, as so on) who require them for an educational plan or to students who are available only at certain times of the day when these structures are made available in the schedule (such as lunch or after school).
Monitoring Structures	Collaborative teams monitor the individual pace and progress of students throughout their learning. School leaders use the information collected on pace and progress to help develop personalized professional development plans for teachers to improve instruction.	Teachers have a shared understanding of what the typical pace and progress of a student should be throughout their learning and use it to monitor individual students.	Teachers work individually to monitor the pace and progress of their students and make instructional adjustments, as necessary. Specialists are included as necessary.

Competency-Based Learning School-Design Rubric: Principle 4

Design Principle 4: Students progress based on evidence of mastery, not seat time.

Big Ideas:

- Policy language supports a model whereby students can advance academically upon demonstration of mastery—regardless of grade level.
- Teachers monitor the pace and progress of each student as they are challenged at their appropriate level.
- Students must produce sufficient evidence in order to be deemed proficient.

Notes:

Indicator	SCALE		
	Performing School meets all characteristics in Developing and improves by . . .	**Developing** School meets all characteristics in Initiating and improves by . . .	**Initiating** School characteristics include . . .
Policy Language	Policies provide students with multiple and varied opportunities to advance upon demonstrated mastery any time, any place, and at any pace, unbounded by a school calendar or clock. They allow students to advance beyond the school that they are in to the next level. At the elementary level, policies support multiage groupings of students and at the secondary level, extensions to higher education when students are ready based on their own learning progression.	Policies allow teachers to meet students where they are by allowing them to access the curriculum that is before or beyond grade level as needed.	Policies support standards-referenced grading and student advancement, which happens at the end of a grade level or course.

page 1 of 2

Indicator	SCALE		
	Performing School meets all characteristics in Developing and improves by . . .	**Developing** School meets all characteristics in Initiating and improves by . . .	**Initiating** School characteristics include . . .
Monitoring of Pace and Progress	The student effectively monitors and self-assesses his or her own pace and progress. A mechanism exists for the school to track student pace and progress such as a personalized learning plan.	Teachers have the ability to manage personalized classrooms with clear academic levels. They can group and regroup students so that they can access units that are before or beyond the grade-level curriculum as needed.	The school calendar drives learning opportunities and monitoring and the start and end times of the school day in each grade level or course.
Evidence of Mastery	The school has an established quality-control system with clearly defined levels of mastery that teachers use to determine when students are ready to move on with teacher input.	Within the existing school calendar, the school has several opportunities for students to advance along their own continuum of learning upon demonstrated mastery through blended and online learning. At the elementary level, this happens through multiage classrooms and at the secondary level, through extended learning opportunities such as apprenticeships, community service, independent study, internships, performing groups, college courses, private instruction, and extended learning opportunities.	Students advance at the end of a grade level or course when they have produced sufficient evidence to be deemed proficient based on grade-level or course standards.

Competency-Based Learning School-Design Rubric: Principle 5

Design Principle 5: Students learn actively using different pathways and varied pacing.

Big Ideas:

- Instruction and assessment of competencies, skills, and dispositions are designed so that demonstration of mastery includes application of skills and knowledge. Multiple and varied opportunities exist to assess these.
- Instructional strategies are learner-centered approaches that promote student agency and deeper engagement with pacing that is varied to meet the unique interests and needs of each student.
- Expanded learning opportunities provide a way for students to personalize how they will demonstrate mastery of lifelong learning skills based on their needs and life experiences in order to help them be college and career ready.

Notes:

Indicator	SCALE		
	Performing — School meets all characteristics in Developing and improves by . . .	**Developing** — School meets all characteristics in Initiating and improves by . . .	**Initiating** — School characteristics include . . .
Learning Outcome and Disposition Design	Instruction and assessment of competencies, skills, and dispositions are ongoing, with students actively tracking their own learning progression within these competencies. Students receive ample opportunities for reflection and growth. Student self-reflection, goal setting, and monitoring are a regular part of the assessment process and students take active ownership in their growth related to these.	Student expectations for competencies, skills, and dispositions are clearly defined by rubrics that provide more opportunity for growth. Teachers assess these on a regular and ongoing basis. Data collected is used by the school to determine a student's college and career readiness.	The school has established learning outcomes that measure application and creation of knowledge as well as the development of important skills and dispositions. One specific rubric does not define the dispositions, which teachers only assess at certain times during the year, limiting active student agency.

page 1 of 2

Unpacking the Competency-Based Classroom © 2022 Solution Tree Press • SolutionTree.com
Visit **go.SolutionTree.com/PLCbooks** to download this free reproducible.

Indicator	SCALE		
	Performing School meets all characteristics in Developing and improves by . . .	**Developing** School meets all characteristics in Initiating and improves by . . .	**Initiating** School characteristics include . . .
Instructional Strategies	Learner-centered instructional strategies that place student interests and needs at the center have wide-spread use at all levels of the system. Such models include project-based learning, workshop instruction, and Universal Design for Learning. The strategies flexibly allow for pacing to be varied to meet the unique interests and needs of each student in an effort to increase student agency and engagement.	Efforts have been made by teachers to shift from teacher-centered to learner-centered instructional strategies on a more frequent basis. Individual student interests and needs have been considered, and in some cases embedded into instruction in several ways.	The majority of instructional strategies prevalent in classrooms are teacher centered, meaning that the teacher is maintaining order and control over the what, when, and how of instruction.
Expanded Learning Opportunities	At the elementary level, students would be able to pursue areas of interest, demonstrating that they are personalizing competencies and have ownership in how they are going to show their mastery. At the secondary level, students are readily able to participate in robust, real-world projects or other inquiry-based learning opportunities where they have the opportunity to apply learning in a new context. These are offered outside of the classroom experience. At all levels, students can exhibit their learning.	The school has established many opportunities for students to engage in real-world projects and other inquiry-based learning opportunities as part of their regular programming.	The extent to which students have the opportunity to engage in real-world projects and other inquiry-based learning varies by grade level and teacher.

Unpacking the Competency-Based Classroom © 2022 Solution Tree Press • SolutionTree.com
Visit **go.SolutionTree.com/PLCbooks** to download this free reproducible.

Competency-Based Learning School-Design Rubric: Principle 6

Design Principle 6: Strategies to ensure equity for all students are embedded in the culture, structure, and pedagogy of schools and education systems.

Big Ideas:

- There exists a collaborative culture with a shared purpose of learning for all, whatever it takes. This strong culture for learning, inclusivity, and empowerment is apparent in all aspects of the school.
- Learning outcomes are completely transparent, and educators work in collaborative teams through a continuous improvement process to monitor and respond to student progress, proficiency, pace, and need.
- Pedagogy promotes student agency because it is based on the most recent scientific research about learning which ensures that all students receive feedback and experiences resulting in powerful learning outcomes.

Notes:

Indicator	SCALE		
	Performing — School meets all characteristics in Developing and improves by . . .	**Developing** — School meets all the characteristics in Initiating and improves by . . .	**Initiating** — School characteristics include . . .
Purpose and Culture	District or school-based leadership have a deep commitment to learning for all, whatever it takes. All educators nurture a strong culture of learning, inclusivity, and empowerment in all interactions and activities. The community has been involved in shaping new definitions of success and graduation outcomes. The school invests in both student and adult mindsets, knowledge and skills.	The school has expanded upon its approach to equity by committing to a belief that high expectations are possible for all students. The school has started to identify and consider the unique set of experiences, strengths, needs, identities, and passions of each student, and use these to make decisions related to school improvement.	The school realizes equity by providing the same resources and educational experiences to all students, and emphasizes equity by holding different students to a shared set of school or district expectations.

page 1 of 2

Unpacking the Competency-Based Classroom © 2022 Solution Tree Press • SolutionTree.com
Visit **go.SolutionTree.com/PLCbooks** to download this free reproducible.

Indicator	SCALE		
	Performing School meets all characteristics in Developing and improves by . . .	**Developing** School meets all the characteristics in Initiating and improves by . . .	**Initiating** School characteristics include . . .
Structure	Equity is realized by all educators in the school through transparency about learning. Teachers work in collaborative teams to continually monitor and respond to student progress, proficiency, and pace, and regularly respond and adapt to student needs using continuous improvement processes.	Educators in the school are actively unpacking the curriculum and looking for ways to ensure that all students are growing at a meaningful pace. The school is developing processes and strategies to measure and monitor student growth based on student performance levels and uncover bias in an effort to provide better learning opportunities for historically underserved students.	The school curriculum is filled with examples of learning targets and rubrics that use language that makes them inaccessible to all students. There exists some scaffolding to provide access for students to the curriculum but it lacks the ability to help them develop proficiency in prerequisite skills. This leads to a strong emphasis by educators to "cover" the curriculum and pass students on at the end of the year to the next grade level without reaching proficiency.
Pedagogy	Educators work in collaborative teams to develop a shared understanding and practice of pedagogies that draw from the most recent scientific research about learning, ensuring all students receive feedback and experiences that result in powerful learning outcomes. This promotes all students to become active learners, fostering their ability for agency, self-direction, and empowerment. All students are held to the same high standards for rigor and excellence, including demonstration of mastery and fluency of foundational skills.	An effort has been made by educators to begin to make use of pedagogical strategies that use a growth mindset model, which recognizes that students start with different sets of academic skills, social and emotional skills, and life experiences in an effort to better meet the needs of diverse learners. These strategies have become more learner-centered and culturally responsive.	Teacher-centered pedagogical strategies that offer little opportunity for students to actively apply their learning are widespread in the school. While formal processes to provide feedback and communicate progress in lifelong learning skills necessary for student agency exist, educators lack support in how to coach or assess the skills in ways that guard against bias. Expectations of what it means to be proficient can look different across grade levels and schools in the system.

Competency-Based Learning School-Design Rubric: Principle 7

Design Principle 7: Rigorous, common expectations for learning (knowledge, skills, and dispositions) are explicit, transparent, measurable, and transferable.

Big Ideas:

- There is a framework of standards, learning progressions, competencies, and dispositions aligned with national, state, or local frameworks.
- Competencies have a high level of cognitive demand and rigor.
- There exists a system to calibrate the competencies and dispositions across grade levels and content areas to ensure a common understanding of proficiency.

Notes:

Indicator	SCALE		
	Performing School meets all characteristics in Developing and improves by . . .	**Developing** School meets all characteristics in Initiating and improves by . . .	**Initiating** School characteristics include . . .
Framework of Standards, Competencies, and Dispositions	Competencies, skills, and dispositions are applicable to real-life situations and require an understanding of relationships among theories, principles, and concepts.	The school has expanded the framework of standards to include competencies, skills, and dispositions with performance assessments and include both academic skills that are transferable across content areas as well as habits of learning behaviors. These are mapped K–12 as a continuum of learning progressions based on the standards so that students know exactly where they are and what they need to do next. The school district has established clear transitional and/or graduation competencies that articulate what it means to be ready for the next level.	The school has developed an academic framework of standards (knowledge and skills) that are aligned with national, state, and local frameworks in the school and are limited to scope and sequence of the textbook, program, or resource. Dispositions are identified by the school but are not easily measurable.

page 1 of 2

Indicator	SCALE		
	Performing School meets all characteristics in Developing and improves by . . .	**Developing** School meets all characteristics in Initiating and improves by . . .	**Initiating** School characteristics include . . .
Cognitive Demand	The cognitive demand of the competencies, skills, and dispositions is high—they require students to have a deep understanding of content as well as application of knowledge to a variety of settings by promoting complex connections through creating, analyzing, designing, proving, developing, or formulating.	The cognitive demand of the competencies, skills, and dispositions is medium—they ask students to show what they know in limited ways through identifying, defining, constructing, summarizing, displaying, listing, or recognizing. Teachers occasionally ask students to create conceptual connections and exhibit a level of understanding that is beyond the stated facts or literal interpretation through reasoning, planning, interpreting, hypothesizing, investigating, or explaining.	The cognitive demand of the competencies, skills, and dispositions is low—they ask for routine or rote thinking and require basic recall of information, facts, definitions, and other similar simple tasks and procedures.
System of Calibration	In collaborative teams, teachers regularly engage in the calibration of the competencies and dispositions across grade levels and content areas to ensure a common understanding of proficiency by looking at student work.	Standards-referenced grading makes it clear what students know and how they are progressing. Teachers have a shared understanding of proficiency for both academic skills and dispositions by grade level and course by looking at student work.	The competencies are very specific to the facts in the content. The school has selected a taxonomy to have common language about depth of knowledge and has started a process to identify the competencies for each grade level, content area, and course. Dispositions are identified by the school, but a common process to collect evidence and report progress on dispositions does not exist in the school.

Unpacking the Competency-Based Classroom © 2022 Solution Tree Press • SolutionTree.com
Visit **go.SolutionTree.com/PLCbooks** to download this free reproducible.

Performance Assessment Template

Unit:	Grade Level:

Essential outcome:
(Why is this learning experience important?)

Competency Statement:
Essential Standards:
21st Century Skills (Communication, Collaboration, Creativity, Self-direction)

Task Summary:	Rubric:

Essential questions to guide learning:	
Students will know (content) and be able to demonstrate (skills): (Teacher-driven)	Students would like to know (content) and demonstrate in their unique way (skills): (Student-driven)
Assessment Schedule (to include CFA and CSA)	Plan for Ongoing Intervention and Extension
Resources:	Considerations for those furthest from accessing learning:
Plan for Post-Intervention and Extension:	
Revisions to task (after administration)	

Sources: Center for Collaborative Education. (2012). Quality performance assessment: A guide for schools and districts. Boston: Author. Hess, K. K. (2012). Learning progressions in K–8 classrooms: How progress maps can influence classroom practice and perceptions and help teachers make more informed instructional decisions in support of struggling learners (Synthesis Report No. 87). Minneapolis, MN: National Center on Educational Outcomes; McTighe, J., & Wiggins, G. (2004). The Understanding by Design professional development workbook. Alexandria, VA: Association for Supervision and Curriculum Development.

Rubric Template

Competency Statement				
Essential Standards	Beginning 1	Developing 2	Proficient 3	Exemplary 4
Standard 1				
Standard 2				
Standard 3				
Skills and Dispositions				

Performance Assessment and Unit Feedback Protocol

Purpose: To review and refine performance assessments and unit design, both pre- and post assessment.

Preplanning:

- Time: Approximately twenty-five to thirty minutes
- Group Size: Two Teams (Size May Vary)
- Necessary Materials:
    - Completed Performance Assessment Template (to include assessment)
    - Accompanying Rubric(s)
    - A Means to Record Observations and Notes
- Recommended Roles: Facilitator, Presenter, Recorder, Timekeeper

Norms:

- Remember, this is someone's hard work. Treat it as your own.
- Actively listen and utilize positive language (I'm wondering about . . .).
- Respect the allotted time and the various roles.
- Constantly consider, How do we strengthen this learning experience for students?
- Ensure time is kept to debrief.

Process:

1. Review the preplanning with the team. (1–2 minutes)

2. Initial Overview: Presenter (or presenting team) shares an overview of the unit, with specific focus on the competencies/essential standards, planned performance assessment and possible formative assessments specific to learning targets, and the rubric. Group members listen. (7 minutes)

    a. Guiding Question to be Considered: Is the *Through Line* Evident? The through line represents consistency in the competencies/standards, what the assessment will elicit, and what the rubric intends to score.

3. Clarifying Questions: Group members are provided the opportunity to ask any questions they may have. (3 minutes)

Unpacking the Competency-Based Classroom © 2022 Solution Tree Press • SolutionTree.com
Visit **go.SolutionTree.com/PLCbooks** to download this free reproducible.

4. Additional Presenter Information Provided: Presenter or presenting team provide additional detail related to the following (7 minutes):

    a. Student engagement and ownership in the learning (Students will be able to show what they have learned by . . .)

    b. Considerations for complexity and rigor (By having the students engage in this way [described], we are able to demonstrate DOK . . .)

    c. Considerations for those furthest from accessing learning (The UDL concepts we included in this assessment are . . . The accommodations/allowable modifications to allow students to access this assessment include . . .)

    d. Potential areas the presenting team is unsure of or wondering about (specifically, where you would like feedback)

5. Group Feedback: The group provides feedback to the presenter/presenting team (5 minutes)

    a. Have you considered . . . ?

6. Presenter Debrief: Presenter shares what they have learned from the process and what changes may be made. (3 minutes)

7. Group Debrief: Group members share what they have learned from the process and how this learning may impact their own work. (3 minutes)

Source: Adapted from Center for Collaborative Education. (2012). Quality performance assessment: A guide for schools and districts. *Boston: Author.*

Student Work Calibration Protocol and Rubric Analysis Tool

Purpose: To calibrate student work and increase collaborative team inter-rater reliability

Preplanning:

- Time: Approximately 45 minutes
- Group Size: 4–6
- Necessary Materials:
    - Student work examples
    - Rubric
    - A Means to Record Observations and Notes
- Recommended Roles: Facilitator, Presenter, Recorder, Timekeeper

Norms:

- Remember, this is someone's hard work. Treat it as your own.
- Actively listen and utilize positive language. (I'm wondering about . . .)
- Respect the allotted time and the various roles.
- Constantly consider, How do we strengthen this learning experience for students?
- Ensure time is kept to debrief.

Process:

1. Review the Preplanning with the team. (1–2 minutes)

2. Initial Overview: Presenter shares a brief overview of the unit, assessment, rubric, and student work to be shared. Group members listen and analyze the artifacts. (5 minutes)

    a. Guiding Question: Is the Through Line Evident? Remember, the through line represents consistency in the competencies/standards, what the assessment will elicit, and what the rubric intends to score.

3. Clarifying Questions: Group members are provided the opportunity to ask any questions they may have. (2 minutes)

4. Individual Assessment: Using the rubric, group members independently read and score the student work, justifying their scores with evidence. (10 minutes)

5. **Sharing Student Work Results:** Team members share their assessment of the work products specific to the categories within the rubric (by standard). (3 minutes)

6. **Group Discussion:** The group discusses consistencies and any variance noted by standard and comes to consensus on where a specific sample would be. (5–10 minutes)

7. **Presenter Debrief:** Presenter shares what they have learned from the process and what changes may be made. (5 minutes)

8. **Group Debrief:** Group members share what they have learned from the process and how this learning may impact their own work. (5–10 minutes)

Source: Adapted from Center for Collaborative Education. (2012). Quality performance assessment: A guide for schools and districts. *Boston: Author.*

Resource for Common Formative Assessments

Team Members:	Unit of Study
What is essential to learn (at the standard level)?	
What are the learning targets that lead to mastery?	
What targets are students interested in pursuing?	
What is the time needed for instruction and assessment of these targets?	
What will the evidence of learning include? Formatively? CFAs? Summatively? Performance Assessments?	
Which student will need additional support How will this occur during Tier 1? Tier 2?	
How will we reassess? Who is responsible?	

Tool 1 in Hess's Rigor Matrices

Revised Bloom's Taxonomy	Webb's DOK Level 1 Recall and Reproduction	Webb's DOK Level 2 Skills and Concepts	Webb's DOK Level 3 Strategic Thinking and Reasoning	Webb's DOK Level 4 Extended Thinking
Remember Retrieve knowledge from long-term memory, recognize, recall, locate, and identify.	• Recall, recognize, or locate basic facts, terms, details, events, or ideas explicit in texts. • Read words orally in connected text with fluency and accuracy.	Use these curricular examples with most close reading or listening assignments or assessments in any content area.		
Understand Construct meaning, clarify, paraphrase, represent, translate, illustrate, give examples, classify, categorize, summarize, generalize, infer a logical conclusion, predict, compare and contrast, match like ideas, explain, and construct models.	• Identify or describe literary elements (characters, setting, sequence, and so on). • Select appropriate words when intended meaning or definition is clearly evident. • Describe or explain who, what, where, when, or how. • Define or describe facts, details, terms, and principles. • Write simple sentences.	• Specify, show relationships, and explain why (such as with cause and effect). • Give nonexamples and examples. • Summarize results, concepts, and ideas. • Make basic inferences or logical predictions from data or texts. • Identify main ideas or accurate generalizations of texts. • Locate information to support explicit and implicit central ideas.	• Explain, generalize, or connect ideas using supporting evidence (such as quote, use examples, include text references). • Identify and make inferences about explicit or implicit themes. • Describe how word choice, point of view, or bias may affect the readers' interpretation of a text. • Write multiparagraph composition for specific purpose, focus, voice, tone, and audience.	• Explain how concepts or ideas specifically relate to other content domains (such as social, political, and historical) or concepts. • Develop generalizations of results or about strategies and apply them to new problem-based situations.

page 1 of 3

Unpacking the Competency-Based Classroom © 2022 Solution Tree Press • SolutionTree.com
Visit **go.SolutionTree.com/PLCbooks** to download this free reproducible.

Revised Bloom's Taxonomy	Webb's DOK Level 1 Recall and Reproduction	Webb's DOK Level 2 Skills and Concepts	Webb's DOK Level 3 Strategic Thinking and Reasoning	Webb's DOK Level 4 Extended Thinking
Apply Carry out (apply to a familiar task) or use (apply to an unfamiliar task) a procedure in a given situation	• Use language structure (pre and suffix) or word relationships (synonyms and antonyms) to determine meaning of words. • Apply rules or resources to edit spelling, grammar, punctuation, conventions, and word use. • Apply basic formats for documenting sources.	• Use context to identify the meaning of words and phrases. • Obtain and interpret information using text features. • Develop a text that may be limited to one paragraph. • Apply simple organizational structures (such as paragraphs and sentence types) in writing.	• Apply a concept in a new context. • Revise a final draft for meaning or progression of ideas. • Apply internal consistency of text organization and structure to composing a full composition. • Apply word choice, point of view, and style to impact readers' or viewers' interpretation of a text.	• Illustrate how multiple themes (historical, geographic, social, artistic, and literary) may be interrelated. • Select or devise an approach among many alternatives to research a novel problem.
Analyze Break into constituent parts, determine how parts relate, differentiate between relevant or irrelevant; distinguish; focus; select; organize; outline; find coherence; and deconstruct (for example, for bias or point of view).	• Identify whether specific information is contained in graphic representations (for example, in a map, chart, table, graph, T-chart, or diagram) or text features (such as headings, subheadings, and captions). • Decide which text structure is appropriate to audience and purpose.	• Categorize and compare literary elements, terms, facts and details, and events. • Identify use of literary devices. • Analyze format, organization, and internal text structure (signal words, transitions, and semantic cues) of different texts. • Distinguish between relevant and irrelevant information and fact and opinion. • Identify characteristic text features and distinguish between texts and genres.	• Analyze information within data sets or texts. • Analyze interrelationships among concepts, issues, and problems. • Analyze or interpret an author's craft (literary devices, viewpoint, or potential bias) to create or critique a text. • Use reasoning, planning, and evidence to support inferences.	• Analyze multiple sources of evidence, or multiple works by the same author, or across genres, time periods, and themes. • Analyze complex and abstract themes, perspectives, and concepts. • Gather, analyze, and organize multiple information sources. • Analyze discourse styles.

Revised Bloom's Taxonomy	Webb's DOK Level 1 Recall and Reproduction	Webb's DOK Level 2 Skills and Concepts	Webb's DOK Level 3 Strategic Thinking and Reasoning	Webb's DOK Level 4 Extended Thinking
Evaluate Make judgments based on criteria, check, detect inconsistencies or fallacies, judge, and critique.	Unsubstantiated generalizations (UGs) are stating an opinion without providing any support for it.		• Cite evidence and develop a logical argument for conjectures. • Describe, compare, and contrast solution methods. • Verify reasonableness of results. • Justify or critique conclusions.	• Evaluate relevancy, accuracy, and completeness of information from multiple sources. • Apply understanding in a novel way and provide argument or justification for the application.
Create Reorganize elements into new patterns and structures, generate, hypothesize, design, plan, and produce.	• Brainstorm ideas, concepts, problems, or perspectives related to a topic, principle, or concept.	• Generate conjectures or hypotheses based on observations or prior knowledge and experience.	• Synthesize information within one source or text. • Develop a complex model for a given situation. • Develop an alternative solution.	• Synthesize information across multiple sources or texts. • Articulate a new voice, alternate theme, new knowledge, or new perspective.

Source: Reprinted from Hess, 2013. Adapted with permission.

Tool 2 in Hess's Rigor Matrices

Revised Bloom's Taxonomy	Webb's DOK Level 1 Recall and Reproduction	Webb's DOK Level 2 Skills and Concepts	Webb's DOK Level 3 Strategic Thinking and Reasoning	Webb's DOK Level 4 Extended Thinking
Remember Retrieve knowledge from long-term memory, recognize, recall, locate, and identify.	• Recall, observe, and recognize facts, principles, and properties. • Recall and identify conversions among representations or numbers (such as customary and metric measures).	Use these curricular examples with most mathematics or science assignments or assessments.		
Understand Construct meaning, clarify, paraphrase, represent, translate, illustrate, give examples, classify, categorize, summarize, generalize, infer a logical conclusion, predict, compare and contrast, match like ideas, explain, and construct models.	• Evaluate an expression. • Locate points on a grid or numbers on a number line. • Solve a one-step problem. • Represent mathematics relationships in words, pictures, or symbols. • Read, write, and compare decimals in scientific notation.	• Specify and explain relationships (such as examples and nonexamples and cause and effect). • Make and record observations. • Explain steps followed. • Summarize results or concepts. • Make basic inferences or logical predictions from data or observations. • Use models and diagrams to represent or explain mathematical concepts. • Make and explain estimates.	• Use concepts to solve nonroutine problems. • Explain, generalize, or connect ideas using supporting evidence. • Make and justify conjectures. • Explain thinking and reasoning when more than one solution or approach is possible. • Explain phenomena in terms of concepts.	• Relate mathematical or scientific concepts to other content areas, other domains, or other concepts. • Develop generalizations from results and strategies (from investigation or reading) and apply them to new problem situations.

page 1 of 3

Unpacking the Competency-Based Classroom © 2022 Solution Tree Press • SolutionTree.com
Visit **go.SolutionTree.com/PLCbooks** to download this free reproducible.

Revised Bloom's Taxonomy	Webb's DOK Level 1 Recall and Reproduction	Webb's DOK Level 2 Skills and Concepts	Webb's DOK Level 3 Strategic Thinking and Reasoning	Webb's DOK Level 4 Extended Thinking
Apply Carry out (apply to a familiar task) or use (apply to an unfamiliar task) a procedure in a given situation.	• Follow simple procedures (for example, recipe-type directions). • Calculate, measure, and apply a rule (such as rounding). • Apply an algorithm or formula (such as area or perimeter). • Solve linear equations. • Make conversions among representations or numbers, or within and between customary and metric measures.	• Select a procedure according to criteria and perform it. • Solve routine problems applying multiple concepts or decision points. • Retrieve information from a table, graph, or figure and use it to solve a problem requiring multiple steps. • Translate tables, graphs, words, and symbolic notations (such as graph data from a table). • Construct models with given criteria.	• Design investigation for a specific purpose or research question. • Conduct a designed investigation. • Use concepts to solve nonroutine problems. • Use and show reasoning, planning, and evidence. • Translate between problem and symbolic notation when not a direct translation.	• Select or devise an approach among many alternatives to solve a problem. • Conduct a project that specifies a problem, identifies solution paths, solves the problem, and reports results.
Analyze Break into constituent parts, determine how the parts relate, differentiate between what is relevant and irrelevant, distinguish, focus, select, organize, outline, find coherence, and deconstruct.	• Retrieve information from a table or graph to answer a question • Identify whether specific information is contained in graphic representations (such as in a table, graph, T-chart, or diagram). • Identify a pattern or trend.	• Categorize and classify materials, data, and figures based on characteristics. • Organize or order data. • Compare and contrast figures or data. • Select appropriate graphs and organize and display data. • Interpret data from a simple graph. • Extend a pattern.	• Compare information within or across data sets or texts. • Analyze and draw conclusions from data, citing evidence. • Generalize a pattern. • Interpret data from complex graph. • Analyze similarities and differences between procedures or solutions.	• Analyze multiple sources of evidence. • Analyze complex and abstract themes. • Gather, analyze, and evaluate information.

Revised Bloom's Taxonomy	Webb's DOK Level 1 Recall and Reproduction	Webb's DOK Level 2 Skills and Concepts	Webb's DOK Level 3 Strategic Thinking and Reasoning	Webb's DOK Level 4 Extended Thinking
Evaluate Make judgments based on criteria, check, detect inconsistencies or fallacies, judge, and critique.	Unsubstantiated generalizations (UGs) state an opinion without providing any support for it.		• Cite evidence and develop a logical argument for concepts or solutions. • Describe, compare, and contrast solution methods. • Verify reasonableness of results.	• Gather, analyze, and evaluate information to draw conclusions. • Apply understanding in a novel way and provide an argument or justification for the application.
Create Reorganize elements into new patterns or structures, generate, hypothesize, design, plan, and produce.	• Brainstorm ideas, concepts, or perspectives related to a topic.	• Generate conjectures or hypotheses based on observations or prior knowledge and experience.	• Synthesize information within one data set, source, or text. • Formulate an original problem to a given situation. • Develop a scientific or mathematical model for a complex situation.	• Synthesize information across multiple sources or texts. • Design a mathematical model to inform and solve a practical or abstract situation.

Source: Reprinted from Hess, 2013. Adapted with permission.

Tool 3 in Hess's Rigor Matrices

Revised Bloom's Taxonomy	Webb's DOK Level 1 Recall and Reproduction	Webb's DOK Level 2 Skills and Concepts	Webb's DOK Level 3 Strategic Thinking and Reasoning	Webb's DOK Level 4 Extended Thinking
Remember Retrieve knowledge from long-term memory, recognize, recall, locate, and identify.	• Complete short-answer questions with facts, details, terms, principles, and so on (such as label parts of a diagram).	Use these curricular examples with most writing and oral communication assignments or assessments in any content area.		
Understand Construct meaning, clarify, paraphrase, represent, translate, illustrate, give examples, classify, categorize, summarize, generalize, infer a logical conclusion, predict, compare and contrast, match like ideas, explain, and construct models.	• Describe or define facts, details, terms, principles, and so on. • Select the appropriate word or phrase to use when the intended meaning or definition is clearly evident. • Write simple complete sentences. • Add an appropriate caption to a photo or illustration. • Write fact statements on a topic (such as, "Spiders build webs").	• Specify, explain, and show relationships (explain why and cause and effect). • Provide and explain nonexamples and examples. • Take notes and organize ideas and data (for example, note relevance, trends, and perspectives). • Summarize results, key concepts, and ideas. • Explain central ideas or accurate generalizations of texts or topics. • Describe steps in a process (such as a science procedure).	• Write a multiparagraph composition for a specific purpose and audience (using specific focus, voice, and tone). • Develop and explain opposing perspectives or connect ideas, principles, or concepts using supporting evidence (such as a quote, example, text reference, and so on). • Develop arguments of fact (for example, "Are these criticisms supported by the historical facts?" and "Is this claim or equation true?").	• Use multiple sources to elaborate on how concepts or ideas specifically draw from other content domains or differing concepts (such as research papers and policy arguments). • Develop generalizations about results or strategies and apply them to a new problem or contextual scenario.

Revised Bloom's Taxonomy	Webb's DOK Level 1 Recall and Reproduction	Webb's DOK Level 2 Skills and Concepts	Webb's DOK Level 3 Strategic Thinking and Reasoning	Webb's DOK Level 4 Extended Thinking
Apply Carry out (apply to a familiar task) or use (apply to an unfamiliar task) a procedure in a given situation.	• Apply rules or use resources to edit specific spelling, grammar, punctuation, conventions, or word use. • Apply basic formats for documenting sources.	• Use context to identify or infer the intended meaning of words and phrases. • Obtain, interpret, and explain information using text features (such as tables, diagrams, and so on). • Develop a brief text that may be limited to one paragraph. • Apply basic organizational structures (introduction, topic sentence, sentence types, paragraphs, and so on) in writing.	• Revise final draft for meaning, progression of ideas, or chain of logic. • Apply internal consistency of text organization and structure to a full composition or oral communication. • Apply a concept in a new context. • Apply word choice, point of view, style, and rhetorical devices to impact readers' interpretation of a text.	• Select or devise an approach among many alternatives to research and present a novel problem or issue. • Illustrate how multiple themes (historical, geographic, and social) may be interrelated within a text or topic.
Analyze Break into constituent parts, determine how the parts relate, differentiate between what is relevant and irrelevant, distinguish, focus, select, organize, outline, find coherence, and deconstruct (such as for bias or point of view).	• Decide which text structure is appropriate to audience and purpose (such as compare and contrast or proposition with support). • Determine appropriate, relevant key words for conducting an Internet search or researching a topic.	• Compare and contrast perspectives, events, characters, and so on. • Analyze and revise format, organization, and internal text structure (signal words, transitions, and semantic cues) of different print and nonprint texts. • Distinguish between relevant and irrelevant information and fact and opinion. • Locate evidence that supports a perspective and differing perspectives.	• Analyze interrelationships among concepts, issues, and problems in a text. • Analyze impact or use of author's craft (literary devices, viewpoint, and dialogue) in a single text. • Use reasoning and evidence to generate criteria for making and supporting an argument of judgment (for example, "Was FDR a great president?" or "Who was the greatest ball player?"). • Support conclusions with evidence.	• Analyze multiple sources of evidence, or multiple works by the same author, or work from across genres or time periods. • Analyze complex and abstract themes, perspectives, and concepts. • Gather, analyze, and organize multiple information sources. • Compare and contrast conflicting judgments or policies (such as Supreme Court decisions).

Revised Bloom's Taxonomy	Webb's DOK Level 1 Recall and Reproduction	Webb's DOK Level 2 Skills and Concepts	Webb's DOK Level 3 Strategic Thinking and Reasoning	Webb's DOK Level 4 Extended Thinking
Evaluate Make judgments based on criteria; check and detect inconsistencies or fallacies; judge; and critique.	Unsubstantiated generalizations (UGs) state an opinion without providing any support for it.		• Evaluate validity and relevance of evidence used to develop an argument or support a perspective. • Describe and compare and contrast solution methods. • Verify or critique the accuracy, logic, and reasonableness of stated conclusions or assumptions.	• Evaluate relevancy, accuracy, and completeness of information across multiple sources. • Apply understanding in a novel way and provide an argument or justification for the application. • Critique the historical impact (policy, writings, discoveries, and so on).
Create Reorganize elements into new patterns and structures, generate, hypothesize, design, plan, and produce.	• Brainstorm facts, ideas, concepts, problems, or perspectives related to a topic, text, idea, issue, or concept.	• Generate conjectures, hypotheses, or predictions based on facts, observations, evidence and observations, or prior knowledge and experience. • Generate believable grounds (reasons) for an opinion or argument.	• Develop a complex model for a given situation or problem. • Develop an alternative solution or perspective (such as a debate).	• Synthesize information across multiple sources or texts in order to articulate a new voice, alternate theme, new knowledge, or nuanced perspective.

Source: Reprinted from Hess, 2013. Adapted with permission.

Tool 4 in Hess's Rigor Matrices

Revised Bloom's Taxonomy	Webb's DOK Level 1 Recall and Reproduction	Webb's DOK Level 2 Skills and Concepts	Webb's DOK Level 3 Strategic Thinking and Reasoning	Webb's DOK Level 4 Extended Thinking
Remember Retrieve knowledge from long-term memory, recognize, recall, locate, and identify.	• Recall or locate key facts, dates, terms, details, events, or ideas explicit in texts.	Use these curricular examples with most assignments, assessments, or inquiry activities in social studies, history, civics, geography, economics, or humanities.		
Understand Construct meaning, clarify, paraphrase, represent, translate, illustrate, give examples, classify, categorize, summarize, generalize, infer a logical conclusion, predict, observe, compare and contrast, match like ideas, explain, and construct models.	• Select appropriate words or terms when intended meaning is clearly evident. • Describe or explain who, what, where, when, or how. • Define facts, details, terms, and principles. • Locate and identify symbols and what they represent. • Raise related questions for possible investigation.	• Specify, explain, and illustrate relationships; explain why (cause and effect). • Provide and explain examples and nonexamples. • Summarize results, concepts, main ideas, and generalizations. • Make basic inferences or logical predictions (using data and text). • Locate relevant information to support explicit and implicit central ideas.	• Explain, generalize, or connect ideas using supporting evidence (quotes, examples, text references, and data). • Support inferences about explicit or implicit themes. • Describe how word choice, point of view, or bias may affect the reader's or viewer's interpretation. • Write a multiparagraph composition or essay for specific purpose, focus, voice, tone, and audience.	• Explain how concepts or ideas specifically relate to other content domains or concepts (social, political, historical, and cultural). • Apply generalizations to new problem-based situations. • Use multiple sources to elaborate on how concepts or ideas specifically draw from other content domains or differing concepts (such as research papers and policy arguments).

page 1 of 3

Unpacking the Competency-Based Classroom © 2022 Solution Tree Press • SolutionTree.com
Visit **go.SolutionTree.com/PLCbooks** to download this free reproducible.

Revised Bloom's Taxonomy	Webb's DOK Level 1 Recall and Reproduction	Webb's DOK Level 2 Skills and Concepts	Webb's DOK Level 3 Strategic Thinking and Reasoning	Webb's DOK Level 4 Extended Thinking
Apply Carry out (apply to a familiar task) or use a procedure in a given situation (transfer to an unfamiliar or nonroutine task).	• Apply basic formats for documenting sources. • Apply use of reference materials and tools for gathering information (do keyword searches).	• Use context to identify the meaning of words and phrases. • Interpret information using text features (diagrams, data tables, captions, and so on). • Apply simple organizational structures (such as paragraph outlines).	• Investigate to determine how a historical, cultural, or political context may be the source of an underlying theme, central idea, or unresolved issue or crisis.	• Integrate or juxtapose multiple (such as historical and cultural) contexts drawn from source materials (such as literature, music, historical events, and media) with intent to develop a complex or multimedia product and personal viewpoint.
Analyze Break into constituent parts, determine how parts relate, differentiate between what is relevant and irrelevant, distinguish, focus, select, organize, outline, find coherence, and deconstruct (such as for bias, point of view, and approach or strategy).	• Identify causes or effects. • Describe processes or tools used to research ideas, artifacts, or images reflecting history, culture, tradition, and so on. • Identify ways symbols and metaphors are used to represent universal ideas. • Identify specific information given in graphics (such as maps, T-charts, and diagrams) or text features (such as headings, subheadings, and captions).	• Compare similarities and differences in processes, methods, and styles due to influences of time period, politics, or culture. • Distinguish relevant from irrelevant information, fact from opinion, and primary from secondary sources. • Draw inferences about social, historical, and cultural contexts portrayed in literature, arts, film, political cartoons, or primary sources. • Explain and categorize events and ideas in the evolution of _____ across time periods.	• Analyze information within data sets or a text (such as the interrelationships among concepts, issues, and problems). • Analyze an author's viewpoint or potential bias (such as in a political cartoon). • Use reasoning, planning, and evidence to support or refute inferences in policy or speech. • Use reasoning and evidence to generate criteria for making and supporting an argument of judgment (for example, "Was FDR a great president?" or "Is this a fair law?").	• Analyze multiple sources of evidence across time periods, themes, and issues. • Analyze diverse, complex, and abstract perspectives. • Gather, analyze, and organize information from multiple sources. • Analyze discourse styles and bias in speeches, legal briefs, and so on, across time or authors. • Compare and contrast conflicting judgments or policies (such as Supreme Court decisions).

Revised Bloom's Taxonomy	Webb's DOK Level 1 Recall and Reproduction	Webb's DOK Level 2 Skills and Concepts	Webb's DOK Level 3 Strategic Thinking and Reasoning	Webb's DOK Level 4 Extended Thinking
Evaluate Make judgments based on criteria; check and detect inconsistencies or fallacies; judge, and critique.	Unsubstantiated generalizations (UGs) state an opinion without providing any support for it.		• Develop a logical argument for conjectures, citing evidence. • Verify reasonableness of others' results. • Critique conclusions, evidence, and credibility of sources.	• Evaluate relevancy, accuracy, and completeness of information using multiple sources. • Apply understanding in a novel way and provide an argument or justification for the application. • Critique the historical impact on policy, writings, and advances.
Create Reorganize elements into new patterns, structures, or schemas; generate; hypothesize; design; plan; and produce.	• Brainstorm ideas, concepts, problems, or perspectives related to a topic, principle, or concept.	• Generate testable conjectures or hypotheses based on observations, prior knowledge, and artifacts.	• Synthesize information within one source or text. • Develop a complex model or symbol for given issue. • Develop and support an alternative solution.	• Synthesize information across multiple sources or texts. • Articulate a new voice, alternate theme, new knowledge, or new perspective. • Create historical fiction drawing on sources.

Source: Reprinted from Hess, 2013. Adapted with permission.

CBL Weekly Lesson Planning Template

Lesson and Unit:	
Lesson Objectives:	Essential Standard (the standard the learning target leads to mastery of): Learning Target (component of the essential standard that this lesson focuses on):
Essential Questions to Guide Learning:	
Considerations for Those Furthest From Accessing Learning:	Lesson Overview and Activities:
Assessment Opportunities (Where will students and adults collect evidence of learning?):	Metacognitive and Feedback Opportunities (Where will students engage in self-reflection, goal setting, monitoring, and adapting through meaningful feedback?):
Teacher Reflections (What worked well? What would you change?):	

Unpacking the Competency-Based Classroom © 2022 Solution Tree Press • SolutionTree.com
Visit **go.SolutionTree.com/PLCbooks** to download this free reproducible.

SMART Goal Team Planning Tool

SMART: Strategic, Measurable, Attainable, Results Oriented, Time Bound
Annual SMART Goal (Based on Benchmark Data):
Essential Standards That Support Day to Day Attainment of SMART Goal:

Data Collected by Benchmark Assessments and Essential Standards			
Marking Period 1	**Marking Period 2**	**Marking Period 3**	**Marking Period 4 (if needed)**

Next Steps Based on the Data Collected			
At the end of the school year: What is your data telling your team? What do you need to consider for next year?			

Making Meaning of Assessment

Purpose: Through an interview, identify the key assessment strategies that allowed you to develop a specific area of skill.

Time: 30 minutes

Introduction: The facilitator asks the audience what the word *assessment* means. The root of *assess* is Latin, coming from the word *assidere* and translates to *sit beside*. The facilitator asks participants to speak to an elbow partner about the role of assessment in their own classroom and how the concept of sitting side by side with students plays into their practice.

Step 1: Introducing and Conducting the Empathy Interview

Participants will pair up and interview each other, sharing a relative area of expertise, or something that they feel very confident in doing. It can be anything (does not have to be based in the education world, but can be). Examples: Skiing, biking, cooking, sewing, surfing, and so on. The following prompts can guide the conversation.

What is something you're quite skilled at?

- How did you originally become interested in that skill?
- What was it like for you when you first began practicing this skill?
- How did you become more skilled over time?
- How did you get feedback? Which type of feedback was most helpful?
- Did you have to go outside of your comfort zone and push yourself to get better?
- Was someone there to support you in doing that? How did they support you?
- How did you know that you had reached a level of proficiency (or beyond)?
- What advice do you have for others in developing this skill?

Step 2: Sharing Key Takeaways

Participants share aloud (through a few examples) responses to the guiding questions. The facilitator should ask participants if there are commonalities in their experiences.

Step 3: Closing the Loop

The facilitator should begin to home in on the specific questions about feedback and support, note the concept of metacognition (self-awareness and monitoring and adapting goals) and how that has a significant impact on the development of any skill.

Step 4: Connecting to Our Craft

The facilitator should allow each teacher the opportunity to reflect, identifying key practices that support meaningful assessment, and identifying key opportunities for growth within their assessment practices. These can be recorded or shared.

REFERENCES AND RESOURCES

Avery, L., Jones, M., Marr, S., & Wenmoth, D. (2021). *Mere engagement: Reflections about the connections between online learning, student agency, and student engagement.* Vienna, VA: Aurora Institute. Accessed at https://aurora-institute.org/wp-content/uploads/Mere-Engagement-web.pdf on July 21, 2021.

Bailey, K., & Jakicic, C. (2012). *Common formative assessment: A toolkit for Professional Learning Communities at Work.* Bloomington, IN: Solution Tree Press.

Bailey, K., & Jakicic, C. (2016). *Simplifying common assessment: A guide for Professional Learning Communities at Work.* Bloomington, IN: Solution Tree Press.

Battelle for Kids. (n.d.). *How we help.* Accessed at www.battelleforkids.org/how-we-help on February 22, 2022.

Black, P., & Wiliam, D. (1998). Inside the black box: Raising standards through classroom assessment. *Phi Delta Kappan, 80*(2), 144, 146–148.

Blauth, E., & Hadjian, S. (2016). *How selective colleges and universities evaluate proficiency-based high school transcripts: Insights for students and schools—Policy spotlight on New England.* Boston: New England Board of Higher Education.

Bloom, B. S. (1956) *Taxonomy of educational objectives, handbook 1: The cognitive domain.* David McKay, New York.

Bristow, S., & Patrick, S. (2014). *An international study in competency education: Postcards from abroad.* Vienna, VA: Aurora Institute. Accessed at www.aurora-institute.org/wp-content/uploads/CW-An-International-Study-in-Competency-Education-Postcards-from-Abroad-October-2014.pdf on December 2, 2021.

British Columbia Ministry of Education (2016). *BC's redesigned curriculum: An orientation guide.* Accessed at https://curriculum.gov.bc.ca/sites/curriculum.gov.bc.ca/files/pdf/supports/curriculum_brochure.pdf on December 2, 2021.

Brookhart, S. M. (2013). *How to create and use rubrics for formative assessment and grading.* Alexandria, VA: Association for Supervision and Curriculum Development.

Brown, C., & Mednick, A. (2012). *Quality performance assessment: A guide for schools and districts.* Boston: Center for Collaborative Education.

Buck Institute for Education. (n.d.). *Why project based learning (PBL)?* Accessed at www.bie.org/about/why_pbl on March 2, 2021.

Buffum, A., Mattos, M., & Malone, J. (2017). *Taking Action: A Handbook for RTI at Work.* Bloomington, IN: Solution Tree.

Buffum, A., Mattos, M., & Weber, C. (2012). *Simplifying response to intervention: Four essential guiding principles.* Bloomington, IN: Solution Tree Press.

Burke, K. (2010). *Balanced assessment: From formative to summative.* Bloomington, IN: Solution Tree Press.

Burns, J. M. (1978). *Leadership.* New York: Harper & Row.

CAST. (n.d.). *About Universal Design for Learning.* Accessed at www.cast.org/impact/universal-design-for-learning-udl?utm_source=udlguidelines&utm_medium=web&utm_campaign=none&utm_content=homepage on January 28, 2021.

Center for Collaborative Education. (2012). *Quality performance assessment: A guide for schools and districts.* Boston: Author. Accessed at www.ode.state.or.us/wma/teachlearn/testing/resources/qpa_guide_oregon.pdf on July 26, 2021.

Chen, B. X. (2009). June 29, 2007: *iPhone, you phone, we all wanna iPhone.* Accessed at www.wired.com/2009/06/dayintech-0629 on February 22, 2022.

Collaborative for Academic, Social, and Emotional Learning. (n.d.a). *Benefits of SEL.* Accessed at https://casel.org/impact/ on February 20, 2021.

Collaborative for Academic, Social, and Emotional Learning. (n.d.b). *SEL is…* Accessed at https://casel.org/what-is-sel/ on February 18, 2021.

Colby, R. L. (2017). *Competency-based education: A new architecture for K–12 schooling.* Cambridge, MA: Harvard Education Press.

Common Core State Standards Initiative. (n.d.). *About the standards.* Accessed at www.corestandards.org/about-the-standards/ on January 13, 2021.

Conzemius, A. E., & O'Neill, J. (2014). *The handbook for SMART school teams: Revitalizing best practices for collaboration* (2nd ed.). Bloomington, IN: Solution Tree Press.

CPO Science. (2007). *Physical science.* Accessed at https://freyscientific.com/FREY/media/downloads/cpo/douglas-county/PSN_Ebook.pdf on July 23, 2021.

Dueck, M. (2021). *Giving students a say: Smarter assessment practices to empower and engage.* Alexandria, VA: Association for Supervision and Curriculum Development.

DuFour, R., DuFour, R., Eaker, R., & Many, T. (2010). *Learning by doing: A handbook for Professional Learning Communities at Work* (2nd ed.). Bloomington, IN: Solution Tree Press.

DuFour, R., DuFour, R., Eaker, R., Many, T. W., & Mattos, M. (2016). *Learning by doing: A handbook for Professional Learning Communities at Work* (3rd ed.). Bloomington, IN: Solution Tree Press.

Dweck, C. (2006). *Mindset: The new psychology of success.* New York: Random House.

Elmore, R. F. (1999–2000). Building a new structure for school leadership. *American Educator.*

Elmore, R. F. (2000). *Building a new structure for school leadership.* Washington, DC: Albert Shanker Institute.

Evans, C. M. (2019). Effects of New Hampshire's innovative assessment and accountability system on student achievement outcomes after three years. *Education Policy Analysis Archives, 27*(10). Accessed at www.education.nh.gov/sites/g/files/ehbemt326/files/files/inline-documents/effectnhpace3years.pdf on July 19, 2021.

Excel*in*Ed, & EducationCounsel. (2017). *Policy, pilots and the path to competency-based education: A national landscape.* Accessed at www.excelined.org/wp-content/uploads/2017/05/CBE.NationalLandscape.Final_.pdf on July 19, 2021.

Gray, A. (2016). *The 10 skills you need to thrive in the Fourth Industrial Revolution.* Accessed at www.weforum.org/agenda/2016/01/the-10-skills-you-need-to-thrive-in-the-fourth-industrial-revolution on February 20, 2022.

Guskey, T. R. (2015). *On your mark: Challenging the conventions of grading and reporting.* Bloomington, IN: Solution Tree Press.

Hattie, J. (2009). *Visible learning: A synthesis of over 800 meta-analyses relating to achievement.* Abingdon, England: Routledge.

Heritage, M. (2008). *Learning progressions: Supporting instruction and formative assessment.* Washington, DC: Council of Chief State School Officers.

Heritage, M. (2010). *Formative assessment and next-generation assessment systems: Are we losing an opportunity?* Los Angeles: National Center for Research on Evaluation, Standards, and Student Testing.

Heritage, M., & Wylie, E. C. (2020). *Formative assessment in the disciplines: Framing a continuum of professional learning.* Cambridge: Harvard Education Press.

Hess, K. K. (2012). *Learning progressions in K-8 classrooms: How progress maps can influence classroom practice and perceptions and help teachers make more informed instructional decisions in support of struggling learners* (Synthesis Report No. 87). Minneapolis, MN: National Center on Educational Outcomes. Accessed at https://nceo.umn.edu/docs/OnlinePubs/Synthesis87/SynthesisReport87.pdf on July 26, 2021.

Hess, K. (n.d.). *Educational research in action.* Accessed at www.karin-hess.com/cognitive-rigor-and-dok on August 7, 2020.

Hess, K. K. (2018). *A local assessment toolkit to promote deeper learning: Transforming research into practice.* Thousand Oaks, CA: Corwin Press.

Hess, K. K., Colby, R., & Joseph, D. (2020). *Deeper competency-based learning: Making equitable, student-centered, sustainable shifts.* Thousand Oaks, CA: Corwin Press.

JumpRope. (2022). *JumpRope Knowledge Base: Explanation—The "Power" of the Power Law.* Accessed at https://help.jumpro.pe/en/articles/650 on March 14, 2022.

Kentucky Department of Education. (2019). *Kentucky Academic Standards: Mathematics.* Accessed at https://education.ky.gov/curriculum/standards/kyacadstand/Documents/Kentucky_Academic_Standards_Mathematics.pdf on January 6, 2021.

Kotter, J. P. (2012). *Leading change.* Boston: Harvard Business Review Press.

Lench, S. C., Fukuda, E., & Anderson, R. (2015). *Essential skills and dispositions: Developmental frameworks for collaboration, communication, creativity, and self-direction.* Lexington, KY: National Center for Innovation in Education.

Lenz, B., Wells, J., & Kingston, S. (2015). *Transforming schools: Using project-based deeper learning, performance assessment, and Common Core standards.* San Francisco: Jossey-Bass.

Levine, E., & Patrick, S. (2019). *What is competency-based education? An updated definition.* Vienna, VA: Aurora Institute. Accessed at aurora-institute.org/resource/what-is-competency-based-education-an-updated-definition/ on July 21, 2021.

Many, T. W., Maffoni, M. J., Sparks, S. K., & Thomas, T. F. (2020). *How schools thrive: Building a coaching culture for collaborative teams in PLCs at Work.* Bloomington, IN: Solution Tree Press.

Marzano, R. J. (2010). *Formative assessment and standards-based grading.* Denver, CO: Marzano Resources.

Marzano, R. J. (2017). *The new art and science of teaching.* Bloomington, IN: Solution Tree Press.

Marzano, R. J., Warrick, P. B., Rains, C. L., & DuFour, R. (2018). *Leading a high reliability school.* Bloomington, IN: Solution Tree Press.

McTighe, J., & Wiggins, G. (2004). *The Understanding by Design professional development workbook.* Alexandria, VA: Association for Supervision and Curriculum Development.

McTighe, J., & Wiggins, G. (2013). *Essential questions: Opening doors to student understanding.* Alexandria, VA: ASCD.

Morehead, J. (2012, June 19). *Stanford University's Carol Dweck on the growth mindset and education.* Accessed at https://onedublin.org/2012/06/19/stanford-universitys-carol-dweck-on-the-growth-mindset-and-education/ on July 19, 2021.

Moss, C. M., & Brookhart, S. M. (2012). *Learning targets: Helping students aim for understanding in today's lesson.* Alexandria, VA: Association for Supervision and Curriculum Development.

Muhammad, A., & Cruz, L. F. (2019). *Time for change: 4 essential skills for transformational school and district leaders.* Bloomington, IN: Solution Tree Press.

National Equity Project. (n.d.). *Educational equity: A definition.* Accessed at https://static1.squarespace.com/static/5e32157bff63c7446f3f1529/t/5f11e9d90cd94734d0079476/1595009497839/Educational+Equity+Definition.pdf on July 19, 2021.

New England Secondary School Consortium. (n.d.). *85 New England institutions of higher education state that proficiency-based diplomas do not disadvantage applicants.* Accessed at www.newenglandssc.org/resources/college-admissions/ on July 21, 2021.

New Hampshire Department of Education. (n.d.). *Extended learning opportunities.* Accessed at www.education.nh.gov/partners/education-outside-classroom/extended-learning-opportunities on March 24, 2021.

New Hampshire Department of Education. (2010). *Competency validation rubric.* Accessed at www.education.nh.gov/sites/g/files/ehbemt326/files/inline-documents/2020-04/validation_rubric.pdf on July 26, 2021.

New Hampshire Department of Education. (2014). *New Hampshire K–12 model science competencies.* Accessed at www.education.nh.gov/sites/g/files/ehbemt326/files/inline-documents/2020-04/science_model.pdf on July 23, 2021.

New Hampshire Department of Education. (2016a). *New Hampshire College and Career Ready K–8 English language arts model competencies.* Accessed at www.education.nh.gov/sites/g/files/ehbemt326/files/inline-documents/2020-04/english-k-8-2016.pdf on July 23, 2021.

New Hampshire Department of Education. (2016b). *New Hampshire College and Career Ready K–8 mathematics model competencies.* Accessed at www.education.nh.gov/sites/g/files/ehbemt326/files/inline-documents/2020-04/math-k-8-2016.pdf on January 3, 2021.

New Hampshire Department of Education. (2016c). *New Hampshire Common Core State Standards–aligned mathematics model graduation competencies.* Accessed at www.education.nh.gov/sites/g/files/ehbemt326/files/inline-documents/2020-04/model_math_competencies.pdf on July 23, 2021.

New Hampshire Department of Education. (n.d). *Extended learning opportunities.* Accessed at www.education.nh.gov/partners/education-outside-classroom/extended-learning-opportunities on December 20, 2021.

New Hampshire Department of Education. (2017). *New Hampshire nationally-aligned K–8 science model competencies.* Accessed at www.education.nh.gov/sites/g/files/ehbemt326/files/inline-documents/2020-04/science-k8-competencies.pdf on July 23, 2021.

New Zealand Ministry of Education. (n. d.). *New Zealand curriculum online: Key competencies.* Accessed at https://nzcurriculum.tki.org.nz/Key-competencies on December 3, 2021.

NGSS Lead States. (2013). Next Generation Science Standards: For states, by states. Washington, DC: The National Academies Press.

O'Connor, K. (2018). *How to grade for learning: Linking grades to standards* (4th ed.). Thousand Oaks, CA: Corwin Press.

Popham, W. J. (2008). *Transformative assessment.* Alexandria, VA: Association for Supervision and Curriculum Development.

Portrait of a Graduate. (n.d.). *Do you have a portrait of a graduate?* Accessed at https://portraitofagraduate.org on February 14, 2021.

Posey, A. (n.d.). *Universal Design for Learning (UDL): A teacher's guide.* Accessed at www.understood.org/articles/en/understanding-universal-design-for-learning on February 20, 2022.

Quebec Ministry of Education. (2001). *Quebec Education Program approved version.* Accessed at www.education.gouv.qc.ca/fileadmin/site_web/documents/PFEQ/educprg2001.pdf on January 4, 2022.

Quebec Ministry of Education. (2021). *The Québec Education Program: Preschool and elementary education.* Accessed at www.education.gouv.qc.ca/fileadmin/site_web/documents/education/jeunes/pfeq/PFEQ-tableau-synthese-primaire-2018-EN.pdf January 4, 2022.

Reeves, D. B. (2002). *The leader's guide to standards: A blueprint for educational equity and excellence.* San Francisco: Jossey-Bass.

Rogers, P., Smith, W. R., Buffum, A., & Mattos, M. (2020). *Best practices at Tier 3: Intensive interventions and remediation, elementary.* Bloomington, IN: Solution Tree Press.

Samaddar, P. (n.d.). *The big ideas.* Accessed at http://pamsamaddar.weebly.com/our-learning-targets.html on February 16, 2022.

Sinek, S. (2009). *Start with why: how great leaders inspire everyone to take action.* New York: Portfolio.

Singapore American School. (n.d.) *Catalyst project.* Accessed at www.sas.edu.sg/academics/high/catalyst on January 4, 2021.

Stack, B. M., & Vander Els, J. G. (2018). *Breaking with tradition: The shift to competency-based learning in PLCs at Work.* Bloomington, IN: Solution Tree Press.

Stuart, T. S., Heckmann, S., Mattos, M., & Buffum, A. (2018). *Personalized learning in a PLC at Work: Student agency through the four critical questions.* Bloomington, IN: Solution Tree Press.

Sturgis, C. (2015). *Implementing competency education in K–12 systems: Insights from local leaders.* Vienna, VA: International Association for K–12 Online Learning.

Truong, N. (2019, June 27). *iNACOL releases updates to the snapshot of K–12 competency education state policy across the United States.* Accessed at aurora-institute.org/cw_post/inacol-releases-updates-to-the-snapshot-of-k-12-competency-education-state-policy-across-the-united-states/ on July 19, 2021.

Visible Learning. (n.d.). *Hattie ranking: 252 influences and effect sizes related to student achievement.* Accessed at https://visible-learning.org/hattie-ranking-influences-effect-sizes-learning-achievement/ on January 18, 2021.

Wallace Foundation. (n.d.). *Expanded learning opportunities models: Expanding time for learning both inside and outside the classroom.* Accessed at www.wallacefoundation.org/knowledge-center/pages/expanded-learning-opportunities-models-expanding-time-for-learning-both-inside-and-outside-the-classroom.aspx on March 27, 2021.

Webb, N. L. (1997). *Criteria for alignment of expectations and assessments in mathematics and science education (research monograph number 6).* Madison, WI: National Institute for Science Education; Washington, DC: Council of Chief State School Officers. Accessed at https://files.eric.ed.gov/fulltext/ED414305.pdf on February 16, 2022.

WestEd. (2021). *Center for Standards, Assessment, and Accountability: Student Agency in Learning (SAIL) course.* Accessed at https://csaa.wested.org/service/student-agency-in-learning-sail-course on December 20, 2021.

Wilhoit, G., Pittenger, L., & Rickbaugh, J. (2016) *Leadership for learning: What is leadership's role in supporting success for every student?* Lexington, KY: Center for Innovation in Education.

Wiliam, D. (2018). *Embedded formative assessment* (2nd ed.). Bloomington, IN: Solution Tree Press.

World Economic Forum. (2016). *The future of jobs: Employment, skills and workforce strategy for the fourth industrial revolution.* Accessed at https://www3.weforum.org/docs/WEF_Future_of_Jobs.pdf on December 20, 2021.

Wormeli, R. (2006). *Fair isn't always equal: Assessing and grading in the differentiated classroom.* Portland, ME: Stenhouse.

Zahidi, S., Ratcheva, V., Hingel, G., & Brown, S. (2020). *The Future of Jobs Report 2020: October 2020.* Geneva, Switzerland: World Economic Forum. Accessed at www3.weforum.org/docs/WEF_Future_of_Jobs_2020.pdf on July 19, 2021.

Zemeckis, R. (Director). (1990). *Back to the future part III* [Film]. Universal Pictures; Amblin Entertainment; U-Drive Productions.

INDEX

NUMBERS

4-point scales, 136–137
21st century skills, 54, 93. *See also* non-academic competencies

A

academic standards. *See also* essential standards; standards
    academics and skills and dispositions, separating, 134–135
    Kentucky academic standards for mathematics, 65, 66
acquisition, 60
active learning (design principle 5)
    Competency-Based Learning School-Design Rubric, 168–169
    reproducibles for, 191–192
    rubrics for, 169–171
ambitious teaching, 77–78
Anderson, R., 57, 62
anytime, anywhere learning, 21–24
applying knowledge/skills, 9, 82–83, 108, 175
assessments
    about, 71–72
    active learning and, 168
    assessment schedules, 96
    classroom assessment-planning template, 92
    co-constructing assessments, 107–108
    common formative assessments, 80–81
    competency statements and, 53–54
    components of a balanced assessment system, 72–73
    formative assessments, 73–77
    formative assessments, ambitious teaching and, 77–78
    lesson planning and, 120
    meaningful assessments (design principle 2), 160–162
    practitioner perspectives, 75–77, 79–80, 83–84, 97–98
    reassessments, 86
    reflection questions, 99–100
    results orientation and, 38–39
    rigor, complexity, and cognitive demand, 86–87
    rubrics and, 87–88, 91
    self-assessments, role of, 78
    summative assessments, 82–86
    unit assessment planning template, 91, 93–99
Aurora Institute, 10

B

Bailey, K., 61, 80, 86
Battelle for Kids, 33
Betton, K., 75–77
big ideas of a PLC, 15, 36–39
Black, P., 73, 78

Blankenship, B., 20–21
Blauth, E., 148
blended learning, 23–24
Bond, S., 109–110
Bonin, C., 144–145
Bourn, G., 63–65
Breaking with Tradition (Stack and Vander Els), 49, 62
Brookhart, S., 61, 74, 88
Brown, C., 87, 160
Brown, S., 7
Buffum, A., 106, 118
building leadership teams (BLT), 28. *See also* guiding coalitions
Burke, K., 74
Butler, P., 97–98

C

Carnegie Unit, 9, 22
Casassa, S., 42–43
CASEL, 54, 57
Center for Collaborative Education (CCE), 82
change, rate of, 6–7
class rank and grade point average, 147–149
classroom assessments, 72. *See also* assessments
co-constructing assessments, 107–108
codesigning learning, 106–107
cognitive demand, 86–87
cognitive rigor, definition of, 86. *See also* rigor/rigor matrices
Colby, K., 86
Colby, R., 53–54
collaborative culture and collective responsibility, 15, 37
collaborative teams
　about, 27–29
　assessments and, 72, 81
　big ideas of a PLC and, 36–39
　critical questions of a PLC and competency-based learning and, 41–45
　differentiated support and, 163
　essential standards and, 88
　practitioner perspectives, 34–35, 39–41, 42–43
　reflection questions, 45
　response to intervention (RTI) and, 104
　shared leadership and, 29–31
　strong foundation/pillars of a PLC, 31–36
collective commitments, 35
Common Core State Standards, 58–60
common formative assessments. *See also* assessments; formative assessments
　in a balanced assessment system, 73
　co-constructing assessments, 108
　measuring where students are, 80–81
communication and grading, 130, 133
competencies, essential standards, learning targets, and learning progressions
　about, 45
　competency statements, 49–58
　essential standards, 58–61
　learning progressions, 62
　learning targets, 61
　metacognition and, 62–63
　practitioner perspectives, 48–49, 63–65, 67–68
　putting it all together, 65–69
　refining the curriculum, 49
　reflection questions, 69
　relationship between competencies, essential standards, and learning targets, 107
　visual for the grain size of competencies, essential standards, and learning targets, 61
competency, definition of, 49
competency statements
　about, 49–51
　active learning and, 168
　assessments and, 53–54, 93, 134
　content relevance and, 51
　evolving policies and, 19
　examples of, 50, 52
　expectations for learning and, 175
　lasting knowledge and, 51, 53
　New Hampshire competency validation rubric, 55–56
　non-academic competencies, 54, 57–58
　rigor and, 53
　rubrics and, 87
competency-based learning. *See also* components of the competency-based classroom
　competency-based learning: a definition, 9–10, 13–14

critical questions of a PLC and, 41–45
design principles, 14. *See also*
Competency-Based Learning
School-Design Rubric
drivers' education as a blueprint for,
150
equity, social justice, and, 15–16
growth of, 10, 13
PLCs and, 15
policy across the United States, 11, 12
popularity of, 1–2
Competency-Based Learning School-Design
Rubric
about, 153
active learning (design principle 5),
168–171
differentiated support (design principle
3), 163–165
equity (design principle 6), 171–174
expectations for learning (design
principle 7), 175–177
final thoughts, 182
how to use the rubric tool, 178–181
Jada's short-term plan: Year 1, 180–181
mastery based on evidence (design
principle 4), 165–167
meaningful assessments (design
principle 2), 160–162
planning your transformation, 155–156
practitioner perspectives, 154–155
student-centered learning (design
principle 1), 157–159
components of the competency-based
classroom
about, 5
anytime, anywhere learning, 21–24
competency-based learning: a
definition, 9–10, 13–14
equity, social justice, and competency-
based learning, 15–16
evolving policies for, 18–20
PLC and competency-based learning
connection, 15
practitioner perspectives, 16–18, 20–21
reflection questions, 24–25
trends in employability skills and
dispositions, 7–9
why now, 6–7
content relevance, 51, 95

Conti, D., 114–115
Couture, D., 125–126
CPS adaptive pacing model, 17
critical questions of a PLC and competency-
based learning, 41–45
Cruz, L., 28
curriculum, refining, 49

D

data-analysis and grading/assessments, 91,
131
Dean, E., 20–21
decaying average, 138–140
design principles, list of, 14. *See also*
Competency-Based Learning
School-Design Rubric
design rubrics. *See* Competency-Based
Learning School-Design Rubric
differentiated support (design principle 3)
Competency-Based Learning School-
Design Rubric, 163–164
reproducibles for, 188
rubrics for, 164–165
Dinkelmann, B., 83–84
Doucet, A., 116–118
Dueck, M., 107
DuFour, R., 27, 30, 37, 111
Dweck, C., 157

E

EducationCounsel, 18
Elmore, R., 29
employability skills, 7–9
enrichments
definition of, 111
extension and enrichment questions,
44–45
equity
equity, social justice, and competency-
based learning, 15–16
mission building and, 31–32
equity (design principle 6)
Competency-Based Learning School-
Design Rubric, 171–172
reproducibles for, 193–194
rubrics for, 173–174
essential outcomes, 93
essential questions, 95

essential standards. *See also* competencies, essential standards, learning targets, and learning progressions
   about, 60–61
   assessments and, 88, 93
   Common Core State Standards, 58–60
   lesson planning and, 119
Evans, C., 19
evidence of learning
   assessments and, 88, 96, 113
   class rank and grade point average and, 147
   grading and, 133
   mastery based on evidence (design principle 4), 165–167
Excel*in*Ed, 18
expanded learning opportunities, 124, 126
expectations and effect size, 31–32
expectations for learning (design principle 7)
   Competency-Based Learning School-Design Rubric, 175
   reproducibles for, 195–196
   rubrics for, 176–177
extended learning opportunities (ELOs), 22–23, 124–126
extensions
   assessment planning and, 96, 98
   definition of, 111
   extension and enrichment questions, 44–45
   at Tier 2, 111–113
external summative assessments, 73. *See also* assessments

F

feedback
   about, 129
   academics and skills and dispositions and, 134–135
   elements of, 78
   formative assessments and, 74
   grading scales and, 135–149
   grading what is learned, 149–151
   grading/what should we grade, 132–134
   grading/why do we grade, 129–131
   practitioner perspectives, 142–143, 144–145
   reflection questions, 151–152
   Tier 2 and, 114

Fernandez, S., 75–77
fixed mindset, 157. *See also* growth mindset; mindsets
Florida Virtual School (FLVS), 22
focus on learning, 15, 37
focused acceleration, 118
formative assessments. *See also* assessments; common formative assessments
   ambitious teaching and, 77–78
   as a classroom practice, 73–77
   grading and, 134, 149
   missing work and, 144
Fukuda, E., 57, 62

G

goals
   formative assessments and, 74
   learning goals, 60
   pillars of a PLC, 36
grade point average, 147–149
grading
   grading what is learned, 149–151
   meaningful assessments and, 161
   what should we grade, 132–134
   why do we grade, 129–131
grading scales
   about, 135–137
   class rank and grade point average, 147–149
   considerations for/what do you notice, 141–142
   decaying average, 138–140
   missing work and, 144
   power law formula and, 137–138
   reassessments and, 146–147
   traditional percentage-based scale, 135
growth mindset, 157–158. *See also* fixed mindset; mindsets
guiding coalitions, 28, 29–31, 36
Guskey, T., 135–136, 141–142, 147–148

H

Hadjan, S., 148
Hattie, J., 74, 78
Heckmann, S., 106
Heritage, M., 62, 74–75, 77
Hess, D., 86
Hess, K., 62

Hingel, G., 7
Holmes, S., 75–77
Howell, T., 16–18
Hume-Howard, E., 67–68
hybrid learning, 23–24

I

I can statements, 67
Inside the Black Box (Black and Wiliam), 78
instruction. *See also* structures and systems to support instruction
    active learning and, 168
    co-constructing assessments, 107–108
    codesigning learning, 106–107
    learner-centered instruction, 168–169
    at Tier 1, 105–106
interim benchmark assessments, 73. *See also* assessments
interventions. *See also* response to intervention (RTI)
    assessment planning and, 96, 98
    characteristics of effective intervention, 112
    intervention and support questions, 43–44
    at Tier 2, 111–113
    at Tier 3, 118–119
introduction
    about competency-based learning systems, 1–2
    about this book, 2–3
    laser-like focus on learning, 3

J

Jakicic, C., 61, 80, 86
Joseph, R., 86
just-in-time assessments, 160. *See also* assessments

K

Kotter, J., 29

L

lasting knowledge, 51, 53
leadership
    definition of, 28
    shared leadership and, 29–31
Leading with Learning (Wilhoit, Pittenger, and Rickbaugh), 30
learner-centered instruction, 168–169
learning goals, 60
learning progressions, 62, 175. *See also* competencies, essential standards, learning targets, and learning progressions
learning targets. *See also* competencies, essential standards, learning targets, and learning progressions
    about, 61
    co-constructing assessments and, 108
    codesigning learning and, 106
    learning progressions and, 62
    lesson planning and, 119–120
    student-friendly language and, 67
Lench, S., 57, 62
Lenz, B., 33
lesson objectives, 119
lesson planning
    competency-based learning lesson plan template, 120
    planning weekly lessons that empower learners, 119–120
    reproducibles for, 217
Levine, E., 14, 168, 175
lifelong learning skills, 134. *See also* skills and dispositions

M

Maffoni, M., 104
Many, T., 104
Marzano, R., 72
mastery based on evidence (design principle 4)
    Competency-Based Learning School-Design Rubric, 165–166
    reproducibles for, 189–190
    rubrics for, 166–167
Mattos, M., 106, 118
meaningful assessments (design principle 2). *See also* assessments
    Competency-Based Learning School-Design Rubric, 160–161
    reproducibles for, 186–187
    rubrics for, 161–162
meaning-making, 60
Mednick, A., 87, 160

metacognition
    role of, 62–63
    student ownership in learning and, 116
    student-centered learning and, 157
mindsets
    fixed mindset, 157
    growth mindset, 157–158
    shifting from adult focused to student focused, 32–33
Ministry of Education, Canada, 19–20, 59
missing work, 144
mission, 31–32
Moss, C., 61
motivation, 130
move-when-ready model/system, 24
Muhammad, A., 28

N

National Equity Project, 13–14, 171
Neihof, J., 34–35
New England Secondary School Consortium, 148
New Hampshire Department of Education, 124
non-academic competencies, 54, 57–58

O

O'Connor, K., 137, 146
Olson, D., 154–155
online schools and programs, 22

P

pacing
    active learning and, 168
    CPS adaptive pacing model, 17
Pappalardo, E., 142–143
Patrick, S., 14, 168, 175
pedagogy
    ambitious teaching and, 77
    competency-based learning and, 14
    equity and, 172
Performance Assessment of Competency Education (PACE), 19
performance assessments. *See also* assessments
    performance tasks, 19, 59, 67, 82, 93
    quality performance assessment cycle, 84–86
    reproducibles for, 197–198, 200–201
    summative assessments and, 82–83
    summative performance assessments, 107–108
    transfer knowledge and, 160
performance-level indicators, 88
personalized learning, 104
Pittenger, L., 30
PLC (professional learning communities). *See* professional learning communities (PLC)
policies
    and competency-based classroom, 18–20
    policy language, 165–166
Popham, J., 75
power law formula, 137–138
practitioner perspectives
    assessments, 75–77, 79–80, 83–84, 97–98
    collaborative teams, 34–35, 39–41, 42–43
    competencies, essential standards, learning targets, and learning progressions, 48–49, 63–65
    design rubrics, 154–155
    feedback, 142–143, 144–145
    structures and systems to support instruction, 102–103, 109–110, 114–115, 116–118, 123, 125–126
professional learning communities (PLC)
    big ideas of a PLC, 15, 36–39
    collaborative teams and, 27–28
    competency-based learning connection and, 15
    critical questions of a PLC, 41–45
    definition of, 27
    pillars of a PLC, 31–36
profiles of a graduate, 33
project-based learning (PBL), 121–123, 160

R

Ratcheva, V., 7
Ray, J., 39–41
reassessments, 86, 146–147. *See also* assessments

Reeves, D., 60
remote learning
    practitioner perspectives, 64, 79–80, 117, 125
    trends in employability skills and dispositions, 8
reproducibles
    CBL weekly lesson planning template, 217
    competency-based learning school-design rubric: principle 1, 184–185
    competency-based learning school-design rubric: principle 2, 186–187
    competency-based learning school-design rubric: principle 3, 188
    competency-based learning school-design rubric: principle 4, 189–190
    competency-based learning school-design rubric: principle 5, 191–192
    competency-based learning school-design rubric: principle 6, 193–194
    competency-based learning school-design rubric: principle 7, 195–196
    making meaning of assessment, 219–220
    performance assessment and unit feedback protocol, 200–201
    performance assessment template, 197–198
    resources for common formative assessments, 204
    rubric template, 199
    SMART goal team planning tool, 218
    student work calibration protocol and rubric analysis tool, 202–203
    tool 1 in Hess's rigor matrices, 205–207
    tool 2 in Hess's rigor matrices, 208–210
    tool 3 in Hess's rigor matrices, 211–213
    tool 4 in Hess's rigor matrices, 214–216
response to intervention (RTI). *See also* interventions
    about, 104–105
    personalized learning and, 104
    RTI inverted pyramid, 105
    Tier 1, 105–108
    Tier 2, 111–118
    Tier 3, 118–119
results orientation, 15, 38–39
revisions and assessment planning, 98
Rickbaugh, J., 30

rigor/rigor matrices
    assessments and, 86–87
    competency statements and, 53
    reproducibles for, 205–216
Rinkema, E., 102–103
Rogers, P., 118
RTI (response to intervention). *See* response to intervention (RTI)
rubrics. *See also* Competency-Based Learning School-Design Rubric
    assessment planning and, 93–94
    assessments and, 87–88, 91
    example of, 89, 90
    rubric template, 87

S

Savage, K., 123
scaffolding
    feedback and, 114
    lesson planning and, 119
    reassessments and, 86
    student-centered learning and, 157
Schinkel, S., 48–49
self-assessments, 74, 78. *See also* assessments
self-direction
    five components of, 58
    frameworks for nonacademic skills and, 57
    grading and, 133
    metacognitive skills framing self-direction, 63
self-paced schools and programs, 22
self-reporting, 78
seven components of the competency-based classroom. *See* components of the competency-based classroom
shared leadership, 29–31
Short, F., 39–41
Singapore American School, 23
skills and dispositions
    academics and, 134–135
    active learning and, 168
    assessment planning and, 95
    competency-based learning and, 10, 49, 156
    expectations for learning and, 175
    instruction and assessment and, 168
    metacognition and, 62
    non-academic competencies, 54, 57–58

skills and dispositions *(continued)*
    self-assessments and, 78
    top ten skills comparison, 8
    trends in employability skills and dispositions, 7–9
SMART goals, 36
Smith, D., 16–18
Smith, W., 118
social and emotional learning (SEL), 54, 57
social justice, 15–16
soft skills, 7. *See also* employability skills
Sparks, S., 104
Stack, B., 49, 62
standards. *See also* essential standards
    academics and skills and dispositions, separating, 134–135
    example academic standards for mathematics, 65, 66
    expectations for learning and, 175
Stinson, I., 79–80
structures and systems to support instruction
    about, 101–102
    lesson planning and, 119–120
    personalized learning, supporting, 104
    practitioner perspectives, 102–103, 109–110, 114–115, 116–118, 123, 125–126
    reflection questions, 126–127
    response to intervention (RTI), 104–119
    school experiences supporting competency-based systems, 121–126
structures for feedback. *See* feedback
Stuart, T., 106, 108
student agency, 158, 172
student ownership, 106, 116
student-centered learning (design principle 1)
    Competency-Based Learning School-Design Rubric, 157–158
    reproducibles for, 184–185
    rubrics for, 158–159
Sturgis, C., 10, 38
success criteria, 74, 107
summative assessments. *See also* assessments
    external summative assessments, 73
    grading and, 134, 149
    missing work and, 144
    quality performance assessment cycle, 84–86
    seeking evidence of transfer, 82–86
    summative performance assessments, 107–108
Szeliga, E., 114–115

T

tasks
    assessments and, 82, 85, 134
    competency-based learning and, 9
    I can statements and, 67
    PACE and, 19
    shared leadership and, 29
    standards and, 59
    task-specific rubrics, 87
    unit assessment planning template and, 93–94, 98
team leaders, 28. *See also* collaborative teams; guiding coalitions
Thomas, T., 104
Tier 1
    about, 105–106
    co-constructing assessments, 107–108
    codesigning learning, 106–107
Tier 2
    about, 111–113
    feedback and, 114
    metacognition and student ownership and, 116
Tier 3, 118–119
tracking progress, 112, 131, 166
transfer/transfer of knowledge
    competency-based learning and, 9, 10, 106
    expectations for learning and, 175
    learning goals and, 60
    performance assessments and, 82, 160
    proficiency and, 87
    summative assessments and, 82–86
Transforming Schools (Lenz), 33

U

unit assessment planning template. *See also* assessments
    about, 91
    section two, 94–97
    selection one, 93–94
    selection three, 98–99
Universal Design for Learning (UDL), 96

V

values, 35
Vander Els, J., 49, 62
Virtual Learning Academy Charter School (VLACS), 22
vision
    pillars of a PLC, 32–34
    values and, 35

W

Wallace Foundation, 124
Webb's Depth of Knowledge (DOK), 53
Wilhoit, G., 30, 57
Wiliam, D., 73, 78, 107
Williams, S., 102–103
Woodruff, L., 114–115
work study practices (WSPs), 63–65, 78
work-based learning, 124, 126
World Economic Forum, 7
Wormeli, R., 136

Z

Zahidi, S., 7

Wait! Your professional development journey doesn't have to end with the last pages of this book.

We realize improving student learning doesn't happen overnight. And your school or district shouldn't be left to puzzle out all the details of this process alone.

No matter where you are on the journey, we're committed to helping you get to the next stage.

Take advantage of everything from **custom workshops** to **keynote presentations** and **interactive web and video conferencing**. We can even help you develop an action plan tailored to fit your specific needs.

Let's get the conversation started.

Call 888.763.9045 today.

SolutionTree.com

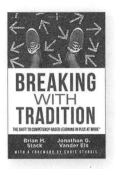

Breaking With Tradition
Brian M. Stack and Jonathan G. Vander Els
Shifting to competency-based learning allows educators to replace traditional, ineffective systems with a personalized, student-centered approach. Throughout the resource, the authors explore how the components of PLCs promote the principles of competency-based education and share real-world examples from practitioners who have made the transition.
BKF780

Learning by Doing
Richard DuFour, Rebecca DuFour, Robert Eaker, Thomas W. Many, and Mike Mattos
Discover how to transform your school or district into a high-performing PLC. The third edition of this comprehensive action guide offers new strategies for addressing critical PLC topics, including hiring and retaining new staff, creating team-developed common formative assessments, and more.
BKF746

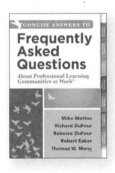

Concise Answers to Frequently Asked Questions About Professional Learning Communities at Work®
Mike Mattos, Richard DuFour, Rebecca DuFour, Robert Eaker, and Thomas W. Many
Get all of your PLC questions answered. Designed as a companion resource to *Learning by Doing: A Handbook for Professional Learning Communities at Work®* (3rd ed.), this powerful, quick-reference guidebook is a must-have for teachers and administrators working to create and sustain the PLC process.
BKF705

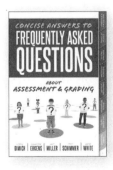

Concise Answers to Frequently Asked Questions About Assessment and Grading
Nicole Dimich, Cassandra Erkens, Jadi Miller, Tom Schimmer, and Katie White
If you have ever asked, "what are the best practices in grading and assessment?" then look no further. Your most challenging questions are answered through this FAQ dialogue that covers how to implement effective and strong assessment practices quickly and easily.
BKG051

Solution Tree | Press — a division of Solution Tree

Visit SolutionTree.com or call 800.733.6786 to order.